MW00340296

LIVED ISLAM

Does Islam make people violent? Does Islam make people peaceful? in this book, Kevin Reinhart demonstrates that such questions are misleading, because they assume that Islam is a monolithic essence and that Muslims are made the way they are by this monolith. He argues that Islam, like all religions, is complex and thus best understood through analogy with language: Islam has dialects, a set of features not shared with other versions of Islam. It also has cosmopolitan elites who prescribe how Islam ought to be, even though these experts, depending on where they practice the religion, unconsciously reflect their own local dialects. Reinhart defines the distinctive features of Islam and investigates how modernity has created new conditions for the religion. Analyzing the similarities and differences between modern and premodern Islam, he clarifies the new and old in the religion as it is lived in the contemporary world.

A. KEVIN REINHART is Associate Professor of Religion at Dartmouth College. He is the author of *Before Revelation: The Boundaries of Muslim Moral Knowledge* and many articles on aspects of Islamic civilization.

Lived Islam

Colloquial Religion in a Cosmopolitan Tradition

A. KEVIN REINHART
Dartmouth College

CAMBRIDGE
UNIVERSITY PRESS

CAMBRIDGE
UNIVERSITY PRESS

University Printing House, Cambridge CB2 8BS, United Kingdom

One Liberty Plaza, 20th Floor, New York, NY 10006, USA

477 Williamstown Road, Port Melbourne, VIC 3207, Australia

314–321, 3rd Floor, Plot 3, Splendor Forum, Jasola District Centre, New Delhi – 110025, India

79 Anson Road, #06–04/06, Singapore 079906

Cambridge University Press is part of the University of Cambridge.

It furthers the University's mission by disseminating knowledge in the pursuit of education, learning, and research at the highest international levels of excellence.

www.cambridge.org
Information on this title: www.cambridge.org/9781108483278
DOI: 10.1017/9781108629263

First published 2020

Printed in the United Kingdom by TJ International Ltd, Padstow Cornwall

A catalogue record for this publication is available from the British Library.

Library of Congress Cataloging-in-Publication Data
NAMES: Reinhart, A. Kevin, 1952– author.
TITLE: Lived Islam : colloquial religion in a cosmopolitan tradition / Dr A. Kevin Reinhart.
DESCRIPTION: 1. | New York : Cambridge University Press, 2019. | Includes bibliographical references and index.
IDENTIFIERS: LCCN 2019030728 (print) | LCCN 2019030729 (ebook) | ISBN 9781108483278 (hardback) | ISBN 9781108629263 (epub)
SUBJECTS: LCSH: Islam – 21st century. | Islam – Essence, genius, nature.
CLASSIFICATION: LCC BP163 .R448 2019 (print) | LCC BP163 (ebook) | DDC 297.09/051–dc23
LC record available at https://lccn.loc.gov/2019030728
LC ebook record available at https://lccn.loc.gov/2019030729

ISBN 978-1-108-48327-8 Hardback
ISBN 978-1-108-70400-7 Paperback

For
Arthur S. Reinhart
Hilma H. R. Reinhart
John Alden Williams
Wilfred Cantwell Smith

اختلاف امتي رحمة

Difference among my community is a mercy

Attributed to the Prophet Muḥammad

Contents

Figures

Preface

This book is an essay in the literal sense of the word. It also tries, in a modest way, to be a manifesto. *Lived Islam* is an attempt more carefully to describe what we ought to mean when we use the term "Islam." While this book claims to describe the situation of Islam as a whole, it subverts itself by pointing to the immeasurable variety of Islam in the world. The book is primarily intended to call attention to the dirty little secret of current Islamic studies – namely that, to the extent we speak of or teach about Islam as a whole, we have been party to a crypto-theological enterprise, and that in fact Islam as a phenomenon is much richer than can ever be embraced in our "Introduction to Islam" courses. It is also a mild and fraternal critique of the work of those who undertake to describe Islam as a lived phenomenon without coming to terms with the full complexity of what they undertake to study. And finally, it is an attempt to provide a model, a heuristic, for talking about the intricate variations of Islam (and perhaps other religions) in a theoretical way. Mine is a model derived from sociolinguistics; other models may be proposed. Perhaps the most valuable works are those that, in the process of being critiqued, bring clarity to a field. This work is above all an invitation to critique.

It is a pleasant duty to thank many friends and colleagues with whose help, in various ways over the many years, this book has, in fits and starts, been written. These ideas have been presented in lecture form at the University of Pennsylvania, Smith College, the University of California at San Diego, the Alliance of Civilizations Institute of Fatih Sultan Mehmet University, and at the Religion Department Colloquium at Dartmouth College, and for this I thank Everett Rowson, Keith Lewinstein, Hasan Kayalī, and their faculty colleagues, Bruce Lawrence and miriam cooke, as well as my own colleagues, particularly those in the Religion Department here at Dartmouth College.

Tracey Maher meticulously copy edited a version of the manuscript. Her eagle eye caught many inconsistencies and failures of clarity. Meredith Wilson, somewhat later, was equally astute and meticulous. I am very grateful for their help. Subsequently the book was read and insightfully commented upon by Maimuna Huq. Linda George and Megan Clark copy edited with discernment and taste. Bruce Lawrence and miriam cooke read chapters of the work, and provided encouragement and helpful critical insight. Patsy Carter, former doyenne of Dartmouth's ILL department, was practically a collaborator on the early stages of this book – so many interlibrary loans did she provide for me. She was the spirit of Baker Library and I miss her help and good nature. Bill Fontaine, also of Baker Library, suffered under a barrage of inquiries about books in our collection, books we do not have in our collection, the location of books mis-shelved in our collection, and so on. His patience was a lesson to me.

Students at Dartmouth, particularly in the seminar "Local Varieties of Islam," helped to stimulate my thinking on these matters. Thanks to Elise Welford, Barbara Seniawski, Clare Choo, and the late Cheryl Pinkerton – a promising and much-lamented student of Middle East studies – from that seminar. Barbara Seniawski later wrote an excellent senior thesis provoked by this model. I have profited from that, and from my discussions with her over the years. Dale Eickelman organized a conference where I first tried to think through (not very clearly) these issues; Clifford Geertz was a charitable and stimulating commentator on that rather murky paper. Ellis Goldberg brought his deep knowledge of contemporary Arab Islam to bear on a very early draft of this argument, and offered important critiques and encouragement. David McMurry was very important in thinking about the issues in the chapter on modern Islam; I had to revise my argument substantially in response to his helpful criticism. Brian Didier was a stimulating colleague and kindly read a chapter when I was in the slough of despond. Above all, James Laine has encouraged this project, suggesting that it has merit not just for Islamic studies but for the study of Religion. His enthusiasm has kept me going when my focus has flagged.

I also have to thank various institutions who have supported my work over the years and made possible my wonderful experiences in Islamdom: the Center for the Study of World Religions at Harvard University, Dartmouth College and particularly its Religion Department, the Fulbright Commission of the DOE, the Social Science Research Committee (especially their Mid-Career Skills Enhancement grant program), the American Research Centers in Yemen, Egypt, and Turkey, under whose auspices I have learned much of what I know about Islam, and also and particularly the Islâm Araştırma Merkezi in Istanbul, which has proved a warm scholarly home abroad.

I am also grateful to Walter de Gruyter/Mouton GmbH for permission to use various quotations from Ibn Taimīya (sic), *Ibn Taimīya's Struggle against Popular Religion: With an Annotated Translation of his* Kitāb iqtiḍā᾽ aṣ-ṣirāṭ al-mustaqīm mukhālafat aṣḥāb al-jaḥīm, translated by Muhammad Umar Memon (The Hague: Mouton, 1976).

Many Muslim friends and acquaintances, from nearly every Arab country, from Europe and America, in Turkey, Iran, Uzbekistan, Bangladesh, India, Pakistan, Malaysia, and Indonesia, over something approaching forty years, have challenged me and engaged me hospitably in discussion, and have taught me to take their tradition with the seriousness it deserves. No one of these named is responsible for the inevitable failings of this work.

The Cambridge University Press has been an efficient and encouraging host for this book, particularly my cooperative and helpful editor, Beatrice Rehl. I am grateful for their dedication to scholarship, efficiency, and good taste.

The book would never have been finished without Marlene Heck's encouragement and support, and her tireless reading and rereading of drafts, and her patient inputting of the index. Her rigorous editorial eye, charitable comments, and intellectual companionship were indispensable.

Finally, this book is dedicated to four people who helped introduce me to the study of Islam and were, in various ways, my guides to Islamdom. The first are my parents, Col. A. S. and Hilma Reinhart, who (over my strenuous objections) took me to Turkey for two years of high school, and encouraged us to live *in* Turkey, and not apart from it. Theirs is surely the formative influence.

John Alden Williams is a teacher, friend, and was a generous mentor during my undergraduate studies and until the present. He taught me to aspire to the widest possible understanding of Muslims, to learn the appropriate languages, and above all to value the humanity, religiosity, and lived commitment of Muslims.

Wilfred Smith is most responsible for my being a "religionist" and, after many agreeable encounters, including in seminar, he agreed to serve as my dissertation advisor, along with Wolfhart Heinrichs and John Carman – they have been models for me of what scholars should be. Wilfred's generous engagement with my work, our conversations, and his invitation in fact for me to revise his *Islam in Modern History* encouraged me to think that expertise in classical Islamic sciences did not disqualify one from thinking about Modern Islam. He believed also that living in Islamdom challenged one to make sense of the living reality of Muslim religious life. I am grateful that in July of the year before he died, he assented with enthusiasm when I mentioned that I'd like him to be among this book's dedicatees.

Note on Text

I have tried whenever possible throughout this book to cite works available in translation, though each of these has been checked against its original. For ease of reading, transliteration from other sources is sometimes silently corrected to conform to the norms of this book. Other changes from published translations are documented in the notes.

Transliteration is according to the Library of Congress with the following changes: *alif maqṣūrah* is written á instead of ā. The *tā marbūṭah* is represented with an "h," and Ottoman is transliterated into a system derived from Birnbaum's rather than into Modern Turkish representations.[1]

[1] E. Birnbaum, "The Transliteration of Ottoman Turkish for Library and General Purposes."

1

Introduction

> [I]t is seldom possible, and still more seldom advisable, to divide a civilization into departments and to attempt to trace their separate developments; life nowhere can be cut in two with a hatchet. And this is emphatically true of the civilization of Islam. Its intellectual unity, for good and for evil, is its outstanding quality. . . . [I]ts life and thought are a unity. So, also, with its institutions. . . . [I]n Muslim countries, Church and State are one indissolubly, and until the very essence of Islam passes away, that unity cannot be relaxed.[1]
>
> Duncan Black MacDonald

Is "Islam a violent religion"? Is it "a religion of peace"?[2] What is "Islam"? What do we mean when we use the term in scholarship? When D. B. MacDonald, the great Scottish missionary-scholar and founder of modern Islamic studies in the United States, used the term Islam, it was clear he referred to a single entity that was indivisible, that encompassed everything Muslims did; in short, it was an essence that would cease to exist only when Islam did – preferably because of Muslims' conversion en masse to Christianity.[3]

What is Islam? Surely this is not a complicated question: Islam is a religion – perhaps the most widespread of religions, with well over a billion and a half adherents on every continent in nearly every country. It is the religion of the "five pillars" – of declaring God's unity, worshipping five

[1] D. B. MacDonald, *Development of Muslim Theology*, 3–4.

[2] "[Islam is mentioned as the official religion in both Afghanistan and Iraq]. Missing . . . is any guidance as to *what kind of Islam* these constitutions are to follow. . . . The references to Islam in both documents ignore the fundamental differences between *violent* and *moderate* interpretations of Islam. Hence the door is left wide open for violence-conducive interpretations." A. Etzioni, *Security First*, 117, my italics.

[3] See the sections on MacDonald in the masterly J. D. J. Waardenburg, *L'Islam*.

times daily, fasting the month of Ramadan, paying charity, and performing the pilgrimage to Mecca. In books of Islamic law the *'ulamā'* (scholars) have spelled out in efflorescent detail how Muslims must act. These specify how a Muslim is to purify himself and pray, how she is to fast and to make the Pilgrimage, but also how to buy and sell, how to dress and to marry, how to slaughter meat and invest money, how to punish miscreants and many other things besides. Consequently, it seems there is a single religious identity that stretches from one end of the map to the other, in which Muslim professionals – the scholars – have been free to travel, to work, and to guide Muslims in North Africa and the Eastern Mediterranean, in India and in Africa, as well as in China, Indonesia, and North America. "Islam is one," Muslims assert. It is "a way of life"; "Islam does not distinguish between Church and State," say Muslim activists and Islam's critics. These all share with Duncan Black MacDonald, whose quotation begins this chapter, the notion that Islam was, and is, an essence plainly revealed in Muslim thought and life, but also in institutions that indissolubly linked what he called Church and State. The civilization of Islam manifests an essence that is seen in the whole of the Islamic world, and surely that means that Islam must be everywhere the same.

But *is* Islam everywhere the same? As an example, let us consider a celebrated real-world case – the medieval religious scholar Ibn Baṭṭūṭah, a classically trained member of the *'ulamā'*, who in the fourteenth century traveled throughout Islamdom and wrote a marvelous account of his travels.[4] His self-description makes it clear that he was a Muslim, and particularly a Muslim-scholar to his very bones.[5] This great traveler journeyed across the breadth of the universal community of Muslims (the *ummah*) – from North Africa to India, at least, and perhaps even to Java and China. As one historian observed, as a Muslim he was always, in a sense, at home wherever he went in Islamdom.[6] As a scholar, a quite ordinary scholar it seems, Ibn Baṭṭūṭah transmitted and embodied the scholarly and universal *'ilm* (knowledge) of Islam. To other scholars wherever they were, it was of little consequence that he was a Moroccan; as an *'ālim* (scholar; pl. *'ulamā'*), a bearer of *'ilm*, he was always one of them.

[4] Ibn Baṭṭūṭah, *Travels of Ibn Baṭṭūṭah.*

[5] He is well known partly because he left us his travel book but also because in it he so clearly shows his nature as an interested man of ordinary intellect – tolerant but far from a cultural relativist. Working as a jurist for the Indian sultan, and married to Indian women, for example, he never ceased for a moment to be a North African Mālikī jurist.

[6] R. E. Dunn, *Adventures of Ibn Battuta*, 7.

For instance, during his travels he attended lectures on Islamic subjects in Anatolia.[7] He studied in Damascus with local scholars and took licenses from professors in every locale to teach books that they had mastered.[8] He wrote *ḥadīths* – authoritative stories from the life of the Prophet Muḥammad – from memory, which were then translated and explained to the less scholarly in Turkish when he was among Turks.[9] Over and over again Ibn Baṭṭūṭah arrived in a town, was received and greeted, fed, supplied, and lodged by other scholars or by the local ruler as a gesture of respect for the scholarship he embodied.

For example, in Maqdashaw[10] Ibn Baṭṭūṭah arrived by boat and young men from the town came on board. Ibn Baṭṭūṭah's companions said of him,

> "This man is not a merchant, but a doctor of the law," whereupon he called out to his friends and said to them, "This is a guest of the *qāḍī*." There was among them one of the *qāḍī*'s men, who informed him of this, and he came down to the beach with a number of students and sent one of them to me . . . He said to me "In the name of God let us go to salute the [sultan]. . . . It is the custom that whenever there comes a jurist or a *sharīf* or a man of religion, he must first see the sultan before taking lodging."[11]

Ibn Baṭṭūṭah was not merely honored throughout Islamdom, but, despite being a Moroccan, Arabic-speaking member of the Mālikī rite of Islamic law, he was appointed to official positions supervising Persian- or Hindustani-speaking members of the Ḥanafī legal rite. When Ibn Baṭṭūṭah arrived in Delhi, far from his home in Morocco, he was given presents, honored, and saluted. The sultan had him eat in his presence. Then the Great King said,

> "Master of the World [the sultan] has appointed you *qāḍī* of the royal city of [Delhi] and has fixed your stipend at 12,000 dinars a year, and assigned to you villages to that amount, and commanded for you 12,000 dinars in cash, which you shall draw from the treasury tomorrow (if God will), and has given you a horse with its saddle and bridle and has ordered you to be invested with a *maḥārībī* robe of honor." . . . I said to him "O Master, I belong to the [legal] school of Mālik and these people are Ḥanafīs, and I do not know the language . . . ."[12]

That did not matter. He was given translators and became the judge of Delhi. When he traveled to the Maldive Islands he was once more appointed

[7] Ibn Baṭṭūṭah, *Travels of Ibn Baṭṭūṭah*, 2:439. [8] Ibid., 1:56–57. See also 4:917 n. 38.
[9] Ibid., 4:441. [10] Mogadishu, Somalia; also Maqdishū. See *EI2* s.v. "Maqdishū."
[11] Ibn Baṭṭūṭah, *Travels of Ibn Baṭṭūṭah*, 2:374–375. [12] Ibid., 3:347.

as judge (*qāḍī*). He was no mere caretaker judge, either, but he rigorously applied the norms of the universal Islamic *sharīʿah*.

> I gave strict injunctions that [worship] was to be observed, and ordered men to go swiftly to the streets and bazaars after the Friday service; anyone whom they found not having [worshipped] I had beaten and paraded. I compelled the salaried [worship]-leaders and muezzins to be assiduous in their duties and sent letters to all the islands to the same effect. I tried also to determine how women dressed, but I could not manage this.[13]

Ibn Baṭṭūṭah was, it would seem, proof of MacDonald's assertion that Islam had a single nature and was indivisible wherever it is found.

And yet – the last sentence of Ibn Baṭṭūṭah's quotation above is a puzzle. He was the Muslim judge; these were Muslims; how was it that he "could not manage" to get the women of the Maldives to cover above the waist? Ibn Baṭṭūṭah confesses,

> I tried to put an end to this practice [of not covering the bosom] and ordered [women in the Maldives] to wear clothes, but I met with no success. No woman was admitted to my presence in a lawsuit unless her body was covered, but apart from that I was unable to effect anything.[14]

Perhaps this neglect of proper Muslim decorum was just the ignorance of the uneducated, or a gesture of gender-resistance to the patriarchy? Yet it was not just in the Maldives and not just from women that he encountered resistance and it was not just from the religiously uneducated. It appears in fact that even a fellow judge differed from Ibn Baṭṭūṭah on what was required of a Muslim:

> One day I called upon the *qāḍī* at Īwālātan [Mali] after he had given permission for me to enter. I found him with a young and exceptionally beautiful woman. When I saw her I hesitated and was going to go back, but she laughed at me and showed no embarrassment. The *qāḍī* said to me: "Why are you turning back? She is my friend." I was astonished at them, for he was a jurist and [had made the pilgrimage to Mecca].[15]

The gender separation that some would argue is an essential feature of Islam, something embedded deeply in Islamic law, could be flouted casually by some Muslims – along with the stinging suggestion that Ibn Baṭṭūṭah's was merely a parochial understanding of Islam.

> One day [when I was in Mali] I called on Abū Muḥammad Yandakān al-Massūfī . . . In the middle of the room was a canopied couch and upon it

[13] Ibid., 4:840–841. [14] Ibid., 827. [15] Ibid., 952.

> was a woman with a man sitting and talking together. I said to him: "Who is this woman?" He said: "She is my wife." I said: "What about the man who is with her?" He said: "He is her friend." I said: "Are you happy about this, you who have lived in our country and know the content of the religious law?" He said: "The companionship of women and men *among us* is a good thing and an agreeable practice, which causes no suspicion; *they are not like the women of your country.*" I was astonished at his silliness. I left him and did not visit him again. Afterwards he invited me a number of times but I did not accept.[16]

Abū Muḥammad flagrantly ignored Ibn Baṭṭūṭah's appeal to Islamic law – in the Mālikī school texts both Ibn Baṭṭūṭah and Abū Muḥammad had studied, it does indeed stipulate gender segregation for those not married or otherwise related to each other. Instead he cites local practices: "among us" "*our* women are not like the women of *your country*," he says. He seems to believe there is more than one way to be a Muslim.

In the end, Ibn Baṭṭūṭah admits as much, though hardly from a culturally relativist point of view:

> Conditions among these people are remarkable and their life style is strange. The men have no jealousy. No one takes his name from his father, but from his maternal uncle. Sons do not inherit, only sister's sons! This is something I have seen nowhere [else] in the world except among the infidel Indians of al-Mulaibār. Nevertheless these people are Muslims. They are strict in observing the prayers, studying the religious law, and memorizing the Qur'ān. Their women have no shame before men and do not veil themselves, yet they are punctilious about their prayers. . . . Women there have friends and companions among men outside the prohibited degrees for marriage, and in the same way men have women friends in the same category.[17]

How are such behaviors to be explained? What are we to make of Abū Muḥammad's reference to "the women of your country," when all Muslims belong to the same "universal" religion?

Read carefully, Ibn Baṭṭūṭah's *Travels* demonstrates that even in "the age of faith" and before modernity's incursions, Islam was understood and practiced in various ways according to place. In fact, local saints and local methods of worship with which he had previously been unfamiliar often attracted Ibn Baṭṭūṭah's attention and approval.[18] The reality was that scholars' religious position on, say, gender relations (as we have seen) differed

[16] Ibid., my italics. [17] Ibid., 951.

[18] Ibid., e.g., 1:44–45, 79–80, 82–83, 139–140, and especially (against the plague) 143–144.

according to locale. As we shall see, even the understanding and practice of the "five pillars" – as well as everything else that comprises the so-called "essence of Islam" – can differ and has differed according to the time and location of the Muslims being observed.

This is not just true of the past. Anyone who has traveled in Islamdom has noticed differences of emphasis and practice, in belief and conduct among Muslims of different locales – as well as of different classes and sexes. Those differences are what keep anthropologists and travel writers in business, whether the sophisticated like Clifford Geertz,[19] the pious, like Michael Wolfe,[20] or the hostile, like V. S. Naipaul.[21] The Muslim differences so prominent in travel literature or ethnography mostly disappear from textbooks and scholarly studies of Islam, however. It is in fact *Muslims* who disappear, to be replaced by some ideal construct, "the Muslim." Such idealism may have a place, but there also ought to be a place in a general study of Islam for *real* Muslims and their particular religious lives.

The Problem

Two facts confront someone studying "Islam." One is the astonishing variety of practices and beliefs that from place to place and time to time are considered to be Islam. The other is that Muslims, despite their manifest differences in practice and belief, tend to recognize each other as fellow Muslims and as distinct from others such as Hindus and Christians.[22] This book is about these two realities that seem to pull in opposite directions.

Many Islamicists, of whatever discipline, have tended, until recently, to keep "Islam" as a vague and nearly contentless sign, so inclusive of religion, government, and culture as to be nearly empty.[23] Their "Islam," as we shall

[19] C. Geertz, *Islam Observed*, comparing Islam in Indonesia and Morocco.

[20] M. Wolfe, *The Hadj*, implicitly comparing his own American Islam to that of Morocco and that of Arabia.

[21] V. S. Naipaul, *Beyond Belief*; *Among the Believers*, comparing (and indicting) Muslims of Iran, Pakistan, Malaysia, and Indonesia.

[22] This perception is amusingly confirmed in a French comparison of Muslims to Englishmen: "From Morocco to China, from South Africa to Siberia, the Muslim of one country feels quite at home in the country of another Muslim, just as the Englishman [feels at home] from Vancouver to Hong Kong, from Cape Town to Nepal. Like the Englishman, too, the Muslim considers himself above all other varieties of the human species. And finally, like the Englishman, once he has finished praying and praising the Prophet, the Muslim has one overriding preoccupation, that of profit." C. Harrison, *France and Islam in West Africa*, 31, citing Le Chatelier, "Politique musulmane," 61–62.

[23] See the first edition of the *Encyclopaedia of Islam* [henceforth *EI1* or *EI2*, depending on edition], which describes itself as "The Encyclopaedia of Islām: a dictionary of the geography,

see in Chapter 2, is an ethereal notion: useful for generalities, useless for particularities, often a term signifying not much more than "them."[24] Islam gives the illusion of being a substantive when we say, "Islam is on the march"; "Islam is growing faster than Catholicism"; "Islam teaches us about finance"; "Islam is the religion of peace"; "Islam is a threat to the Egyptian government"; "Islam expanded in the ninth century." But to what, in fact, does "Islam" in these phrases refer? To a set of beliefs? To an empire? To a religious practice? To a people? To a political movement? In the study of both religion and culture, "Islam," unfortunately, remains a basic and mostly unproblematic term of analysis and description.[25]

Some scholars, confronted by Muslim diversity, have, in effect, chosen among Islamic phenomena and, like Muslim dogmatists, asserted that some practices are "authentically" or "essentially" Islamic. Other religious practices or beliefs are called *popular* or *local* religion, and are said to result from *outside* or *autochthonous* influences which, these scholars assert, are foreign to the real Islam – or these local religious features are said to be indisputably native, genuine, and authentic, compared to the imported Islam.

As the anthropologist Abdul Hamid el-Zein cleverly has shown, this cutting off of the "local" from the "genuine" by Westerners or by Muslims is a kind of theology.[26] Like theologians, these academic students of Islam in effect decide what is "really" Islam and what is not. Worse, to separate the local and particular from the universal and the official is like slicing into the body of lived Islam and pointing to only the lungs or pancreas as the "real essence," the true body of Islam, while ignoring the face and frame that are equally part of the patient. For these vivisectionists, the "real" or "orthodox"

ethnography and biography of the Muhammadan peoples . . ." Even in the second edition it is clear that "Islam" is first of all a place, and city/country descriptions get much more space than descriptions of religious practices or beliefs; kings likewise get more space than many or most religious figures. See also the brief discussion under "The Study of Islam after 9/11" in Chapter 2 on Bernard Lewis's *What Went Wrong*.

[24] M. G. S. Hodgson, *Venture of Islam*, 58–59. Certainly the sociology of Islamic studies plays a part in the resistance to precise terminology. We Islamicists are few and far between, and are often expected to teach about and comment upon Israel and the Palestinians, though our training be in medieval theology, or about Islamic law, though we be political scientists who studied nation formation in Syria. Hence the notion of a hegemonic "Islam" legitimates our omnicompetence. It also justifies Eurocentric educational institutions in their choice to have one person responsible for all of "Islam," one for "China" (and ten for United States history). Hodgson's distinction between "Islamic" (to refer to the religion proper) and "Islamicate" (to refer to features of the cultures where Islam is the culturally dominant religion) subverts the notion that we are omniscient of all Muslims do and have done, and, for that reason alone, it ought to be the standard usage of our field.

[25] See Chapter 2 where data on use of the word "Islam" in book titles is discussed.

[26] A. H. M. el-Zein, *Sacred Meadows*.

Islam is composed of textual norms: knowledge of the Arabic Qur'ān, Islamic law (*sharī'ah*), the "five pillars" – affirmation of a single God with the messengerhood of Muḥammad, the five daily prayers, welfare contributions, fasting during the month of Ramadan, the pilgrimage to Mecca. Everything else is "not Islam." This approach drills through the rich layers of practice and worldview, and keeps a "core" as "Islam" while its lived context is – depending on the discourse – "blameworthy innovation," "vital affirmation of local culture," a contamination by local influences from paganism and animism, or exogenous "borrowings" from Judaism, Christianity, or liberalism.

Though dissection may reveal the constituents of a living Islam, it does not help in understanding the Islam of its practitioners for whom – and this is the point – *it all is Islam*. To hive off "popular custom" from "real Islam" either excises thousands of practices and ideas that to the devout, self-identifying Muslim are part and parcel of *their* lived Islam, or denies that the life lived by millions of Muslims, perhaps indeed all Muslims, is Islamic at all – whatever they might say about themselves.

To say that someone is Muslim in fact tells us virtually nothing of his economic worldview or her political allegiance, and most importantly it tells us less than we think it does about what this Muslim does religiously, or believes. The reality is that she may pray regularly, or not; he may affirm the value of sexual segregation or she may not; he may have only one God as the object of his allegiance, or one god and many demigods; she may ask the Prophet, or a saint, or no one for intercession. He may know Arabic, but probably does not. She may follow *sharī'ah*, she may follow tribal law, she may know only the law of the state. Of course, for any of the options above, we may also substitute "both/and" for "either/or," since the most common Muslim life is lived amidst a congeries of various laws and norms. What value then is there to a term like "Islam," which points so imprecisely to a variety of practices and notions that when we label a person "Muslim," we know so little of their actual religious life?

Introduction to the Book

This small essay aims to clarify a large topic: What do we mean and what ought we to mean when, as scholars and students, we use the term "Islam"? I will argue that the seeming "naturalness" of the object of our study rests on a mistake – namely, the belief that this set of practices and even creedal commitments that we call Islam constitutes a real object in the world. What we *can* study is Islam as Muslims practice it in the world. This *Lived Islam*[27] ought to be the proper object of our references when we casually and without qualification use the term "Islam." *Lived Islam* has certain features that mislead scholars in Islamic studies. Once these misapprehensions are corrected, a whole series of interesting research possibilities and agendas reveal themselves, as well as a better understanding of such topics as practice versus theory in Islamic law, the role(s) of women, and, of course, so-called Islamic fundamentalism.

Chapter 2 briefly describes assumptions that have shaped the ways in which Islam has been studied – by historians of religion and theologians, by historians, and by anthropologists and colonial administrators – and it offers a critique of these approaches. It then makes the case for a renewed attention to "*Lived*" or "*Colloquial*" *Islam* – Islam as it exists in the world, as opposed to Islam as it is talked about by professional Muslims. I argue that Islam, as practiced, can be considered as a conversation, or, more concretely, as a living language. Living languages are composed of diverse elements that can artificially be separated, but which, to the native speaker, altogether make up what the speaker understands to be his or her native language. In the case of Islam, elements unique to localities, elements unique to scholars, and elements shared among diverse Muslim groups together make up the *Lived Islam* of a given community.

Chapter 3 then turns to the differences among "islams" and proposes that their distinctive local features (while nonetheless important parts of *Lived Islam*) be regarded as *Dialect* features of Islam. Here, we will also consider the particular features of *Standard Islam* that facilitate the formation of Islamic dialect practices.

In Chapter 4 we discuss those features of Islam shared among most Muslims of most locales and circumstances, and suggest that they function as the koiné, or *shared* language, of Muslims. Observers and practitioners are likely, however, to overestimate the extent to which the *meaning* of the practices is shared along with the practices themselves. We demonstrate this for several of the "five pillars," and then consider what other elements of Islamic practice seem widely to be shared.

Chapter 5 considers the antithesis of *Dialect Islam* – *Standard Islam*, the Islam of Cosmopolitan Muslims. This is the Islam of books, of scholars, of

[27] This term is used also in an interesting edited volume containing papers from a 2002 conference. The participants seemed unaware of the term's use in the study of religion. It appears that for the authors and editors, the term refers to "syncretic and liminal positions as well as accommodation of Islam in South Asia." See I. Ahmad and H. Reifeld (eds.), *Lived Islam in South Asia*, ix.

high theory and law; it is taught in Islamic institutions of learning, and is the focus of most scholarship about Islam – by Muslims and by non-Muslims as well. It is the language of professional Muslims, we might say. We will assert, however, that like *Standard English*, *Standard Islam* is no one's native dialect. We will also try to see the distinctively religio-mythic features of Cosmopolitan Islam.

In Chapter 6 we consider special features of Islam in the modern period and how these connect in a particular way to the aspects of Islam we have already described. It appears that some features of the modern world are flattening out the dialects of Islam, while others are hardening the lines that define local Islamic dialects.

Readers familiar with Islam in the world will not be surprised when told that *Lived Islam* is more than book-Islam; and academic Islamicists will hardly be astonished to be told that Islamic learning matters. What I hope to contribute is a set of categories, or tools, to clarify the way in which, in the particular case of Islam, the ideal and the particular together construct the phenomenon we call "Islam." Perhaps Muslims too will find reassurance in the empirical fact that the thriving, growing religion to which they are committed is now and always has been both plural and universal, local and cosmopolitan, and that a certain openness and receptivity has been a feature of Islam at its strongest.[28]

To close this introduction, it is important to state, and we will reiterate, that to say Islam is *like* a language is not to say that it *is* a language. These features of Islam that we isolate heuristically are not real; they have no ontology. By the artificial exercise of considering them separately, I hope we can better understand that which *is* real – Islam in the world, *Lived Islam*.

[28] Citation will for the most part be only of works that have immediately influenced my argument. There will be few of the "for X see A, B, and C" defensive citations. It would be unwieldly to list all the wonderful scholarship, or for that matter all the wonderful and collegial conversations, from which I have benefitted in writing this book.

2

How Scholars Study Islam

Lived and Colloquial Islam

Critiquing Essentialism

The study of Islam depends on what "Islam" is. Is it a thing with a stable essence, or is it a different thing according to where and for whom it exists? Is it a feeling,[1] or a way of regarding the world that is imposed anonymously on the faithful, a "discourse," so to speak?[2] It has become the fashion to criticize essentialism,[3] but the only alternative until recently was the "islams" approach, the assertion that there as many islams as places where Islam was found, or even that there are as many islams as there are Muslims.[4] As a result, the assertion that Islam is always and everywhere the same, at a deep level at least (as we saw in D. B. MacDonald's quotation, Chapter 1), is essentialism, as is the belief that everything done by Muslims is shaped by something called "Islam." Essentialism is improbable because of the sheer diversity of environments where Islam is found.

On the other hand, practitioners of the "islams" approach have had far too little to say about what is found in common among Muslims. Worse, the "islams" approach ignores what most Muslims affirm – that they consider themselves to be members of a single community sharing something called "Islam" with other Muslims, wherever they may live.

Essentialism is too seldom defined, even by those who disdain it, and so an attempt at definition is in order. Essentialism may be simply described as the belief that the thing under consideration is what it is because of

[1] G. Marranici, *The Anthropology of Islam*, 8. [2] S. Mahmood, *Politics of Piety*, 32.

[3] "Pernicious essentialism," G. Marranici, *The Anthropology of Islam*, 7. See also, e.g., S. Haj, *Reconfiguring Islamic Tradition*, 2–3.

[4] D. F. Eickelman, "Changing Interpretations of Islamic Movements," 19, and sources cited there. It is called by Waardenburg the "disaggregation approach." J. J. Waardenburg, "Changes of Perspective." See also Waardenburg's thoughtful reflections on the term "Islam" in J. J. Waardenburg, *Muslims as Actors*, 29ff. Also R. A. Lukens-Bull, "Between Text and Practice," 46. See also just below for my definition of essentialism.

certain stable and irreducible characteristics. Things that have these characteristics are linked, so that all forms of that object share an identity. Finally, essentialism assumes that essence, in the abstract, precedes its historical or particular existence. As a result, the thing under consideration may be perfected in one form, not yet perfected in another. Nonetheless, because of the underlying essence, an unperfected form of the thing, as we find it in the world, is always on its way to becoming the perfected form required by the essence. The philosophical terminology that shapes this definition allows us to say concisely what we will see in various forms when we discuss of the concept of Islam, below.

In the last decades there have been several excellent discussions of precisely the problem of Islam's plurality, coming, not surprisingly, from anthropologists.[5] This book comes from the other side of the humanities/social sciences divide, that is, from a historian of religion and Islamicist, confronted by the variety of Islamic practice that confounds any kind of essentialism, but also one confronted with the datum that Muslims insist that "Islam is one," or "all Muslims have the same religion." What we offer below is not a history or a methodological analysis of the study of Islam, but instead a simple account of four trends that have predominated in our field. The goal is to orient the reader to the general problem from which this book offers a way forward.

The Problem: How to Study Islam

One way to illuminate how Islam has been studied – and here we are limiting the discussion to the English-language studies – is to survey a list of book titles, which will suggest a shorthand presentation of their subject matter and approach. (Whether the title was chosen by the author or the publisher can be ignored for the purposes of this discussion.) A survey of the books bought since the 1920s by the University of California libraries suggests that titles of books on Islam can, for the most part, be sorted into three groups: "Islam and ..." (or "... in Islam"); "Islam in ..." which are the older and the younger form of essentialism; and a regionalist ("islams") approach that uses adjectives modifying "Islam" to suggest the focused particularity of the study – *Moroccan Islam, Persatuan Islam, Indonesian Islam, Iranian Islam*, etc.,

[5] Notably for Indonesia, J. R. Bowen, *Muslims Through Discourse*. For West Africa, R. Launay, *Beyond the Stream*. For the East Coast of Africa, M. Lambek, *Knowledge and Practice*. More generally, see G. Marranici, *The Anthropology of Islam*.

or that plainly refers to "Islams" (or "islams").[6] "Islam and" and "Islam in" both suggest an elemental "Islam" existing apart from time, location, and practitioners. The titles using an adjective of locality to modify Islam suggest (in the works surveyed) that the Islam of Indonesia, for example, is really an Indonesian phenomenon rather than an Islamic one. These works spend little time discussing the "Islam" part of the formulation, and are ultimately parochial in their approach. The most recent articulation of this approach is the "islams" approach, to be discussed below.

"Islam and . . ." – Naked Essentialism[7]

The "Islam and . . ." approach takes no notice of where Islam is located. It "reifies" or "makes a thing" of Islam.[8] This classical approach in many ways still dominates the field, and is especially characteristic of Islamic studies specialists, historians of religion, and comparative religionists (see Figure 2.1). It assumes *an* "Islam," with a stable essence relatively uninflected by time or place. Hence, these book titles link the abstracted or reified "Islam" to other abstractions. This is the oldest and best-established approach, and led our scholarly forebears to entitle their books *Islam and Christianity, Islam and the West, Islam and the Arabs.* This reified Islam is a parallel to other abstractions such as "politics" or "development,"[9] or to the West[10] or modernism,[11] or to the army,[12] or Britain.[13] In its very vagueness, it is the conceptual parallel of both the particular and the unspecified – of oil and turmoil, of France and Pan-Turkism, and, of course, as the parallel to Christianity,

[6] I have used the University of California's unified catalog, first, since it reflects the purchases of the (mostly) well-funded entire University of California system, a system that has a number of first-rate schools where Islam has long been studied and taught. These catalogs should, therefore, give us a fair picture of what has been published and taken seriously by scholars. The collection is, of course, not as strong in pre–World War II titles as Yale, Harvard, Chicago, or Princeton collections might be. Nonetheless, its sample seems quite good, so I am confident that what we find is representative, if not in a statistical sense, then in a "ball-park" sense of work in the field. I have confined myself to English-language books, and to their first editions.

[7] The University of California collection includes approximately 1,190 English-language works published between 1920 and 2018 with the word "Islam" in the title. Of these, nearly 34 percent (399) used the phrase "Islam and . . ." There is a steady increase in this usage between the 1930s and 1980s, followed by a mammoth spike in this usage during and following the 1990s (36 percent).

[8] W. C. Smith, *Meaning and End*, 103–110.

[9] J. L. Esposito (ed.), *Islam and Politics*; J. L. Esposito and H. Askari, *Islam and Development.*

[10] B. Lewis, *Islam and the West.*

[11] V. A. Martin, *Islam and Modernism.*

[12] N. Green, *Islam and the Army in Colonial India.*

[13] R. Geaves, *Islam and Britain.*

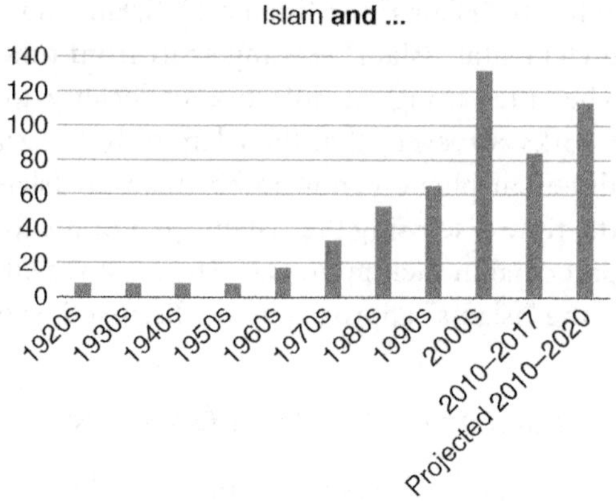

Figure 2.1 "Islam and . . ." in book titles.

Judaism, and so on.[14] Islam was and is for these scholars a given, though its boundaries and content are never clearly defined.

As a method, essentializing scholars for the most part studied the inevitable effects of the Platonic, unchanging, essential Islam on real, contingent, historical variables. Hence, it is "a significant force" whose "strength and interaction . . . has often been overlooked or underestimated."[15] It is a "system."[16] It is an "autonomous political force."[17] It "addresses itself to many aspects of economic development"[18]; it "has given life and form to the Saudi state,"[19] and the Saudis "use Islam to facilitate reforms"[20]; it is "a powerful force that unites the region against outsiders and directs the lives of most Middle Eastern peoples. Together, oil and Islam symbolize life in the Middle East, past and present."[21] "It is indeed the equivalent of the Middle East."[22] "Islam appears as the champion of the people and challenger of established . . ." Yet "Islam has time and again proved too powerful to be shoved away in . . . a simple manner. . . . Islam [was] a fourth 'force' contending for power, along with the army, communists and Sukarno."[23]

[14] C. R. Haines, *Islam as a Missionary Religion*; C. Harrison, *France and Islam in West Africa*; M. G. Peletz, *Adat and Islam*; S. A. Zenkovsky, *Pan-Turkism and Islam*; S. R. Ali, *Oil, Turmoil, and Islam*; D. H. Dwyer, *Law and Islam in the Middle East*.

[15] J. L. Esposito and H. Askari, *Islam and Development*, ix.

[16] J. S. Trimingham, *Islam in Ethiopia*, 42. [17] D. Pipes, *In the Path of God*, 4.

[18] J. L. Esposito and H. Askari, *Islam and Development*, xi. [19] Ibid., xv. [20] Ibid.

[21] S. R. Ali, *Oil, Turmoil, and Islam*, 2.

[22] Ibid.: "The Middle East is of utmost importance to the world for at least two reasons. One is oil, the other Islam. The two may be considered separately or as a unit."

[23] B. B. Hering, *Studies on Indonesian Islam*, 20, 32, 33, 37, 38.

Islam – as an undefined monolith – is frequently responsible for whatever certain authors do not like, and so we constantly see the pathetic fallacy in which "Islam" acts – on persons, on nations, or on events:

> Islam . . . gave direction to governments . . . influenced electoral politics . . . and posed important challenges to Communist regimes. . . . Islam heightened domestic tensions . . . and it defined rebellions against the central government. . . . It fueled international conflicts . . . [and] helped account for the nature of Arab resistance to Israel's existence, the intense involvement of such distant countries as Iraq and Libya, and the meaning of the call in the Palestine National Covenant for the establishment of a "secular and democratic" state in Palestine.[24]

The contingent nature of at least some Islamic practice has not interested these classical essentialists. The assumption that Islam is an entity (always conveniently undefined), indeed, is what gives university professors their professional identity. So, for example, the utter diversity of Islam as understood and practiced in Constantinople, Fathipur Sikri, and Isfahan disappears in summaries such as this:

> [The Ottoman, Safavi, and Mughul empires] each carried over the basic features of Islamic state and society. Islam provided legitimation, political ideology, and law; it informed the principal institutions of government. The head of state . . . was an absolute monarch, ruling his empire as head of its military through a strong central government.[25]

Yet Ṣafavī Shāh Ismāʿīl was legitimated by his claim to be the protégé of God and the Twelfth Imām redivivus; the Ottoman sultan was legitimated by claims to be the designated successor of the Abbasid caliphate and a member of the family's dynastic founder, Osman; the Mughul emperor was legitimated in part by the achievements of the putative forebear of the dynastic family, Timur (Tamerlane). Two of these were Sunnī states, the other was Imāmī Shīʿī; the shock troops of one were members of a heterodox Sufi order, another used local Hindu troops in battle. Two patronized saints, one suppressed their veneration; Ottoman Islam was shaped by Christian heterodoxy, the Mughuls by Hindu orthodoxy. It seems simply false to history to ascribe a timeless quality to phenomena so diverse as Islam in India, Iran, and Asia Minor/Eastern Europe, even within a single century.

One of the scholars quoted above notes, "Islam, like modern civilization, itself is characterized by diversity" and one must not underestimate "the vitality of Islam," but must "realize that the unity of Islam manifests itself in

[24] D. Pipes, *In the Path of God*, 3. [25] J. L. Esposito (ed.), *Islam and Politics*, 24.

different countries and situations in diverse ways."[26] Exactly so. Yet, when in fact this diversity is encountered, it leads to weirdly theological arguments such as that "Indonesia is not a Muslim country" (because *santri* – devout Muslims – are only 30 percent of Indonesian Muslims but *abangan* – nominal Muslims – are the majority) and that "... there was never a real Muslim state in Indonesia."[27] This struggle to "explain" diversity leads to overt theological interventions such as "On the coast of Kenya it is Islam that has become intertwined with traditional customs and beliefs. Abungu ... records that many of the people who are involved in spirit propitiation nevertheless see themselves as Muslims, *although this is a very un-Islamic practice, since Allah must only be approached directly.*"[28] A Western academic anthropologist asserts that these Muslims are wrong when they believe that what they are doing is Islam!

Those who study Islam as essence focus particularly on texts and the class that produces them. Yet, as Bowen says,

> [a]lthough the field of Islamic studies does focus on shared Muslim traditions, it does so in such a way as to render it weakest precisely where anthropology is strongest: in the study of how rituals take on locally specified social and cultural meaning. Islamicists ... are, of course, well aware of the diversity of Muslim religious and cultural lives. But the discourse of Islamic studies—which itself is, explicitly or otherwise, embedded in a framework of comparative religious studies—assumes generalized or essentialized images of Islam that may be set alongside other, similarly essentialized, religious traditions. ... Islamicists base their general accounts of Islam largely on scripture and on a relatively narrow range of Middle Eastern social forms. These forms are assumed to play out, more or less accurately, a single, scripturally embodied Islamic culture.[29]

"Islam" is sometimes the domain in which Muslims live, sometimes the religion minimally defined, sometimes a supposed universal culture that is composed of discrete elements subsumed under "Islam." The view of Islam as universal and all-encompassing allows one to concentrate confidently on constituent aspects of that Islam.

Muslims, of course, also talk about Islam as a single essence, though this kind of language makes sense when they write theologically or make legal stipulations or produce a revivalist pamphlet. Muslims, after all, have to

[26] J. L. Esposito and H. Askari, *Islam and Development*, xix.
[27] B. B. Hering, *Studies on Indonesian Islam.*
[28] D. L. Carmichael et al. (eds.), *Sacred Sites*, 3, Introduction, my italics.
[29] J. R. Bowen, "On Scriptural Essentialism," 656.

decide for themselves what to do or believe, and they may try and persuade others that *this* practice conforms to God's dictates while *that* practice does not. It is worth noting, however, that as Jane Smith demonstrated, this use of "Islam" as a reified authority is something of a historical novelty.[30] A consequence of Muslim essentialism is that "Islam" itself can become the object of faith, replacing the more troublesome and obscure "God."[31] Yet it is worth noting that Muslims themselves, or at least until very recently, have mostly been open to the notion of diverse interpretation of Islam, perhaps following the Prophetic *ḥadīth*: "in diversity there is a mercy." So all but the most intransigent Salafis have accepted that there are four acceptable Sunnī legal schools. Sunnī Muslim legists allowed for the possibility of divergent legal interpretations based on the recognition that most legal knowledge was "suppositional" (*ẓannī*) rather than certain. Sunnīs and Shīʿīs have mostly accepted each other as Muslims, insofar as each denomination is made up of "people who pray in the same direction" (*ahl al-qiblah*). For most of Islam's history there was a wide variety of spiritual practices acceptable to the mass of Muslims. In other words, Muslims themselves have been religiously pluralistic at most times and in most places.

The strange reality is that, as el-Zein has shown, essentializing is a kind of theological discourse whether it is done by Western academics or Muslim apologists. It is a theological enterprise because it always, ultimately, entails separating the *real* from a *false* Islam. As a general rule, for essentialists, whatever is dynamic and different – as we saw in the anthropologist's description of an African Islamic practice above – is not "the real Islam."[32]

"Islam in . . ." – The Regional Manifestation Approach

Perhaps an approach that tries to describe different localities might remedy the essentialism of the essentializing approach described above? One tried-and-true method scholars use we will call the "Islam in . . ." approach, for example, Islam in Ethiopia, Islam in Java, Islam in Egypt.[33] This approach seems to belong particularly to local historians and anxious colonial administrators (see Figure 2.2). The image is of some cargo dropped into a remote location, or brought in piece by piece until

[30] J. Smith, *Study of the Term Islam*.

[31] C. Geertz, *Islam Observed*, chapter 3; W. C. Smith, "The Historical Development in Islam."

[32] A. Rahnema, *Superstition as Ideology in Iranian Politics*. The author distinguishes between "superstitious" Shīʿism and "some other kind."

[33] M. Berger, *Islam in Egypt Today*; J. S. Trimingham, *Islam in Ethiopia*; M. R. Woodward, *Islam in Java*. For this trend, see discussion in R. Launay, *Beyond the Stream*, 4–6.

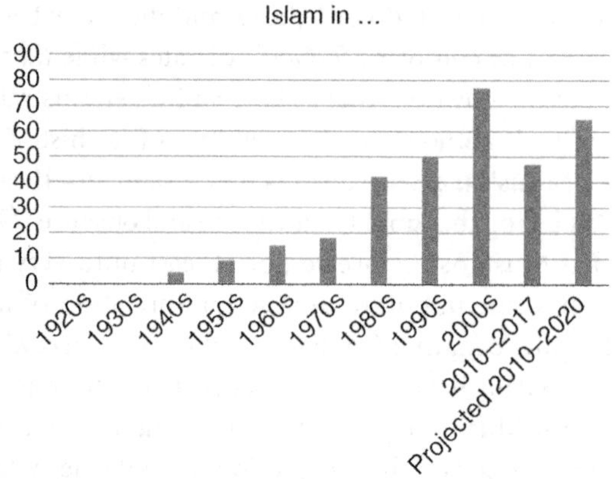

Figure 2.2 "Islam in . . ." in book titles.

it has all arrived and is fully "Islam."[34] In the majority of cases, "Islam in" refers to places in which Islam is one religion among others. This approach to the study of Islam seems to lend itself particularly to the study of "peripheral locales" – Islam in India, Islam in Indonesia, Islam in Africa – peripheral that is, if one ignores the fact that these are the places where the majority of the world's Muslims live, peripheral only to someone who believes that the real, authentic, or essential Islam is found only in the Middle East.

As an example, Francis Robinson, critically reviewing Imtiaz Ahmad's *Ritual and Religion Among Muslims in India*,[35] complained that anthropologists, and "those who feel they have anthropological insights, [emphasize] that Muslim society . . . particularly in India, is much more Indian in its beliefs and practice than has been thought in the past."[36] Robinson says that "[t]he suggestion seems to be that the co-existence of high Islamic and custom-centered religious traditions developed in the past, is established in the present, and is the distinctive, unique, pattern of Indian Islam which will probably persist into the future."[37]

Robinson, the historian, counters that anthropologists suffer from their disciplinary focus on the synchronic view, the snapshot, the provincial. "[A]ll Islamic societies contain a mixture of local pre-Islamic practice and high Islamic culture."[38] We can distill Robinson's argument to the following form.

To understand Islam in India,

[34] For an example of this teleological view of Islam, see discussion in R. Launay, *Beyond the Stream*, 16.

[35] I. Ahmad (ed.), *Ritual and Religion Among Muslims in India.*

[36] F. Robinson, "Islam and Muslim Society in South Asia," 185. [37] Ibid., 187. [38] Ibid., 189.

> one must understand how Islamic history moves. Islam offers a pattern of perfection for man to follow. It is contained in the Quran ... It is also contained in the traditions which relate what the Prophet ... said and did. It is summed up in the law ... [W]e should not be deceived by the fact that in many societies non-Islamic practices had acquired the force of law in Muslim minds. This is often a matter of imperfect knowledge or temporary expedient ... Nevertheless, such is the desire to follow the true path ... that, as knowledge of the law has grown more widespread, its provisions have tended to oust false practice.[39] [I]ncreasing contact with cultures which are thought to represent more fully the pattern of perfection, cultures in which Islamic knowledge is more widely spread and manifest ... often seems to draw [them] towards higher Islamic standards.[40]

The state too plays a role.

> Where some form of the holy law has come to be applied by the modern state, with all its great coercive force and power of social penetration, we may be sure that large groups of Muslims have probably come closer to the pattern of perfection than ever before.[41] [I]f this process is slow, we should also recognize that the combination of many such processes, wherever Islam has gained a footing, from the seventh century to the present, has brought, as Marshal Hodgson declares, perceptible movement towards similar beliefs, similar forms of behavior, and similar religious practice.[42]

In summary,

> [i]n Islamic history, in general, there has been a movement towards, or occasionally away from, the pattern of perfection ... The historian's extended view suggests that there is ... movement between visions of perfect Muslim life and those which ordinary Muslims lead.[43]

It would seem then that the study of Indian Islam, though restricted to a particular locale, is informed by a universal *telos* as Muslims inevitably gravitate toward "higher Islamic status," to "the pattern of perfection," toward better realizing Islam's essence. An Islam that is truly local is not only *imperfect* in the synchronic sense but it is also *preliminary* in the teleological sense. Islam in India will eventually, the implication would seem to be, become indistinguishable from Islam in Egypt or Islam in Indonesia. Of course Francis Robinson is too fine a scholar to believe this, but it is hard to see his argument leading to any other conclusion.

A reader sees this over and over when reading books that take the "Islam in ..." approach: "Islam" is both imperfect but also on an inevitable track to

[39] Ibid., 190–191. [40] Ibid., 192–193. [41] Ibid., 194. [42] Ibid., 196. [43] Ibid., 201.

the Middle Eastern, "orthodox" Islam. There is an important truth here that will be discussed later – that inasmuch as the people of a locale identify themselves as Muslims, their religious life is permeable to influences from elsewhere, particularly when the summons is to elements believed to be shared with other Muslims. Yet the notion that to the extent they are "orthodox" they cease to be "local" is demonstrably a mistake.

The "Islam in . . ." approach became common, even normative, in the 1960s and 1970s and especially after 9/11, and shows no signs of abating.[44] An efflorescence of all forms of essentialism followed the Iranian revolution, particularly in political science, a discipline one of whose goals is a level of abstraction.[45] The result of the "Islam in . . ." approach might *seem* to be more precise, more specific – since the author's focus is geographic – but the "Islam" modified by the adjective of place remains a vague and unexamined spectre hovering over Egypt, Ethiopia, Java, and the like. (In the language of medievals, the essence is mingled with, but remains unmodified by, accidents of time or space.) For the "Islam and . . ." scholars, it is often the program to show that, unlike an imagined *Somewhere Else*, Islam, as it is manifested in *Wherever*, is shaped by local economic, social, gender, and other attitudes. Where there is an Islam uninflected by these local forces is never specified. Surely *every* Islam manifests itself somewhere: Where then is the universal unchanged norm from which the regional variety deviates?

The obvious poverty of this use of the term "Islam" – at least by others than Muslims writing as Muslims – is in theory well known and has been criticized by anthropologists, but also by religionists.[46] Many of the good scholars whose works are cited above as examples would wish to deny that they are essentializing and would repudiate essentialism. Still, using the term "Islam" to mean an identity, a set of practices, an allegiance uninflected by time or place, misleads. It suggests – and many Muslim apologists are comfortable with this assertion – that it is to the name "Islam" itself that

[44] Nine titles with "Islam in" in the 1950s; 15 titles in the 1960s; 18 in the 1970s; 53 in the 1980s; 65 in the 1990s; and 132 in the first ten years of the new millennium.

[45] Searches for "politics," "policy," "democracy," "international," "nation," "nationalism," "social," "society," among academic titles also with the word "Islam" yielded 238 bibliographic "hits." That the religious and the political scientists are the major users of an essentialist notion of Islam would seem to confirm Lévi-Strauss's assertion that much of the work that used to be done by myth is now done by history. C. Lévi-Strauss, *Myth and Meaning*, 42–43. It also reminds one of the quip (by Jacques Barzan?) that "abstraction is to sociology what references are to history."

[46] E.g., from the perspective of religion studies in the classic W. C. Smith, *Meaning and End*; from the perspective of the social sciences, in the brilliant article of Zein, A. H. M. el-Zein, "Beyond Ideology and Theology"; and J. Cesari, *When Islam and Democracy Meet*.

these various peoples have committed themselves. Yet it is absurd to say that Malcolm X and a thirteenth-century *ghāzī*-warrior were converts to the same unchanging entity. The relative absence of Islamic sectarianism, and our own unawareness of the variety and transformations of Islam's history, makes us complacent about Islamic essentialism as we would never be to the assertion that Joel Osteen and Hildegard of Bingen preach the same Christian message.

There is a still more serious problem, however, with this essentialism. Not only does it obscure the various configurations of "Islam" that have appeared in history, but the observer and the Muslim both miss seeing what *really is* common to the *ghāzī* and the African-American convert and activist. They miss understanding the situational attractiveness of various islams and the malleability of its forms, beliefs, and practices. We shall argue below that while there is not an "Islam" that can be pointed to across the ages and continents, there may be Islamic logics, structures, and "cognates" whose arrangement and significance are creatively and appositely constructed in particular locales and times.

The "Islams" Approach – Regional Parochialism

The third approach to the study of Islam – now very much in vogue among culture critics and anthropologists – is the "islams" approach. The "islams" approach suggests implicitly that there are as many "islams" as there are places, or "there are as many Islams as there are situations that sustain it."[47] A characteristic book title of this group is *X-ian Islam* where X is a people or a locality, for example, Persatuan Islam, Moroccan Islam, Indonesian Islam, Indian Islam, and the like.[48] Certainly this more contemporary approach, one often reflecting sophisticated fieldwork and methodology, avoids the obvious

[47] A. Al-Azmeh, *Islams and Modernities*, 1. What Eickelman calls the "islams" approach. Eickelman's discussion of the history of the term. D. F. Eickelman, "Changing Interpretations of Islamic Movements," 19, cites A. H. M. el-Zein, *Sacred Meadows*, 172, though this seems to be a mistake. The term "islams" occurs only in A. H. M. el-Zein, "Beyond Ideology and Theology," first on p. 231. On p. 242 he says: "the greater the reflection on experience, the greater the order in the systems of meaning. . . . The local *islams* involve accepted taken-for-granted experiences, and little directed reflectivity." The term has become something of a nonce word: "One should therefore begin by speaking about Islams rather than Islam." E. Said, "Impossible Histories," 70. See D. M. Varisco, *Islam Obscured*, and G. Marranici, *The Anthropology of Islam*, for good accounts of the history of the anthropology of Islam. And for an unsophisticated appropriation of the "islams" approach, see A. W. Hughs, *Theorizing Islam*. For data on usage of the term, see note 60 below.

[48] P. Mayer, *Tombs and Dark Houses*; J. L. Peacock, *Muslim Puritans*; *Purifying the Faith*; D. F. Eickelman, *Moroccan Islam*; H. M. Federspiel, *Persatuan Islam*; B. B. Hering, *Studies on Indonesian Islam*; K. A. Steenbrink, *Dutch Colonialism and Indonesian Islam*.

pitfalls of essentialism and recognizes the importance of particularity in the study of Islam. Indeed, it often makes a fetish of it, the author reveling in the disparity between this local islam and the very idea of an Essential Islam. "Orientalists" are often the whipping boys, if not the dead horses beaten in such works. Much of this literature appears to deny any universalism to "islam" at all.

In reply to the essentialist claim of Francis Robinson, who argued that Muslims' differences are attributable to "imperfect knowledge" of the "true path," though Muslims are inexorably moving toward "the pattern of perfection," Veena Das and Gail Minault, both distinguished social historians, objected to what they saw as a stifling normativity but also a mistaken teleology in the study of Indian Islam.

Veena Das objected in the fashion characteristic of the "islams" group. "Can we think of Islam as a single unified tradition? . . . Does a single, true Islam exist at all? . . ."[49] She then makes the case that should be familiar by now, that interpretative variation means differences in Islam.[50]

Gail Minault, also responding to Robinson's article, asserts that he sells short the book under review. She is convinced that "these volumes highlight what is Indian about Muslims in India, the degree to which Islam in India is unique, and the degree to which it is a composite of different regional cultures, customary observances, and sectarian loyalties."[51] She believes "[t]he direction and outcome of . . . change, are uncertain."[52] She agrees that

> the growing awareness of the sense of *ummah*, the international community of Islamic believers, as the result of the global movement of Islamization, [is] undeniable. But there is another dimension to the question which [Robinson] does not consider, and that is the fact that Islamic revivalism may create divisions among Muslims as well . . . The divisiveness of Islamic reassertion is a problem that the proponents of reassertion have not adequately addressed.[53] Islamisization, [she also suggests,] may . . . encounter resistance precisely because of the value placed on cultural uniqueness.[54]

If Robinson sees a *telos*, Das and Minault see randomness and disaggregation. If the essentialists value only what Muslims share, anthropologists have tended to study only what the different "islams" do not share. It is saints – *velis sīds*, marabouts and holy women, and exotic rituals (exorcism, healing, agricultural rituals) – that dominate works on the anthropology of Islam,

[49] V. Das, "For a Folk-Theology," 293. [50] Ibid., 295.
[51] G. Minault, "Reflections on Islamic Revivalism," 301. [52] Ibid., 303. [53] Ibid., 304.
[54] Ibid., 303.

or Islam in local contexts. The "anthropologists of Islam" are aware that, in describing the Islam of their villages, there is something that remains when saints, shrines, exorcisms, spirits, and holy women have been presented and analyzed. That something is usually called "Orthodox" Islam, or some vague, and yes essentialist, equivalent. Yet, the practices and beliefs that the Islam of *Wherever* shares with the Muslims of *Somewhere Else* are excluded for the most part from their purview and analysis. This exclusion is usually done by some kind of reference to the Great Tradition/Little Tradition dichotomy. This view of religion is not without its problems and has been criticized in the literature. Yet implicitly or explicitly it remains a staple in the ethnographic description of Muslims.[55]

Unlike our criticism of the "Islam and . . ." and "Islam in . . ." approaches, the critique of the "islams" approach is not that its practitioners do badly what they set out to do; it is rather that the task they set themselves is too limited; they are content to be parochial. In their determination to avoid essentialism and to focus on the local, anthropologists tend to ignore or take for granted important aspects of the religious lives of their subjects. In the process they miss the mark that some of them – at least to judge by their book titles – aim for. (1) They obscure an important fact of religious life when they neglect the Islamic rituals shared with other Muslims. As Munson points out,

> Geertz [the ethnographer of Morocco who is the particular object of his attention] is not alone in neglecting the basic rituals of Islam. Most anthropologists have—as have most students of the political role of Islam in other disciplines.[56]

(2) They have historically missed the opportunity to discern what normative Islamic rituals mean locally. There are a number of fine ethnographies of religious life in Islamicate regions. It is rare that anthropologists turn their attention to "normative Islamic rituals" and when they do, the results are often extremely rich.[57] Surely the point of ethnography is to locate particular meanings – even of practices shared with those of other localities that call themselves "Islamic."[58]

[55] Redfield's argument is found in R. Redfield, *The Little Community, and Peasant Society and Culture*.

[56] H. Munson, *Religion and Power in Morocco*, 116.

[57] D. F. Eickelman, *Moroccan Islam*, on Ramadan; on sacrifice, see J. R. Bowen, "On Scriptural Essentialism"; on *ṣalāh*, see J. R. Bowen, "Salat in Indonesia" and S. Mahmood, "Rehearsed Spontaneity."

[58] Consider the collection of articles in A. Strathern and P. J. Stewart, *Contesting Rituals*. In seven articles, not a single one considers the normative or koiné rituals of Islam!

In any case, the "islams" folk leave those of us interested in "Islam" as uninformed about the full reality of Islam in their villages and towns as the essentialists do about Islam in *Wherever*. In fact, ethnographers also essentialize *an* Islam, just not the *islam* in "my village," or "my neighborhood." When they turn to Islam elsewhere, "orthodox Islam" remains a single entity, though for ethnographers that Orthodox Islam is never theirs, it is the Islam of Others. Yet by neglecting the way "orthodox" rituals, symbols, and ideas are locally understood, they fail to understand a crucial feature of local Islam – the way it connects to Islam outside the village. If one is going to "go local" one might ask, why retain the term "Islam" at all? Why not go all the way, and simply write about, for example, *The Religion of Java*?[59] Without some clear notion of the nature of this "islam" that is indigenous to the locality – one among many, presumably – and how it connects to some other islam, there is no reason to use the term "Islam" at all.

The choices available to students of "Islam," as they have presented themselves so far, have been between a kind of "capital I" Islam, or the belief that to every group there is an islam, which leads quickly to the unhelpful notion that there are as many islams as there are Muslims.[60]

The Study of Islam after 9/11

If the Islamic Revolution of 1979–81 led to a burgeoning of the study of Islam, the terrorist attacks of September 11, 2001, led to a tsunami in the field. Leaving aside the ideologues and unqualified activists who feasted like ticks on the study of Islam, and the hacks who worked Grub Street of Islamophobia,[61] the result of 9/11 was to increase the mass of serious scholars who studied Islam, and to give Islamic studies an urgency it had not had before. Because Euro-America experienced Islamic terrorism, and as Euro-America responded with the invasions of Afghanistan and Iraq (and with often draconian and indiscriminate measures against Euro-American

59 C. Geertz, *Religion of Java*; for a discussion of the "religion of Y" approach from a different perspective, see R. Launay, *Beyond the Stream*, Introduction.

60 The use of "Islams" in the plural is relatively recent. A. Tayob, "Dialectical Theology in the Search for Modern Islam," 161–162, is the only discussion of the term's history, aside from the Eickelman mention cited above (note 47). Checking both English and French, it appears the first use of "islams" in titles is in the 1980s with two mentions. By the 2000s there are nine uses of the term, and for 2010–2020 there are a projected eleven mentions. The term is used less and less ethnographically and more and more as a gesture toward the pluralism of Islam without having to actually engage with the problem, it seems to me.

61 Robert Spencer and Daniel Pipes being the most notorious.

Muslims and Muslim organizations), 9/11 altered the reflexivity of Islamicists.

Since 9/11 the study of Islam has been shaped on the margins by cultural converts or actual converts repudiating their "defective" heritage,[62] and more centrally by Muslims who have become part of the Euro-American academic enterprise – some from outside the boundaries of Euro-America, others the children of emigrants or converts.[63] It is too early fully to assess work written or published in the shadow of 9/11 but some tendencies are clear.

This new climate immediately revitalized the essentialist approach to Islam, this time critical in an often frank and self-aware way. This new essentialism drew strength in part from the Islamic activists' and terrorists' claim that they were acting in the name of Islam, doing what Islam required, or reclaiming Muslim lands for Islam. The terrorists' converse equivalents, the essentialists, tried to figure out the underlying cause of Islamdom's social failures, particularly in the Arab world – "what went wrong" – and the answer proposed was "Islam."[64] Without a doubt Bernard Lewis was the most prominent spokesman for the new essentialism, and remains a prominent target for those who oppose it. Lewis was a figure whose stage was not merely the academy, but the odeons of Washington DC and Whitehall. The neo-conservatives of the G. W. Bush administration, many reabsorbed into the Trump administration, seemed to view the world through lenses he had ground over the previous thirty years in works where he coined the phrase "clash of civilizations," and asked repeatedly "what went wrong." The response was always "Islam."[65]

[62] Among the best known, "Ibn Warraq [pseud.]," Ayaan Hirsi Ali, and in Evangelical circles, the Caner brothers.

[63] Inter alia, Kecia Ali, Ibrahim Moosa, Omid Safi.

[64] Not just essentialism, but the reductive explanation for whatever flaws one finds in Islamdom, and their attribution to "Islam," draws on a long discourse dating back to the imperial movements of France and Britain and articulated by people like Renan. The argument has been that Islam retards society, in Renan's case, due to the limits of "the Semitic mind," or according to others, due to the rigidity of Islamic law, the failure to continue the early engagement with Greek philosophy, and so on. For an excellent study that looks at early Muslim responses to Renan and his ilk in the nineteenth century and its ramifications in contemporary Islamism, see I. F. Gesink, "Chaos on Earth." There are indeed ethnic Muslims who affirm that for things to "go right," in all cases it is Islam that must be changed or limited or eliminated. This is not just the position of the overt polemicists like Hirsi, or Ibn Warraq, but also secularist critics of Islamism, such as Timur Kuran. See T. Kuran, *The Long Divergence*.

[65] Despite the whole thrust of his argument, in both the magazine article and the book, Lewis inserts a caveat that the cause of "Islam's" decline, couldn't be "Islam," because "... to blame Islam as such is usually hazardous and not often attempted. Nor is it very plausible. For most of the Middle Ages it was neither the older cultures of the Orient nor the newer cultures of the

But what is this "Islam" that has "gone wrong"? For Lewis, like the early twentieth-century essentialists, Islam seems to be the sum total of ideas, beliefs, and cultural practices within Islamdom; it is everything Muslims do. Yet at the same time, perplexingly, it is an agent that shapes the history and culture of Muslims.[66] It has armies[67] and merchants.[68] Subtle, complex, and multisided debates among Muslim scholars are reduced to "the jurists said,"[69] as if there were no variety among judicial opinions, no disagreements among scholars, and as if no one ever ignored the opinions of Islam's specialists. And of course "Islam" means the Middle East. The case of Indian Islam, with its complex history of interaction with both Europeans and non-Muslim Indians, has no place in Lewis's account of "Islam." The medieval terms such as "infidel" and "unbeliever" are used to represent Muslim views of non-Muslims, but Europeans regarding Muslims use contemporary terms such as Egyptian, Turk, Persian, or Muslim rather than heretic, renegade, and pagan.[70]

What is most striking is the exoticization of Islamdom: on every page of Lewis's book he includes a quote or example from some European traveler remarking on the backwardness of Muslims who don't speak Italian, don't have watches, or brass bands, or some other indispensable feature of civilization. Lewis's understanding of cultural change is unaffected by the large and complex body of literature – even within Islamic studies – on modernization and cultural transformation. In every paragraph, Islam and the Muslim is unequivocally the Other, the different, and so on. This approach, famously derided by Edward Said as "Orientalism," has already been appropriately eviscerated, and what *scholarly* reviews there are of *What Went Wrong* were appropriately critical.[71]

West that were the major centers of civilization and progress but the world of Islam." B. Lewis, "What Went Wrong?," 156. However, he implies, that was then; this is now.

66 "Islam in contrast created a world civilization, polyethnic, multiracial, international, one might even say intercontinental." B. Lewis, *What Went Wrong?*, 6. Perhaps "Islam" is a people? See B. Lewis and B. E. Churchill, *Islam: The Religion and the People*.

67 "Islam represented the greatest military power on earth." B. Lewis, *What Went Wrong?*, 6.

68 Islam "trad[ed] in a wide range of commodities through a far-flung network of commerce and communications in Asia, Europe, and Africa; importing slaves and gold from Africa, slaves and wool from Europe, and exchanging a variety of foodstuffs, materials, and manufactures with the civilized countries of Asia." Ibid.

69 E.g., ibid., 36, 37, and *passim*.

70 That this is a contemporary re-presentation of an older tradition seems confirmed by the fact that not only are the sources overwhelmingly Turkey-centric, but there are very few academic sources cited that date from after 1975 or so.

71 See, e.g., F. Robinson, "What Went Wrong? (Book Review)."

What is most important for us is that Islam in the world is becoming less and less the Other, and more and more just "us"; "we" in the West are more intimately involved with Muslims both elsewhere and at home than ever before. Yet the essentialist view of "Islam" as an indeterminate entity that acts, reacts, inherits, and retards still obscures the variety of "Islam" at all times and in all places. Paradoxically, essentialism conceals the actual way in which a common identity has been constructed and shared by Muslims.

It might be objected that the essentialism of Lewis and other journalistic treatments of Muslims is passé, and no longer a part of the scholarly study of Islam. A much better, though no doubt less influential, book[72] nonetheless reminds us that essentialism still lives in the more respectable neighborhoods of the academy. Lawrence Rosen, a distinguished anthropologist, has written a work in which he presents himself as someone "who is sincere in [his desire to understand] something about Islamic cultures ..."[73] Rosen derides the "splitters" who refuse to recognize commonalities among subjects, and so he breaks with the ethnographic parochialism characteristic of contemporary anthropologists. Rosen has worked in Morocco; but his observations purport to apply to all Arabs. His elegantly written book is also essentialist, but here the essentialism is the essentialism of mono-causality and a-temporality. Whatever the issue – a grossly inconsiderate neighbor of Arab (we assume) origin, the Arab world's "economic, political, and scientific" backwardness, or suicide bombing – it is ultimately explained not by reference to the sort of explanations we would use to account for the backwardness of Mississippi, or Queens, or Bulgaria (lack of education, poverty, control by a Great Power, absence of legitimate democratic structures) but by referring to a special set of cultural features peculiar to Arabs.[74]

For example, in the Arab world, we are told, "the 'self' was never rendered divisible. In addition, doubt about fundamentals has always been equated with unbelief and premonitory chaos."[75] That this is primordially so is proven by the citations which are exclusively to sources about the ancient past: a work on classical madrasas, one on "lies in medieval Islam," a book on medieval Muslim philosophy, and an

[72] Lewis's book, alas, spent roughly nineteen weeks on *The New York Times* Best Sellers list. It debuted on January 27, 2002, and remained there through May 15, 2003. That means it was the primary text on "Islam" read by Americans as they tried to make sense of 9/11 and as the administration invaded Afghanistan and began to turn to Iraq. By the time the United States invaded Iraq, Lewis had produced another bestseller, *The Crisis of Islam*.

[73] L. Rosen, *Varieties of Muslim Experience*, 1.

[74] The frequency with which Rosen footnotes Islamic texts or studies of them makes it clear that all Arabs are Muslims, even if, unimportantly, not all Muslims are Arabs.

[75] L. Rosen, *Varieties of Muslim Experience*, 23–24.

encyclopedia article on a second–fifth Islamic century theological school, and further to pre-Islamic wine poetry, a book of games in classical Islamic sources, and to some confirmatory contemporary "Islamic anthropology," as well, of course, to the Qur'ān. Surely it would be a surprise if someone seeking to understand criminals in Mississippi or Naples referred to the New Testament, Boethius' *Consolation of Philosophy*, and works on medieval *chansons*. Nor would lessons learned from the Algarve be indiscriminately applied to "Europe."

In Rosen's *Varieties*, Islam is defined as simply the opposite of the West (which is Judaism and Christianity):

> The contrast to the West, of course, could not be sharper. Where Judaism underscores the distinctive components of the self by separating the qualities of God from those of humans except through metaphorical linkages, and Christianity underscores the inevitable separation of aspects of the self by their unique unification in Christ alone, Islam offers unity as both the given of this world and its perpetuation into eternity. Each moment, in the dominant philosophy of Islam, incorporates the whole creation of the world, rather than, as the losing philosophers of the medieval period held, a fractionated set of creations that might seem to undermine the unity that suffuses every level from the self to the community of believers to Allah himself.[76]

It is hard to know where to start with the farrago of imprecision except to exclaim "shoemaker stick to your last!" But aside from the utterly garbled account of quite arcane Muslim metaphysics (Rosen presumably refers to the occasionalism of the Ash'arī school of theology) one is struck by the ease with which Rosen slides from the West as a class to Islam as its Other. What of Muslims in the West? What of Christian Occasionalists like Malebranche? But in addition, to explain Arabs' understanding of the self by reference to truly obscure medieval metaphysics is akin to accounting for Americans' love of fast food by reference to debates over transubstantiation. This sort of argument would be ridiculous in any context, but it is not ridiculous in one that essentializes an Arab/Muslim *geist* across the ages, throughout diverse regions. Worse, such an argument explains Muslims utterly apart from other more down-to-earth factors that we ordinarily invoke when accounting for the history and society of fellow human beings. This is Muslims as "ontologically other," to use Said's phrase.

[76] Ibid., 25.

Discursivists

It is fair to say that academic essentialists deploy their arguments for the most part on the right of the political spectrum. And it is fair to say that they represent an approach that has a long academic history. The other major post-9/11 methodological movement would surely locate itself on the political left,[77] and though it too has a history, most of its scholarly output dates from the new millennium.

The most influential voice of the discursivists, really the founder of this approach to Islamic studies, is Talal Asad. The founding document of discursivism is Asad's brilliant 1986 piece, "The Idea of an Anthropology of Islam," which is for the most part a critique of the sociologist/anthropologist Ernst Gellner. (Both earlier and later Asad trained his guns on another anthropologist of Islamdom, Clifford Geertz.) This is not the place for an extensive discussion of discursivism, but here we can say that it has two main targets: essentialism (as we've described it above) and "liberal-humanism," by which Asad and his epigones mean particularly the notion that "religions" are entities apart from politics, or other human domains, that "religion" is a real object, as opposed to a construct of liberal modernity itself. Following W. C. Smith, in this regard, Asad and his followers recognize that the invention of "religion" in the seventeenth and eighteenth centuries is part of a distinctly European cultural shift to exclude the religious from participation in the domain of (particularly state) power. So, part of the discursivist enterprise is to "deconstruct" or "expose" the notion that is "natural," or essential to development, to separate religion and politics. All of this seems sensible assertion, and perhaps even indisputable.

However, what is particularly to the point for us here is that the object we call "Islam" is defined by Asad (and his followers) as "a discursive tradition that connects variously with the formation of moral selves, the manipulation of populations (or resistance to it) and the production of appropriate knowledges."[78] This definition is manifestly a criticism of the essentialists because Asad's understanding of discourse assumes a dynamism incompatible with essentialism.[79] A discourse is something taught authoritatively by various agents – *ʿulamāʾ*, Sufi shaykhs, even parents – and when that teaching is enforced through an alliance of one sort or another with power, the result is "orthodoxy."[80]

[77] Though I am not entirely convinced that that is unambiguously where they should be placed.

[78] T. Asad, *Anthropology of Islam*, 7. [79] Ibid., 16.

[80] Ibid., 1. The notion of "orthodoxy" as an Islamic category is interrogated in, inter alia, M. B. Wilson, "The Failure of Nomenclature," and sources cited there.

But Asad also critiques the "islams" advocates. Since "a tradition should not be regarded as essentially homogenous ... heterogeneity in traditional practices is not necessarily an indicator of the absence of *an* Islamic tradition."[81] Note that Asad uses the singular here and elsewhere, because in his view there are boundaries to the Islamic tradition. For Asad and the Asadians, Islam is

> a discursive tradition that includes and relates itself to the founding texts of the Qur'ān and Hadith. Islam is neither a distinctive social structure, nor a heterogeneous collective of beliefs, artifacts, actors, and morals. It is a tradition.[82] [For] those who have been taught to regard essentialism as the gravest of intellectual sins, it is necessary to explain that certain things are *essential* to that project... some of its constitutive elements are essential to its historical identity and some are not.[83]

Indeed, Asad is surprisingly "orthodox" himself in his definition of what is really Islam, and it turns out to be the Islam of "jurists," "premodern Islamic jurists," "most Muslim jurists," "Muslim scholars," and the like.[84] Perhaps it is a reflex of the discursivists' quasi-Foucauldian focus on power that, rather than practice, Asad and his followers attend overwhelmingly to discourse, which privileges the jurists, the revivalists (*dāʿiyāt* in the lamented Saba Mahmood's first monograph[85]), or the preachers (*khuṭabāʾ* in Hirschkind[86]) and others of the Muslim "chattering classes." Since authority is what concerns them, the discursivists study authorities and their texts (written and oral). This seems perfectly reasonable, but from our point of view it has at least two problematic aspects.

The first we have already pointed to. The authoritative texts are a reasonable topic of study, but surely an account of Islam or Muslims that leaves out or marginalizes the understandings and practices of *hoi polloi* is incomplete. Discursivist anthropology recognizes that the discursive tradition is appropriated in different ways, but that appropriation is always ascribed to the authoritative figures, rather than to the laity (*ʿawāmm*), who, in the Asadian view, are being lectured to, written about, preached to. Sometimes Mahmood, for instance, notes the variation between the doctrine prescribed by an authoritative figure and the reaction of a consumer of that prescription, but if space allotted is a measure of the importance of the

[81] T. Asad, *Anthropology of Islam*, 16, my italics. [82] Ibid., 14.

[83] T. Asad, *Genealogies of Religion*, 18. A very good account of Asad's approach, and a defense by a disciple, is found in O. Anjum, "Islam as a Discursive Tradition."

[84] T. Asad, *On Suicide Bombing*, 28. [85] S. Mahmood, *Politics of Piety*.

[86] C. Hirschkind, *Ethical Soundscape*.

subject, it is the authorities who are by far the most important figures in these ethnographies.[87]

It is also the case that the features of what we ordinarily call Islam are not described in any larger context. This means, for instance, that Arabic is privileged as a domain of Islam (even Mahmood, a Pakistani, does her ethnography in Egypt), but also that what gets lost is that among Muslims in different localities, "Islam" itself is a topic and source of the discursive tradition as much as Qur'ān and *Ḥadīth*. Indeed, it can be argued, as we did above, that for some Muslims Islam itself is the object of veneration, rather than God.[88] This shift in focus seems not to be grasped by the discursivists who also, despite Asad's critique of parochialists, remain rooted in Arabic texts and, as far as I can see, in Arabic-speaking countries. These Arabs are at most a fifth of the world's Muslims (if we count the populations of non-Arabic speaking Berbers, Kurds, and so on, with the Arabs). Why (unless one is a crypto-Arab nationalist) should the discourse of Arabs define Islam?

What interests me, as a historian of religion, is not just the discourse of (and about) Islam, but the set of practices and allegiances that help to construct the "object" we call "Islam," and in particular the structural relations among those elements that are also constitutive. For a number of reasons, I don't think we should restrict our inventory of Islamic practices and discourses to those traditionally recognized by ethnographers and colonial officials as authoritative. The variability of the discourses that are revered or taken for granted across Islamdom and throughout Islamic history, and the staggering variety of figures who have been taken to be authorities, preclude such a ruthless pruning of religious data.

No one can deny that even the *ʿulamāʾ* are imbedded in the culture of their time and place, and those particularities are interesting. Equally interesting, as we shall see, is the aspiration of at least some *ʿulamāʾ* to present themselves as dis-embedded from the inauthenticities of their time and place and disembodied from quotidian interests. In addition, with its focus on the Islamic chattering class, the mass of Muslims loses its agency. Yet in fact, most Muslims choose whom to obey, they elect views of Islam that suit them, and they construct a *bricolage* Islam from the Islamic and other notions and practices they find around them – like all the religious, Muslims have always been creators and also consumers of their religion, not blank slates on which their religious lives have been written by others.

A number of new approaches to the study of Islam have appeared, as the fruits sown by Hodgson have matured, and as 9/11 has given a new urgency to

[87] S. Mahmood, *Politics of Piety*, 106–113. [88] See notes 30 and 31 above.

Islamic studies. Works by (or edited by) Bulliet, Feener, Marranici, Lincoln, Varisco, among many others, have begun to incline the field of Islamic studies to stop taking its object of study for granted, and to see it as both universal and particular.[89] Really, for most scholars, it is scarcely news that Islam in Egypt is different from Islam in India. But, once we are committed to trying to think about Islam wherever it is found, once we are committed to look at the full range of practices ascribed by Muslims to Islam, once we are determined to include all Muslims' religiosity in our account of Islam, then what?

The purpose of this book is to make explicit what most students of Islam know: that Islam is more various than references to Arabs or *ʿulamāʾ* allow, that all Muslims create Islam, and that Islam in the world is fecund and diverse; at the same time Muslims believe the term "Islam" to be a profoundly meaningful one, and that the term "Muslim" has an actual referent.

Lived and Colloquial Islam

As academic disciplines merge and cross-fertilize, the study of the past, called history, and the study of contemporary peoples, called anthropology, have come increasingly to inform each other. One outcome is that the study of religion, both of the past and of the present, has been enriched by attending to the religious lives of ordinary members of the faithful. The study of the history of ordinary persons' religion is beginning to alter our understanding not only of religion, but of how to study religion. One influential work has referred to this new field as "Lived Religion."[90]

Lived Religion is an approach that studies the religiosity of those who don't write books, though it studies also the religiosity of clerics that isn't expressed in their books. It looks at what the clergy share with the laity, rather than assuming that the laity will be imperfect or unrealized versions of the clergy. It focuses also on day-to-day religion and not just the liturgical moment – the cosmology of the ordinary and not just scriptural cosmology, for instance. The concept of Lived Religion has been developed by those who

[89] R. W. Bulliet, *View from the Edge*; *Islamo-Christian Civilization*; R. M. Feener, *Islam in World Cultures*; B. Lincoln, *Holy Terrors*; G. Marranici, *The Anthropology of Islam*; D. M. Varisco, *Islam Obscured*; *Reading Orientalism*.

[90] D. D. Hall (ed.), *Lived Religion*. The editor offers no single definition of "Lived Religion," but in his introduction he offers a number of observations on the targets of "lived religion" research. See the Introduction, vii–xii. "Lived Religion" is a *calque* from the French "*religion véçue*" (from "*vivre*"). Robert Orsi's works – particularly R. A. Orsi, *The Madonna of 115th Street*; *Gods of the City*; *Between Heaven and Earth* – are also associated with this term.

study Christianity, but it proves useful too for the study of Islam. The study of Lived Religion, one might say, is the study of *colloquial* religion. Lived Religion is to theology what ordinary speech is to books of normative English grammar. Colloquial speech is what everyone uses when not in a situation that requires particular linguistic care; colloquial speech is always locally inflected. So too, Lived Islam is always locally constructed and so, locally inflected. What we mean here by Lived Islam, then, is the Islam of ordinary Muslims, and of the *ʿulamāʾ* "when they are at home." "Lived Islam" refers not so much to the Islam we see in books by Muslim scholars telling Muslims how to be Muslims (though, as we shall see, those too have a place in our study) as to what we learn of Islam when we observe Muslims, converse with them, live with them, and so on, whether in Iraq or North Carolina, whether among illiterate tribal folk or Azharī scholars. This includes what we *would have* seen in previous times as well, since Lived Islam exists not just now but describes the *actual* or *lived* situation of Muslims at any time, in any place.

It is perfectly reasonable for Islamicists to study history, or literature, or gender, but surely one of their goals ought to be to understand the reality of the object of their study – Islam. An ideal Islam, or a partial Islam, cannot substitute for the *Lived* Islam, which is distinct from an Islam of texts, or Islam as it ought to be, or Islam in the mind of God. The task of this book is to suggest an alternative way of thinking about "lived" Islam – an alternative particularly to the approaches we have just discussed.

It is a useful beginning point to grasp that every Muslim lives somewhere, and the place where he or she lives shapes and constrains his or her practice of Islam.[91] There are other constraints as well – gender being among the most significant of them – but "place" seems a particularly important predictor of the range of beliefs and actions that constitute a Lived Islam.[92] For Islamicists – whether in anthropology, political science, religion, or sociology – there can be no denying the reality of regional differences.

[91] J. R. Bowen, *Muslims Through Discourse*, 3: "I soon learned, however, that Gayo [Sumatrans] . . . had developed much of their 'local' knowledge about the world by elaborating, transforming, and adapting elements from broader Muslim traditions." "Place" refers of course not just to physical location in geographical space but to other factors such as sex, class, gender, education, and other determinants of subjectivities and life-worlds.

[92] A woman's Lived Islam varies as greatly from locality to locality as that of any other group and in ways more or less consonant with the local Islam of other groups in that locality. In our account we focus on locality and give gender short shrift. This is, in part, because the work on premodern gendered Islam has not been done (and will be very difficult to do, though Marion Katz among others is trying). Given these limitations, to give gender its proper place would require more speculative construction of premodern women's Islam than scholarship to date would support.

Anyone who has traveled in Islamdom, or even in different neighborhoods in a given region, will know that Lived Islam varies from place to place. The Qur᾽ān is important wherever one goes, but the chapter *Yā Sīn* has a talismanic prominence in Turkish Islam I seldom observed in contemporary Egypt. When one visits some place in Islamdom, one doesn't know, for instance, what percentage of Muslims goes to mosque for afternoon prayer. Do women attend mosque at all on Fridays? Are Qur᾽ān classes something one is more likely to attend as a child or as an adult? The answer to these questions differs from place to place, and surely, from time to time. *Each difference is a variety of Islam. Yet each local variety is, for those who reside there, nothing other than their Lived Islam, or for short, their "Islam."* So Islam is always locally inflected, locally appropriated, and this, of course, is how it is possible to have people both Indonesian and Muslim, and North American and Muslim. We will discuss below how even the most central practices of Muslims vary in the way they are appropriated, and these different "uptakes" require the assertion that Lived Islam is always a vernacular or colloquial Islam.[93] Once this fact is recognized, much of the confusion we identified above goes away.

It may be useful to look across the academy to find a model for the study of phenomena both local and widespread. If Lived Islam is like colloquial speech, perhaps it is to variations in speech – to Sociolinguistics – that we should look for models of how to study something like Islam. More than other social scientists, sociolinguists have had to think about identity and difference, regional variation and central prescriptivism, as well as change and stasis. It seems a useful heuristic to imagine Islamic practice and belief as a kind of language spread across most of the world. Muslims, wherever they are, "speak Islam," and what divides and unifies Muslims in their religious life seems analogous to what separates and joins speakers of a language as widely spread as English or Spanish.

To begin, then, I will suggest that regional varieties of Islam be understood as colloquials, and it must be grasped from the start that everyone *speaks* some kind of colloquial, no matter their education or class. It is not impossible, theoretically, to speak "standard" English, but no one does.[94] And even

[93] We will use these terms – vernacular and colloquial – both in the sense of colloquial language (the everyday, the native or indigenous) and in the sense of vernacular architecture, pertaining to the domestic or the functional, rather than to the monumental. Colloquial Islam is the everyday Islam of ordinary Muslims – in Islamic scholarly terms, the Islam of the *ʿawāmm* rather than of the *khawāṣṣ*.

[94] Perhaps here is the place to acknowledge that my first real knowledge of sociolinguistics, and my appreciation of its power to describe, came from Anne Royal. In the short time we were together, her deep commitment to the discipline and the clarity of her thought impressed me

if someone spoke only normatively, she would still have to make choices in vocabulary. She drinks a milkshake but, in Boston, a "frappe"; she puts a suitcase in the "boot" in Britain, but in the "trunk" in the US; she rides in a "lift" or an "elevator," depending on where she ascends. No one is exempted from speaking a regional form of the language, because there is no alternative. Yet whether I ride a lift or an elevator, I speak about it in a language both my Texan relatives and my Edinburgh friends recognize (some reluctantly) as English.

Islam too is regionally shaped, first for the simple reason that Muslims live in some particular place, and their lives, including their religious lives, are shaped by the concerns of the moment – which will naturally differ in place and time from other Muslims. One can imagine, as a simple example, that Muslims in a dry climate – southern Morocco, say – are more familiar with *istisqā'* (the canonically determined prayer for rain) than Muslims in the rain forests of Malaysia.[95] The prayer – its form and content stipulated in every major book of normative Islamic practice – may or may not be part of the *Lived* Islam of Muslims who are never in need of rain. (There is no prayer for drought.)

It is not just the unlettered or "laity" whose Islam is shaped by where they live. Even a Muslim scholar (*'ālim*) lives a life constrained and conditioned by locality. Surely it makes a difference whether his madrasa is an arm of the state – as in Egypt – or of political parties – as in Pakistan. The power and status of an *'ālim* surely differs between India – a non-denominational state – and Iran, where some *'ulamā'* have great power in the state system. Similarly, the epitome of textual Islam, the *muftī*, had quite different roles in Ottoman Turkey and in Zaydī Yemen.[96]

Lived Islam, then, is always *colloquial* Islam because it is the "native," "domestic," Islam that people live, just as it is always the local colloquial that they speak. Everyone lives somewhere, and where they live shapes their linguistic norms and expressions; so too it shapes their religious norms and expressions. This is why there is much to be learned from books about *Moroccan Islam* or *Islam in Ethiopia*. What must be understood is that the Islam of *Wherever* is not unique because

with an appreciation of her field. There is no doubt that when I tried to think about variety and unity, my instinctive move toward linguistics was a result of her abiding influence.

95 Even this canonical feature is used creatively in Africa, where it is invoked not only for rain, but to prevent or provide relief from epidemics. See P. J. Ryan, "*Imale*: Yoruba Participation in the Muslim Tradition," 165.

96 Compare H. Gerber, *State, Society, and Law in Islam*, chapter 3, to B. Messick, "The Mufti, the Text and the World."

it is Wherever-ian, but that all local islams are similarly unique in their localism.

Linguists have had to understand how varieties of English (or other widespread languages) both vary and cohere throughout their zones of use, how regionalisms both are distinct and remain part of English. We are going to do the same with Islam and suggest that Lived Islam has three aspects that we do well to recognize: the Dialect (features unique to a particular place, whether geographical, temporal, or otherwise locative), the Koiné (a form of the language shared among different kinds of speakers), and the Cosmopolitan or Standard (the equivalent of the English of grammar books). Each can be found within a given colloquial Islam, but all three are always present and in ways more significant than scholars have usually recognized.

3

Dialect Islam

The Islam of Differences

Introduction

Everyone knows that English differs from place to place. Not everyone recognizes that religion does too. In linguistics, the general term for these differences is *dialect.* In the UK, the committee *are* against a proposal; in the US, the committee *is* against it (grammar difference). In Canada, one goes *aboot* one's business; in the US, one goes *abowt* it (phonological or pronunciation variant). One can take a *lift* or an *elevator* and still get to the tenth floor. You can drink a *frappe* or a *milkshake* and still be refreshed (lexical or vocabulary difference). Religions too differ according to their location, and this is as true of Islam as it is of, say, Hinduism.

Linguistic variations mark someone's location – in terms of physical location (Canada, the US, New England, Texas) – but also in terms of factors like class and education (*isn't/ain't*), or "linguistic heritage" (*he cold, he be cold/he is cold*). Some of the differences, depending on how much one has traveled, can be mutually intelligible (most Americans and British would understand the Canadian *aboot*). Some differences are mutually unintelligible (*jimmies* (chocolate sprinkles) in Boston; *cullen skink* (smoked haddock soup) in Edinburgh).

In some cases differences will line up with political boundaries (English on one side of the Channel, French on the other). In other cases, within a country, a dialect or language feature shades off and is found by degrees less often as one moves through space or class, until it disappears. In some parts of the UK one says "give me it"; in other parts "give it me"; in still other parts, "give it to me." Similarly in the Northern Plains states of the US for refreshment you'll order a bottle of "pop"; in the Southeast and Texas you'll order a "coke" which refers to all sorts of carbonated drinks, not just Coca-Cola. And in New England and California, you'll ask the waiter for a "soda." Again, there are regions that are solidly "soda," but that usage shades to regions where one can choose "soda" or "pop," as in mid-Pennsylvania. These differences in regional usage can be plotted onto a map.[1]

In reality, there is no sharp line between "give it me" and "give it to me," no sign on the road saying "welcome to 'soda-land.'" Rather, in a certain area "give it to me" is the only natural way to demand a thing, then as one moves to the boundary of the linguistic custom "give it to me" is a free choice with "give it me"; beyond that, "give it me" becomes an idiosyncrasy and finally it is unheard and, when encountered, seems "wrong." Sociolinguists use the term "isogloss" to refer to the boundary line separating one "linguistic landscape" or "dialect landscape," where some particular feature predominates, from a region that favors alternatives. New England is a linguistic landscape where we find the word "jimmies" used to refer to sweet bits of candy sprinkled over ice cream. New England is also a linguistic region that uses "wicked" as an emphatic adverb, as in "wicked good." Those variations, and hundreds of others, comprise the dialect of New England (within which, of course, there are features peculiar to Mainers, distinctive vocabulary choices found in Vermont, or phonological features peculiar to New Hampshire).

Religions too vary by region. Historians of religion, influenced by doctrinal commitments, have tended to essentialize religion and to describe some essential feature or belief as "real" or "core" or "orthodox" or "the Great Tradition," of Islam, for instance, wherever the religion is found. In this scheme, Islam has variants that are called "popular" or "marginal" or "local" or "heterodox," "the Little Tradition." But finding the *essence* of Islam (or any other religious tradition) is no more possible than finding the "essence of English" would be. It is doubtful if there is any single feature – lexicographical, grammatical, morphological – that is found among every single English speaker. Similarly there is or has been some group of Muslims somewhere or at some time that does not know, or does not care to practice, some "essential" feature of Islam, whether fasting, praying, or giving children "Muslim" names. And of course in local versions of Islam there are features as odd to other Muslims as "cullen skink" to a Texan or "dirty rice" to an English speaker in Singapore. In this chapter we are going to focus on the features of Lived Islam that can be identified as Dialect landscapes, that is, those beliefs or practices of Islam that are found in one place but not in another.

Obviously, when a Turk or an Arab or an English Muslim makes a private prayer of petition – *duʿāʾ* in Islam's canonical language – it will generally be

[1] As at http://popvssoda.com. I owe this reference to Megan Clark.

muttered in Arabic among Arabs, in Turkish among Turks, in English among Americans, and so on. While obvious, such differences in language are not necessarily trivial. The word *duʿāʾ* itself is connected to lots of ordinary words for an Arab, and so its field of meaning draws from those other usages: "a request, to please, a good wish, an imprecation, a curse" are all possible meanings of *duʿāʾ*. But in addition, summoning, calling, and inviting, but also appointing, alleging, being pretentious, and so on (also meanings of the root), may float about somewhere as an Arab Muslim imagines him- or herself making a "prayer of petition," that is, asking God for something in Arabic. However, the equivalent in Turkish, *dua*, does not connect to other Turkish concepts; it is a technical term, a term used only for a sacral activity, as arcane as *Introit* or *Kyrie*. In my experience American Muslims differ from Turks and Arabs; they use the standard English word "pray"; to use *duʿāʾ* (as some do) is a prestige-marker, or a pretension.

There are other more substantial instances of difference, however, and it is some of these that have provoked the writing of this book. The political boundary between Iran and Turkey (with some exceptions) defines the Islamic landscape of Sunnī Islam (Turkey) and Imāmī Shīʿī Islam (Iran). There are certainly Alevis in Turkey, who are devoted to the Twelve Imāms and whose religiosity is Shīʿah-ish – in Turkey, and most Turks esteem the founding figures of Shīʿism – ʿAlī, al-Ḥasan, and al-Ḥusayn. Nonetheless, the denomination of Twelver, or Imāmī, Shīʿism is located firmly in Iran and not in Turkey. Consequently, the visual piety – what is written on the back windows and bumpers of cars, as well as what is written on mosques, what is on television and radio; and the temporal piety – the holidays for instance; the auditory piety – the homiletic style of preachers – all this changes abruptly as a bus crosses from Iran to Turkey. It is visibly, audibly, and palpably a different Islam from Iran to Turkey, despite there being in both places a call to prayer, mosques and minarets, and Friday prayers. These kinds of changes are not denominational only – between Shīʿī and Sunnī – they are perceptible between Eastern and Western Turkey, between Iran and Iraq, not to mention between India and Morocco. To move between Islamic localities can feel as different as it must have felt to go from Germany to Italy, when religion still mattered to Europeans.

Dialect Islam

Difference among Muslims and among "islams" is not just a matter of denominational and doctrinal difference. In every Islamic locality there are differences that other Muslims, from elsewhere, would find deviant or abhorrent, or just plain odd. Here we are in the domain of the traditional anthropologist when he or she studies Islamdom. These "dialect practices" of Islam have constituted the focus of most anthropologies of Islam.[2] These local forms of Islam used to elicit an anthropologist's preface conceding that these practices are not "real" Islam, or "orthodox Islam," or that "it is the Islam of the ignorant" or the "rural Islam," or "it's cultural Islam," or "a cultural survival," just as "I'm fixin' to go" might elicit the comment "that's not (proper) English." However, "fixin' to" is a productive and common feature of Texan English, just as these Islamic dialect features are a productive and important part – often the most important part – of a local Lived Islam.[3] And as we have seen, just as some sociolinguists' approach to linguistic variation is, essentially, "it's all good," many current anthropologists of local islams defend the differences of "their" Muslims as just one islam among many, or a local resistance to "orthodoxy," or authentic local practice. While we do not disagree with the sentiments of these provincial (in the non-pejorative sense) anthropologists, we want to argue here that they have missed the point.

It is not simply that people naturally differ from place to place. It is not simply that there are always local appropriations. We want to argue instead that certain features of what we will discuss below as Standard/Cosmopolitan Islam, and the shared, "core" Islamic practices and beliefs of what we will call Koiné Islam, structurally give rise to, provoke, and create a space within which the rich dialect features of local Lived Islam can thrive. In addition, these local practices shore up the Koiné and Standard Islam, root it, and make it relevant.

"Standard Islam" Promotes the Formation of "Dialect Features"

The rituals and beliefs of Islam shared by most Muslims are what we will call Koiné Islam. Another aspect of Lived Islam – the prestige form, the

[2] Almost any anthropology of Islam is about regional differences and local practice; the unique practices of a local Islam are thought to define that Islam. Consider also the chapter titles of R. C. Martin (ed.), *Islam in Local Contexts*, one of the first books in Islamic Studies proper to consider Islam in particular localities: "The Function of Institutional Sufism in the Islamization of Rajasthan, Gujarat and Kashmir"; "Local Perceptions of the Shrine of Bābā Farīd, Pakpattan, Punjab"; "Islam and Custom in Nineteenth-Century India"; "Islam in the Chinese Environment"; "The Qur'ān in China"; "Ritual and Symbolic Aspects of Islam in African Contexts," etc. [titles abridged and excerpted].

[3] See D. A. DeWeese, *Baba Tükles and Conversion to Islam*, 53ff., for a rebuttal to the assumption that rural Islam is merely "ignorant," that different Islam is "merely nominal" Islam. See also p. 54, n. 39, for a useful observation that "survivals" are nothing "other than normative religious practices of a community whose self-understanding of being a 'Muslim' immediately 'Islamizes' those 'survivals.'"

normative form, inasmuch as it is taught in classrooms – we will call Standard Islam (and normative because it is also linked to various forms of power, or Cosmopolitan Islam, since the works produced by the bearers of this prestige form of Islam are often read throughout Islamdom without regard to the place of origin). Dialect Islam is local and particular, Koiné Islam is shared by most Muslims, Standard or Cosmopolitan Islam is the sophisticated, prestigious, academic aspect of Islam. Several features of the Koiné and Standard Islam that help to construct Lived Islam help give rise to Dialect Islam.

The first structural feature is that the *ritual* language of Koiné Islam (the "Islam shared by everyone"), and the *scholarly* language of Standard Islam, are in both cases Classical Arabic – a language incomprehensible to the overwhelming majority of the world's Muslims now, and arguably, for most of Islam's history. And even within the Arab world, Classical Arabic is as far from spoken Arabic as Latin is from Italian. This distance between the vernacular language and the religious language creates a space for local understanding and appropriation of the shared Muslim rituals and beliefs that is undisciplined by the texts and scholars of Standard and standardizing Islam.

Secondly – and a feature generally overlooked in overviews of Islam – the Islam of texts (and introductory textbooks) is really quite spare in its ritual content and prescriptions. Most observers are struck by Islamic law's luxuriance – the stipulations not only for the minutia of worship, but how to clean the teeth, write a contract, slaughter beef, and divorce a husband, among many thousands of regulations. Yet the actual scope of Standard Islamic *religious* ritual is quite meager. We will elaborate below. But in short, there are only two Standard Islamic festivals. There are also few – and very minimal – rituals of the life cycle.

Finally, the scope of misfortunes that can be ritually prevented, or desiderata that can be ritually facilitated – even with the most uncritical embrace of the oceanic *ḥadīth* corpus – is quite limited. The religious demography of belief is likewise limited: a single (often quite remote-seeming) God, complemented by angels, devils, and creatures, of uncertain nature, called jinn. There is this quotidian life and an uncertain future life either in a good state or a bad state. Cosmopolitan Islam's austere set of rituals and beliefs is much less luxuriant than most ritual and supernatural traditions – particularly in the premodern period. This religious Lean Cuisine leaves a lot of room on the plate for local beliefs and rituals – rituals preexisting Islam's arrival or that have developed after a population became Muslim. A few examples can illustrate just a fraction of the teeming set of Dialect Islamic practices found throughout Islamdom. Since for so many, religion is defined by "belief," Dialect Islamic beliefs begin this brief survey.

Beliefs

In Standard Islam, to convert to Islam the new Muslim recites only the *shahādah* – the declaration (in Arabic) that there is no god but God, and Muḥammad is the Messenger of God – with intent to become a Muslim, and the transformation is done. It is that simple, and that low key. Nominal conversion to Islam of the Islamically unlettered is both easy and common, because the set of beliefs essential to Standard Islam, though profound in its implication, is limited in its content. Even the modern bureaucracies of embassies and ministries that certify conversion require only the signing of a document that one "believes (or has faith) in God, His angels and His prophets." Yet this minimal set of Islamic beliefs has been gilded, altered, even displaced by rich streams of local beliefs about the seen and unseen.

As an example, in Afghanistan, Muslims have an elaborate theology of "*jinnd*."[4] These *jinnd* may be either benign or malevolent; the malevolent or black *jinnd* cause illness, snake-bite, scorpion-bite, and other afflictions. They can drive souls from bodies and produce melancholia, or they can possess a person, paralyzing and convulsing him or her. They can haunt houses, pull pranks on the inhabitants, stone them, or cause other kinds of harm. The *jinnd* can be controlled and propitiated only by a local sacred technician called a *malang*, who, by various imprecations, rituals, and techniques, can expel the *jinnd*, or moderate their behavior. Though the austere God of the Qur'ān and Islamic theology does not involve Himself in such matters, these local semi-deities (who may inherit attributes of the pre-Islamic divinities *al* and *div*) shaped the religious lives of Muslims in Afghanistan before the Russian invasion. No doubt, even after the Taliban they are still part of many Afghans' Lived Islam.

Nineteenth-century South Indian Islam was enriched by

> malignant spirits, fairies, Narasinha, the lion incarnation of Vishnu, [and] Mātā, the Mother goddess. . . . Some [Muslims] . . . in order to obtain their wishes, pray[ed] to His Majesty Sikandar or Iskandar, Alexander the

[4] M. H. Sidky, "*Malang*, Sufis, and Mystics." The term is derived from the Arabic *jinn*, who are beings referred to in the Qur'ān. (See, for instance, 24:12, 14.) This Afghan spiritology and thaumaturgy is much more elaborate, and in some ways quite at variance with Qur'ānic and other normative descriptions of jinn.

> Great . . . vowing that if their desires [would be] accomplished they [would] offer horses in his name.[5]

Egyptian Muslims, for instance, would have no idea of the significance of "Mātā," but for the South Indian Muslim of Jaʿfar Sharif's time (c. 1832), this belief in Mātā, and the rituals attached to her, was very much a part of being a South Indian Muslim. "Extra-Islamic" beliefs are found equally in the Arab world – the guardian serpents that protect each quarter of Cairo, for example, or the *ghūl*s who eat both the dead and the living.[6]

A better-known supernatural force – widely believed in across Islamdom as well as in Greece, Eastern Europe, Southern Italy, and elsewhere – is the "eye," or the "evil eye," sometimes (with a nod to the Qurʾānic *sūrah* 113) called "envy." The evil eye is not found explicitly in the Qurʾān, though there are references to it in some *ḥadīth*.[7] It is, and has been, a powerful force in the lives of Muslims (as well as Christians and Jews) throughout Islamdom. In both Morocco and Lebanon the praise of children must be deflected ritually by saying "*ismāllah*" [*sic*] (name of God; i.e., "I was talking about God, not little Fāṭimah"), so as not to attract "the eye."[8] Loeffler's Iranian informant describes the evil eye quite elaborately:

> The evil eye is the most dangerous of all things. It can bring harm and damage to anything: an animal, a house, a tool, a rug, a child. It makes people ill and causes them to have accidents . . . There are some whose evil eye is so strong that when it hits something, this will die instantly and no written prayer can protect against it. We had one such person here in the village; he died recently. When he happened to look at a cow saying, "This is a good cow," the cow would drop dead. In this way he even caused damage to his own possessions. . . . When a child gets sick, it is mostly due to the evil eye of the father and mother. The child smiles, they are happy and pleased, they feel joy, they love it, it is sweet to them. So they cast the evil eye onto their own child.[9]

For the Egyptian, Iranian, Turkish, Moroccan, or whatever sort of Muslim who believes in the "eye," these beliefs are as much a part of her cosmology as a Supreme and Solitary God Who Created Adam. That they are part of the universe of Islam is proved by the Islamic technology by which one counters

[5] J. Sharif and G. A. Herklots, Qanūn-*i-Islām*, 139.

[6] E. W. Lane, *Manners and Customs*, 226–267. [7] See *EI2*, "ʿ*Ayn*."

[8] By following praise words directed toward the child, such as "handsome, smart, tall," with *ismallāh*, or reference to the child as "ugly," or "stupid." See E. W. Lane, *Manners and Customs*, 57–59, 249–250. See also (exhaustively) E. Westermarck, *Ritual and Belief in Morocco*, vol. 2, chapter 8.

[9] R. Loeffler, *Islam in Practice*, 123.

the eye – saying "name of God" or using items such as "the hand of (the Prophet's daughter) Fāṭimah" prophylactically.

Elaborate alternative creation accounts are central to some Muslims' understanding of how God has worked in the world. For example, the well-known American Nation of Islam account of a man, Allah, who created a Meccan paradise of Black humans that was subverted by the machinations of the evil scientist Mr. Yakub and his demonic white race.[10] In many places there were Gnostic cosmogonies that paralleled and complemented the Qur'ānic account of creation.[11] An Inner Asian Muslim oral tradition that began "when land became land and water, water, there were the infidels, Sons of Six Fathers, and the Muslims, Sons of Three." The hero, Almanbet, was conceived "through the intercession of the saints" and the Muslim God (*azrät Alda*).[12]

Beliefs held by Muslims that are not found or are even condemned in the Standard Islamic texts fill volumes, and collecting them has been the quest of missionaries and ethnographers alike. These local beliefs are particular to a given Islamic locale but foreign to other Muslims. To the academic student of Islam, their idiosyncrasy does not make these local beliefs un-Islamic. It is only if one imagines that there is an "Islam" to which these beliefs are supererogatory that these beliefs become "superstition," *super-stitio*, "beliefs added."

Rituals: The "Bare Walls" of Standard Islamic Ritual Life

The weaving of the dialect inseparably into a colloquial Islam is clearer still when we look at Muslims' ritual lives. The trans-regional, Koiné and Cosmopolitan Islamic laws of ritual (*'ibādāt*) might strike the non-Muslim (and non-Jewish) observer as remarkably full. There are the five daily acts of ritual worship, and the ablutions that precede them. The prescriptions of Islamic law ritualize nearly all of life itself and sacralize all domains of human existence. Yet, despite the universalizing scope of Islamic stipulations of ritual and life, two salient facts remain. The first fact is that the detailed prescriptions of the *'ulamā'* are known only to varying degrees by the non-scholarly Muslim. Parts of the *sharī'ah* stipulations may be known, others are not known, still others have been forgotten or suppressed. As a result, the *idea* of a *ritualized life* often is more potent than the actual prescriptions of

[10] For this see Malcolm X, *Autobiography*, and in more detail E. E. Curtis, *Black Muslim Religion*, 67ff.

[11] For example, see Rāzī, *Path of God's Bondsmen.*

[12] D. A. DeWeese, *Baba Tükles and Conversion to Islam*, 60.

the normative Islamic life. Muslims often practice a colloquial version of the *sharʿ* (or *shraʿ* as in Morocco[13]) – whose content is, in fact, local law not shared by all Muslims – as we will see below. The second observable fact is that, all these guidelines notwithstanding, compared to other societies, the ritual Islam of scholars is in fact rather sparse.

Scholars have usually categorized rituals according (a) to the time of their occurrence and (b) to their ostensible purpose. (a) Time: Rituals often occur in such a way as to periodize the year, or to mark transitional moments in people's lives, or to mark times of crisis. Consequently, across the world there are rituals to define the seasons: harvest rituals in the autumn, winter solstice rituals in the darkest parts of the year, rituals at the new year, spring rituals, planting rituals, summer solstice rituals – all these reflect some concern, some need, or some structuring principle located in absolute calendrical time.

Similarly, many societies have rituals that mark transitional moments in the life cycle – rituals of birth and of birthdays, rituals of puberty and adolescence, marriage and consummation rituals, and, of course, rituals of the dying and the dead. Whatever the explanation – that these rituals address crises of transition or commemorate the structures of life-time, or some other explanation – it is a fact that they are very common around the world. This is so even in less ritualized cultures, such as the contemporary Euro-American world, and every minister and rabbi has "customers" who never come to church or synagogue, but nonetheless insist that the clergy perform at a birth or coming-of-age ritual (circumcision, baptism, christening, bar or bat mitzvah), at their marriage, and at a funeral – when they are hatched, matched, and dispatched – as the clerical joke has it.

(b) There are many rituals that have an immediate purpose, that are functional in the strict sense of the word, that procure or prevent some event – cure an illness, procure success on an exam or in conceiving a child, produce a good harvest, or exorcise a demon. These shade off into magic, depending on the degree of certainty they are said to provide, but nonetheless these have all the features of ritual and are responses to crises or attempts to involve some transcendent power in a particular situation.[14]

As far as (a) calendrical and life cycle rituals, surprisingly, the Islam of scholars, particularly Sunnī scholars, has little to offer. Of absolute calendrical rituals it is utterly bereft, since Islam's calendar is a lunar calendar. Such

[13] D. F. Eickelman, *Moroccan Islam*, 131.

[14] There is no intent here or above to examine the rich field of ritual theory. For our purposes, the causes, meanings, significances, or explanations of ritual do not matter here. It is only their observable existence that matters.

rituals by definition cannot be seasonal rituals; there is no Standard Islamic spring festival, no standard Islamic solstice observance, no Standard Islamic harvest ritual, and so on, since Islamic dates float backwards each year by eleven to thirteen days. Ramadan may occur in the summer, but before long the Ramadan fast is in the spring, and then, three years later, it occurs in late winter.[15]

Likewise, there are very few life cycle rituals. At birth there is the *ʿaqīqah* ceremony, but it is recommended, not required, and until recently it did not seem to matter to anyone other than the very Islamically observant. In Standard Islamic law, marriage is a contract for the exchange of responsibilities and obligations. Like all contractual relations, there are forms of practice that make a marriage valid: a contract is signed, the consent of both parties is confirmed, there is a transfer of property from the groom to the bride. But there has been no *Islamic* ritual form by which marriage is accomplished, if by Islamic we mean "stipulated in the works of the *ʿulamāʾ*." For funerals, there is rather more, as we might expect from an eschatologically oriented religious tradition. Rules for the cleansing of the body, its wrapping, and the forms of prayer to be said for the departed are all specified. The rules for entombing the dead are also found in the *fiqh* works, though these are recommended, not required. A number of ritual practices, such as keening, are explicitly forbidden. Consequently, one would expect that all Muslim funerals would be the same. But they are not.

Standard Islamic rituals of prevention and promotion are likewise very limited. There are modified forms of the ordinary ritual worship (*ṣalāh*) for lunar and solar eclipses, and a somewhat theatrical form of *ṣalāh* for seeking rainfall in times of drought. *Sūrah*s 113 and 114 may be read as prophylaxes against enchantment. Otherwise the Qurʾān in particular offers very limited "spiritual technology" to accomplish this-worldly aims. The Qurʾān is focused on the big picture – the single God, the gratitude and obedience owed Him, His dictates for attaining salvation, and the fate of those who do and do not observe these His requirements. This "ritual thinness" is far from a liability, I would argue. It is the space that allows local needs and practices to be inscribed so that Islam is not a foreign import but a living, relevant, and local tradition wherever in the world it is found.

[15] This feature is not a drawback, but a powerful feature in the creation of a distinctively Islamic time.

Rituals of Time in Islamic Dialects

Notwithstanding the non-fit between the Muslim ritual calendar and a solar, seasonal calendar, the meaningful times of the year have been observed by Muslims as much as anyone. These rituals were not tied to the Islamic calendar for reasons we explained above, but they were observed nonetheless.

To take spring as only one example, according to Ibn Taymiyyah, the fourteenth-century Muslim reformer (on whom see Chapter 5), medieval Syrian Muslims observed spring with a series of rituals that they shared with Christians and no doubt Jewish countrymen that involved the painting of houses and even animals.

> In course of time . . . many Muslims, during non-Muslim festivals, such as this Maundy Thursday, . . . took to the habit of congregating in large assembly places, coloring eggs, cooking milk, marking their beasts in red, preparing foods such as they would hardly prepare during an Islamic festival, and exchanging gifts as are exchanged during the pilgrimage season. . . . this Christian festival coincides with spring season which marks the beginning of the solar year when meat, milk, and eggs are found in abundance . . .[16]

Egyptians (2016) still observe *Shamm al-nasīm* on the first day of the southern winds – the *khamsin* – which begin the Monday after Coptic Easter, though Lane notes that scholars, the custodians of Standard Islam (presumably to separate *Shamm al-nasīm* definitively from the Christian observance), asserted that it took place on the first three days of the spring quarter, a time called *Nawrūz* (in the original Persian, *Nowrūz*).[17]

In Iran and the Persianate world, the New Year spring festival, *Nowrūz* (Turkish: *Nevruz*), is very much a part of Muslim identity, despite the opposition from secularist and Islamist Turks and Islamist Iranians.[18] *Nowrūz* observances mark the coming of spring and require jumping over a fire and eating seven things that begin with "s" (in Persian) – including garlic, fruits, grain sprouts, rue, etc.[19] It is something that this group of

[16] Ibn Taymiyyah, *Ibn Taimīya's Struggle*, 213–215. See below, Chapter 5, where such rituals are discussed in the context of Ibn Taymiyyah's objections to them.

[17] E. W. Lane, *Manners and Customs*, 488–489.

[18] Muslims in areas where Persian culture was predominant, such as Turkey, Northern and Western India, and Afghanistan, all observed, and for the most part still observe, *Nowrūz*. In fact, it is very much a part of the identity of Alevi Muslim Turks, and increasingly so, as Islamists seek to suppress its observance.

[19] See Shapur Shahbazi, "NOWRUZ ii. In the Islamic Period," *Encyclopædia Iranica*, online edition, 2016; and "HAFT SIN," available online at www.iranicaonline.org/articles/haft-sin.

Muslims do as Muslims, and it is understood as a way to invoke God's blessings on the coming seasons.

Dialect Life Cycle Rituals

In many parts of Islamdom, the rituals of the life cycle are quite elaborate and involved; yet these rituals are idiolectically unique – they are found only in one place, and might seem bizarre and certainly "un-Islamic" to Muslims from elsewhere.

In India, part of being a Muslim was to observe the ritual of "*basmallāh*" when a child reached the age of four years, four months, and four days.[20] Girls had their hair parted in an uneven number of braids, scented powder was rubbed onto the body of the child by women whose husbands were alive,[21] and the child licked the written "*Fātiḥah*"[22] off a plate and repeated the "*basmallāh.*"[23]

Dialect rituals are a feature not only of historical Islam. Local islams still generate new rituals that are important to local circumstances but are far from universally observed. At present, in the Koko section of Korhogo, Ivory Coast, Muslims marry with a quite recently invented ritual, one that involves the married couple "placing one foot on a loaf of French bread on the ground. At the same time, bride and groom each press their lips to another loaf of French bread which they hold between them."[24] Since there is no canonical Islamic ritual of marriage, these Ivorian Muslims have developed a Muslim form of marriage that is both fully local and, for them, fully Islamic. In other Muslim countries the white veils and dresses familiar to Euro-Americans are worn by brides, and the Wagner and Mendelssohn wedding marches accompany her arrival or departure. There are many elaborate local Muslim marriage customs, but the point is that while in a given case there is usually no Standard Islamic ritual, there are many and diverse Muslim marriage rituals around the world.

Despite the specificity of death rituals in Standard Islam which one might expect to find uniformly among Muslims everywhere, it is an observable fact that funerals in Yemen, in Turkey, in Egypt and Morocco, all differ from

[20] I've been unable to determine whether these practices are still to be found in Indian Islam.

[21] This emphasis in rituals on women whose husbands are living is surely a characteristic of Indian Islam and religion in India, generally. See, for example, J. Sharif and G. A. Herklots, *Qanūn-i-Islām*, 37.

[22] The first *sūrah* of the Qur'ān.

[23] The words "in the name of God, the Merciful, the Compassionate." See J. Sharif and G. A. Herklots, *Qanūn-i-Islām*, 44–45.

[24] R. Launay, "Birth of a Ritual," 150.

each other. In Yemen, for example, I have seen processions to the graveyard accompanied by a boys' choir chanting Qur'ān.[25] In Egypt, burials are deep, and the body is placed in a niche in the side of the grave's wall, whereas burials in Turkey used to be relatively shallow, with the deceased not in a niche, but turned to face the *qiblah*.

In the US, the Muslim blogosphere, at Muslim chat-sites and even Twitter, is filled with discussions of how to observe – in a Muslim way – the Fourth of July, Thanksgiving, and even Christmas. It is clear that this is a process – sometimes deliberate, sometimes unconscious – of creating an American Islam no less Muslim for being American, for people who are no less American for being Muslim.

Dialect Rituals of Prevention/Promotion

Rituals and practices of efficacy shade off into technology and magic. It is not relevant here where the boundaries, if there are any, are to be located that separate religion, technology, and magic.[26] The fact remains that throughout Islamdom, though in markedly different ways, Muslims seek to use Islamic symbols and figures associated with Islam to procure good health, wealth, and success, as well as to avert illness, failure, and affliction.

In addition to the practices against the evil eye mentioned above, we might look at the large body of Qur'ān healing rituals. In Nigeria, for example, there are a number of divinatory practices that invoke Islamic symbols, but that do so in ways particular to Nigeria, and that are, at any rate, unrecognized by *ʿulamā'* and other official Muslims.[27] For example, a practice,

> meant largely to elicit a positive or negative response to a client's question or proposal is known as Kala Musa (Arabic: "Moses said"). . . . It consists of a rectangular sheet of paper folded to form a book of two pages facing each other. The exterior is covered with opaque paper so that the contents cannot be read from the outside when the book is closed. The opened book reveals eight chapters . . . four on one side reading from top to bottom and the opposite only readable by turning the book over. Closer perusal

[25] Ibn Baṭṭūṭah, in his fourteenth-century travel work, describes what is clearly, to him as a Moroccan, an unusual (and admirable) Damascene funeral custom of processing to the gravesite, men in front, while Qur'ān reciters follow chanting in an ornamented style. There are other subsequent local rituals. He also discusses Indian Muslim funeral practices. Ibn Baṭṭūṭah, *Travels of Ibn Baṭṭūṭah*, 2:153.

[26] On this distinction, see R. Styers, *Making Magic*, especially chapter 1. I owe this reference to my colleague Ehud Benor.

[27] I draw this account from P. J. Ryan, "*Imale*: Yoruba Participation in the Muslim Tradition," 165–176.

> reveals that there are only two chapters, repeated alternatively. From each chapter a string or tassel extends so that, when the book is closed, eight indistinguishable strings can be offered to the client. The *alfa* (Muslim diviner) proffers this book, the client picks a string and the *alfa* reads the chapter to which the string is connected. The alternating chapters are each one verse of *Sūrat al-Zalzalah* (Qurʾān 99:7–8):
>
> {And whoever does good, even an atom's weight, will see it then. And whoever does evil, even an atom's weight, will see it then.}
>
> If the client picks the first of these verses, his plans are considered approved or a positive response given to his question. If he picks the second, the opposite is true . . . No real literacy in Arabic is demanded of the *alfa* who employs this technique, as long as he can tell the difference between the two chapters, which only differ by the change of the words "good" and "evil."[28]

There are many more divinatory practices used in Nigeria, all with some sort of Muslim quality to them. Nigerians too practice "slate-washing," where, to heal various ailments, Qurʾānic verses are washed off of a slate on which they are written and the water is drunk. "Lessons" from the Qurʾān are also mixed with a "soap" to heal bites, shooting wounds, and various aches.[29]

When Lane was in Egypt in the mid-nineteenth century, the Qurʾān was used similarly:

> The most approved mode of charming away sickness or disease [was] to write certain passages of the Qurʾān on the inner surface of an earthenware cup or bowl; then to pour in some water, then stir it until the writing is quite washed off; when the water, with the sacred words infused in it, is to be drunk by the patient. These words [were] as follow: {And He will heal the breasts of a people who are faithful (9:14)}.

Again, it is important to see that the "ritual thinness" of Standard Islam is an adaptive advantage. Islam, once it arises in a certain place, grows around what is there as a tree grows to surround a wall or iron fence. It is not just that practices already present are Islamicized, however. It is also the case that on the featureless plain around Standard Islamic practices, new local creedal and ritual flora spring up to fill the ecological niches left by Standard Islam's disciplined simplicity. In all cases, however, the Standard Islam is situated amidst, and interpenetrated by, local religious life forms.[30] In a given locale

[28] Ibid., 166. [29] ibid., 178.

[30] Richard Eaton's *Sufis of Bijapur* is the best "on the ground" description of how people come to be Muslim that I know of. In chapter 6, especially pages 159–164, for example, he describes how wonder-working Sufis wrote mnemonic grain-grinding songs that layered Islamic dogma on

this amalgamation of the normative and the dialect, the shared and the idiosyncratic, constructs the only Islam there is, the local colloquial Islam – Lived Islam for that locality. Variables like class and gender likewise are "localities" that shape, enrich, and prune the features of Islam that Muslims elsewhere would most readily recognize as "Islam." These aspects of social life too are "locations" that shape Lived Islam. Physical place, however, has decisively and distinctively shaped Lived Islam throughout its history and across its geography.

The Importance of Place

The importance of location to the experience of Lived Islam is clearest, not surprisingly, in the prominence that Dialect Islam has often ascribed to particular places. In contrast, as we shall see, to "Cosmopolitan Islam," Dialect Islam is particularly attentive to localities and their numinous importance. Yet the general principle that some places are sacred while the rest are profane has been central even to Standard and Koiné Islam. Mecca and Medina are visited by all Muslims who are able, in the rituals of hajj and *ziyārat qabr al-Nabī* (visiting the Prophet's tomb).[31] Both Mecca and Medina are Standard Islamic locales par excellence and the example of these holy sites rhetorically justifies local sites of power and grace. While Standard Islam restricts access to Mecca and Medina to Muslims alone, and denies efficacy to any non-Muslim sites, in its localism Dialect Islam often tends to blur the boundaries between what outsiders and Cosmopolitan Muslims would call "the Islamic" and "the non-Islamic," seeing "place" as more important than creedal citizenship. The geographers, travelers, and local historians have too many references to cite here, but there can be no denying that places outside of Arabia have also resonated for Muslims from the beginning of Islam's history.

Such places form the sacred geography of Dialect Islam. These sites can be not just historical *aides mémoires*, but are also sites of religious power and presence. Most often a saint's burial place is a locus of devotion – although presently many Muslims vociferously reject the legitimacy of such devotion (historically only a tiny Sunnī group categorically objected to observances at places other than Mecca, Medina, and Jerusalem – these Ḥanbalīs are the foundation of the later Wahhabis who now rule Arabia). Throughout

top of the indigenous piety of the women who sang the songs while making flour. These songs are of course absorbed by the children, who then grow up taking Islamic cosmology for granted.

31 For the scriptural justification for these practices (in Sunnī Islam), see M. J. Kister, "Only Three Mosques," 4.

Islamdom, shrines, *dargahs*, *sīds*, *mashhads*, and the like, drew Muslims to pilgrimage and devotion. In Bombay, pilgrims visited the tomb of Makhdūm Faqīh, close to the shore. On the anniversary of his death, devotees drank water "which [had] been waved over the tomb, and [ate] the ashes of incense burnt there. The Saint enjoyed high reputation for the cure of hysterical and other spirit-possessed patients."[32] In Tanta, Egypt, the tomb of Sayyid al-Badawī and its cultic observances are widely observed and supported by the state religious authorities, as well as by local officials and influential persons.[33]

Thanks to the ethnography of Westermarck, we have an encyclopedic gazetteer for Islamic sacred space in Morocco. There, it is, and was, assumed that the *barakah*, or grace of a saint, could be transferred to the spiritually needy Muslim through visitation to the saint's place of internment. By that logic, a place perceived to be auspicious *had* to contain the bodies of saints, however uncertain his or her identity, or there had at least to be souvenirs of mythical visits by saintly persons to explain the numinousness of a locale. As a consequence, the saint associated with some places has only a generic name like Saint Goodluck (Sīdī Maymūn) or Saint He-Takes-Care-of-Needs (Sīdī Maqḍī Ḥājah/Sīdī Qāḍī Ḥājah) or Saint Hidden-One (Sīdī al-Ghā'ib).[34] The burial place of a saint – called a "home," "room," "courtyard," or "garden"[35] – and a sanctified zone around it called *ḥorm* (using the same root that denotes the sanctified zones around Mecca, Medina, and Jerusalem) is naturally the site of visitation, and of various rituals and restrictions. Yet so place-oriented are some forms of the Moroccan dialect of Islam that sometimes even springs are sacred, as are trees, river rapids, pierced rocks, and mountains.[36] Associations of particular saints with particular localities and natural features continue and can be seen now, for instance, at the grave of Sīdī ʿAlī, which is associated with a spring (*al-ʿayn al-kabīr*) and the grotto of the female jinn ʿĀ'ishah Qandisha.[37] In all of these examples and many more, it is place that signifies: the saint is *here*, not there, and his or her effects can be perceived in *this* place, not everywhere.[38]

[32] J. Sharif and G. A. Herklots, *Qanūn-i-Islām*, 142.

[33] E. B. Reeves, "Power, Resistance, and the Cult of Muslim Saints," 314.

[34] E. Westermarck, *Ritual and Belief in Morocco*, 1:49–50. [35] Ibid., 65. [36] Ibid., 65–88.

[37] V. Crapanzano, *The Hamadsha*, 64–66.

[38] The importance of particular place is obvious in the story a Muslim told me at the shrine of the Jewish saint Rabbi Amran, in Wazzān, Morocco. When I asked him why Muslims made visitation to the shrine of a Jewish saint he replied, "They only say he's Jewish because he died in the Jewish quarter." In my informant's view, the place of death determines the deceased's religious identity.

When place is emphasized, the identity of the individual believer may be subordinated to the power of the locale, and it is not surprising to observe that, in the Dialect practices of Islam, at local shrines Muslims and non-Muslims are frequently religious together. In Wazzān, Morocco, headquarters of a Sharifan-lineage family of great scholarly dignity, Muslims nonetheless visit the tomb of the Jewish saint Rabbi Amran. Bābā Lāl, a Hindu who taught the syncretist Indian Mughul King Dāra Shukoh, was revered as a saint by some Muslims.[39] Also in India, Ghāzī Miyān was revered as a martyr by Muslims and as one of the "youthful heroes" by the Hindus.[40] Mīrān Ṣāhib's tomb in Karnal, India, was a site of pilgrimage and vow-making both by Muslims and Hindus.[41] In Nagore, Tamilnadu, the saint Shahul Hamid is buried in a shrine on land given him by the Hindu ruler, and the shrine was subsequently patronized by Hindu rulers. "[S]ixty percent of the premises have been built by Hindus and about fifty [to] seventy-five percent of pilgrims on any given day are Hindu."[42] In such circumstances, it is not surprising that, when forced to declare a religious identity, 200,000 Gujaratis in the 1911 Indian census declared themselves "Mohammedan Hindus."[43]

In Kosovo, "until very recently, Muslims and Christians of different ethnic backgrounds visited one another's sanctuaries, worshiped one another's saints and ignored the evident theological objections of religious orthodoxies."[44] In these places, "Muslim and Christian forms of pilgrimage and saint veneration have amalgamated and formal religious divisions have become blurred."[45]

For both the typical Muslim reformer and the essentialist academic alike, this muddling of categories is disruptive, but for Syrians, Egyptians, Indians, Eastern Europeans, Moroccans, and West Africans, it has made, and can make, perfect sense as part of their Lived Religion. Why should access to the sacred, to healing, fertility, restitution, or Power in general, be limited by denominational labels? Only the fanatic would refuse a physician because she was of the wrong religion. A fortiori, saints' powers are invoked by all who need them, whatever religious identity is ascribed to saint or supplicant.

39 J. Sharif and G. A. Herklots, *Qanūn-i-Islām*, 140. 40 Ibid., 141. 41 Ibid., 142.

42 V. Narayanan, "Shared Ritual Spaces," 15.

43 G. Viswanathan, *Outside the Fold*, xii, citing A. Nandy, "The Politics of Secularism," 70.

44 G. Duijzings, "End of a 'Mixed' Pilgrimage," 1.

45 Ibid.; see also F. W. Hasluck, *Christianity and Islam Under the Sultans*, on shared sacred spaces in the Ottoman World.

Local Rituals of Religious Identity

It should not be supposed, however, that all idiolectic Islamic rituals are nondenominational. Some local Islamic rituals are mainly celebrations of Islamic identity. Yet these rituals are not canonically prescribed, nor universally recognized by other Muslims; they too are local practices of the Islamic dialect. In the Madagascar culture of Mayotte, dancing is among the most important *Islamic* rituals – the *daira*, *mulidi*, and *maulida shengy* – all are dance rituals that are part of being a Muslim in Mayotte. The *maulida shengy* is primarily something women do and it involves the chanting of the *Barzanji*[46] – a poetic devotional text commemorating the Prophet's cosmological significance.[47] The *daira* and *mulidi* are recitations of God's names and attributes, which are preceded by the recitation of the *Barzanji*. The *daira* is "fast-paced and arduous," the *mulidi* is "slower and more graceful." These are not, however, the enthusiasms of a few devotees, or religious *virtuosi*, but rather the performances of these rituals "are open to and supported by everyone."[48] This is a practice that is part of being a Muslim in Mayotte, and it is only for Muslims.[49] Lambek describes these dances as "intense, vivid, total experiences, syntheses of sacred words, music and movement." He adds, "performances draw on enduring sacred values, yet have a tremendous immediacy, bringing people an experience of the beauty and power of their own and the collective faith. The performances are exhilarating. As one participant put it, 'Performance is a means of gaining strength from God.'"[50] But none of these practices is shared with Muslims elsewhere in Islamdom, and these are not variations on a shared Islamic theme. They are, rather, local, idiomatic practices found only in Mayotte and surrounding regions, yet they exist to celebrate and perform the fact that one is Muslim. They are the religious equivalent of Scottish Caleigh or Texas Line Dance – a cultural feature unique to a place and celebrated as a marker of identity but imbued with far deeper significance and meaning.

[46] On which, see A. Rippin and J. Knappert, *Textual Sources*, 6–7, 66–68.

[47] M. Lambek, *Knowledge and Practice*, 149–155. [48] Ibid., 153–154.

[49] Ibid., 150: "'This dance is for Muslims only,' he said. . . . 'If you want to join us, you have to dress properly. Go and put on a *kanzu be* [long gown] and a *kufia* [hat].'" This dress too is part of being a Muslim in Mayotte; perhaps in its distinctiveness, it is sufficient to establish Muslim identity.

[50] Ibid., 155.

Conclusion

For those who would imagine a single essential Islam from Indonesia to Morocco, these dialect practices are disturbing. As an Edwardian academic might have supposed that there was English (*his* English, the "King's English") and that the rest was mere dialect or provincial solecism, Muslim scholars and Western academics both have left Islam's dialects to anthropologists – who wrote about religion in Upper Egypt or Nubia, Java or Turkmenistan, and who were by definition "not writing about Islam at all." For the last fifty years or more, if these local practices were discussed within the context of Islam, it was, explicitly or implicitly, within Redfield's paradigm of the Great Tradition ("Orthodox Islam"), and the Little Tradition.[51] One of the most accomplished and self-aware ethnographers of Islam, the late Richard Antoun, tried to make sense of the Great/Little Tradition in the context of Jordanian Islam.[52] He says that anthropologists' task is to concentrate on the local, and they therefore face "the impossibility of studying social organization of the [Islamic] tradition ... in a generalized or globalized manner."[53] Fair enough. Yet the religious contrast to the palpable reality of his villagers' Islam is the "Islam of the Big City," "orthodox Islam," in short, another "Islam of Nowhere." Ethnographic reality is contrasted with a Platonic ideal. In effect, like so many anthropologists, despite what they profess to assert, he implicitly endorses the belief that village Islam is an imperfect version of a more authentic Islam. He is writing, he says, about "the mediation of Islam to a locality" by "cultural brokers." This top-down view may reflect self-image of rurals daunted by the metropole, but it does not reflect the village view of Islam. For the villager, what s/he does is Islam. And, more importantly, even the official Muslims of Amman practice, as we will see below, a locally inflected Islam.

Models like "Little Tradition" don't work "because [such a distinction] omits upper class [and clerical] participation in popular culture ..."[54] and, as William Christian points out in his rich study of sixteenth-century Spain, "the style of life of some rural notables and parish priests was not so different from that of the peasants around them," and the same is true for Muslims

[51] R. Redfield, *Peasant Society and Culture*; *The Little Community, and Peasant Society and Culture*.

[52] Antoun has a very persuasive analysis of the Great Tradition/Little Tradition dichotomy in R. T. Antoun, *Muslim Preacher*, 35–41. He notes Zein's disparagement of the Great/Little Tradition distinction, but in the end, he accepts it (43).

[53] R. T. Antoun, *Muslim Preacher*, 41.

[54] P. Burke, *Popular Culture in Early Modern Europe*, 24.

everywhere and always.[55] Christian points out that studies that distinguish sharply between the equivalent of the Great and Little Tradition there is "an exaggerated distinction between city and country, with cities representing civilization and culture in the face of rural—'popular'—ignorance."[56] And this is true for the study of Islamic localism. The urban disdain for the rural masses is utterly inconsistent with the respect that Antoun and ethnographers generally show for their subjects. Why then think of the subjects' religion as "Little" anything? The "subjects" do not. All that is left, in short, is the Little Tradition, which, seen in the aggregate, amounts to "Islam." The problem remains how to think of the regionally particular as constituent of the aggregated whole.

An implicit invocation of the Little Tradition approach is James Grehan's brilliant study of eighteenth- and nineteenth-century religion in Syria and Palestine.[57] His wide-ranging research demonstrates that for Muslims in eighteenth- and nineteenth-century Greater Syria (as well as for Christians and Jews too), religious life was quite distinct from the Great Tradition as it was generally described in Damascus or Aleppo; he refers to these rural practices as "folk religiosity."[58] Mosques were few and far between, and in 1870 "more than a thousand villages held virtually no trace of official Islamic architecture whatsoever."[59] Muslims were mostly illiterate and so, rather than media to convey Great Tradition religious information,

> books were objects of wonder ... remote, incomprehensible, and recondite ... quasi-magical ... [and] were used for divination and blessing. ... The vast majority knew very little about religious law and doctrine.[60]

The locus of religious immanence was wonder-working saints (chapter 2) whose ongoing site of power was the tomb (chapter 3). They revered saints and groups of saints about whom, in some cases, they knew next to nothing.[61] They venerated sacred stones, caves, streams, springs, trees, and other

[55] W. A. Christian, *Local Religion in Sixteenth-Century Spain*, 28. [56] Ibid., 8.

[57] J. Grehan, *Twilight of the Saints*. I'm very grateful to Leslie Pierce, who first called this very valuable book to my attention.

[58] Ibid., e.g., 191.

[59] Ibid., 33. It should be noted that Ottoman demographers may have failed to recognize Nusayrī, Druze, or other religious groups sufficiently, and thus identified populations or villages as "Muslim" that were not. As Deringil and Türkyılmaz have shown (S. Deringil, *Well-Protected Domains*; Z. Türkyilmaz, "Anxieties of Conversion"), such minorities were viewed by Ottoman officials not as distinct groups but as bad Muslims. Of course Nusayrī areas, such as the inlands of Latakia to which Grehan refers here, had no mosques. At the bottom of the page he shows he is aware of this problem.

[60] J. Grehan, *Twilight of the Saints*, 53. [61] Ibid., 112–113.

distinctive features of the landscape, very much like Westermark's Moroccans (chapter 4). They believed in spirits tangentially related to Standard Islamic spiritual demography, or not related at all (chapter 5). They had distinctive rituals of oaths and vows, and like those of Turks and Central Asians, these quasi-magical commitments were cemented by various rituals including, particularly, animal sacrifice. The villagers consecrated the animals with water, prostrated themselves before the animals, prayed to them on beads, and circumambulated them. The boundaries between religious communities were blurred as saints' sites and artifacts were used irrespective of their denominational origins (chapter 6).

I have summarized this excellent book not only because it is a terrific piece of research that gives a brilliant historical view of what more contemporary ethnographers have also described synchronically. It is also an instance of what I believe to be a misunderstanding of Lived Islam. *Twilight of the Saints* ends as it began, with an argument that while Muslims remain Muslims at some (relatively unimportant) level (and Christians, Christians; and Jews, Jews), what mattered to everyone outside the cities was what he calls "agrarian religion." This is different, he says, from Islam, and is the real religious substrate; Islam itself is an epiphenomenal superstructure.[62] Grehan's larger point is to argue that the existence of this substrate, shared across denominations, makes the "religious clashes" explanation of conflict in the Middle East untenable – and of course in that he is correct.

I summarize the book, however, because Grehan, despite his argument, in fact demonstrates that Dialect practices did not make Muslims of Greater Syria non-Muslims or bad Muslims or Little Tradition practitioners. They were Muslims, and nothing in *Twilight of the Saints* suggest that *ṣalāh*, Ramadan, the Qur'ān, or the *idea* of *sharīʿah* were not also often key components of those Muslims' religious views and practices. And indeed, Grehan does not claim that Muslims ceased to be Muslims, though disappointingly he downplays Muslim practices as "formulaic prayer, reflexively uttered ..."[63] Why *ṣalāh* should be more formulaic or reflexive than the "agrarian religious rituals" is not clear. In fact, given his description of religious life, the presence of those "formulaic prayers" suggests a real tenacity of identity and belief in Islam and in being Muslim.

Even an account that downplays the "Islam" part of Muslim religious life cannot escape, amidst all the "agrarian religion," ongoing and widely

[62] I am paraphrasing and condensing a complex argument. See the introduction, and consult the index under "agrarian religion."
[63] J. Grehan, *Twilight of the Saints*, 190.

distributed references to components shared among Muslims – mosques, the Qurʾān, jinn, prophets, prayer (communal and individual), the Day of Judgment, Sufism, and so on.[64] This mélange of the "folk" and the "actually Islamic" suggests that, as anything other than a superficial heuristic, the islams approach – in which there is no Muslim aggregate, only the individual local islams – is deeply misleading. The notion that local Islam (presented always as *sui generis*) is comprehensible when studied in isolation is belied by the very present elements of Koiné Islam, by deference to Standard Islam, and here even by the ethnography of Grehan for Syria, and of Westermark for Morocco. Grehan's important book not only subverts his underlying argument, but, implicitly, those who would confine themselves only to the "differences" of Dialect Islam. It remains the case that Lived Islam is Local Islam and almost all "Lived Islams" have dialect features. Yet the parochialist approach to Islam amplifies the distinctive features of "their" particular, local, Islam but it seriously underplays the "Great Tradition" aspects of the local practice. The particular and idiosyncratic is exaggerated, if only by omission. And thus in the ethnographers' accounts, what is shared by Muslims disappears from the rural, or the lower-class environment – just as urban religious elites allege! As importantly, if one takes a diachronic point of view, the "islams" approach or the Great/Little Tradition approach downplays the dynamism of "orthodox" Islam and indeed of Dialect Islam as well.

However, this intriguing blend of historical Cosmopolitan approval and Dialect enthusiasm is complicated by the current reality that the institutions of the modern state, but more importantly the modern Standard Islamic Establishment, is, in most places, wary of or hostile to Sufism, to sites of religious piety, and particularly hostile to saint veneration.[65] It is safe to say that in many places in Islamdom, the reverence for saints is now mostly exclusively a domain of Dialect Islam, that is it has few defenders among Cosmopolitan Muslims or even the average Aḥmad on the street.

Recall that what makes something a Dialect feature of Islam, or of the Koiné, or of Cosmopolitan Islam, is how it is used. Dialect features are those features that seem different or strange to other Muslims. Arguably the veneration of saints, so widespread in the premodern period, was a Koiné and Cosmopolitan feature of Middle Period Islam. It is now, I think, primarily a Dialect practice (except perhaps in Morocco and in Greater India).

[64] Ibid. See index for these topics.

[65] F. D. Jong and B. Radtke (eds.), *Islamic Mysticism Contested*; L. V. J. Ridgeon, *Sufis and Salafis*; and see below Chapter 6.

But all along, throughout Muslim history, the *way* in which a saint was venerated was localized, from *ayazmik* drinking from springs, to *darshanic* "viewing," from *maraboutic* animal slaughter to *shamanic* saintly ecstasy – these had the potential to surprise Muslim visitors from Elsewhere.[66]

So, then, does saint-worship belong to islams, to the Great Tradition, or the Little Tradition? Surely it is, to an academic observer, an inseparable part of many Muslims' Islam whether it is emphasized in a Pakistani *dergāh* or derided in a Pakistani madrasa. It is mostly dialectal at present, and because of its link to particular place, has always been expressed through local idioms. At the same time, however, those Dialect practices have been justified by reference to High Tradition legal, theological, ethical, and pietistic literature, by reference both to overt discussions and to Koiné models that asserted the reverence for place and for persons (alive and dead).

These local forms deserve attention because, for many Muslims, they have been, and still are, the vibrant center of their experience of religious life – the domain of both collective effervescence and personal piety. Academics who have failed to recognize these factors as Islamic, or have disdained them as ignorant or marginal, have failed to understand Lived Islam. And it is not just that these Dialect practices and beliefs have mattered to local Muslims. It is rather that for many Muslims they are part of the warp and woof of what they mean by Islam itself.

The absence of certain kinds of "Islamic" rituals invites the Muslim of a place to fill the void with practices that both make Islam at home in that place, but by emulation and contrast, these local and "heterodox" practices simultaneously highlight the structural significance of, for instance, the Ramadan fast, the two festivals, and the daily worship – the rituals that are not local but transcendent, in all senses of the word.

The shared Islamic elements have kept Muslims "Muslims" and allowed them to recognize in other Muslims their own Islam: if for Muslims from elsewhere the Dialect was strange, the Koiné language of Islam was still comprehensible. This mutual comprehensibility remains to be explained. Nonetheless, as we will argue in the next chapter, even those structural features of Islam – the "universals of Islam" its "essential features" like five-fold worship, fasting, Pilgrimage, allegiance to the Qur'ān and Prophet – these too are locally inflected and a proper understanding of Lived Islam requires us to see the shared Islam as manifestly shared but at the same time tacitly local as well.

66 See the Conclusion below.

4

Shared Islam

The Koiné Islam

DIALECTS ARE ABOUT DIFFERENCE; ORDERING A "REGULAR" COFFEE in Idaho gets you a black bitter cup of java; in Boston "*regyaleh*" is a sweet, milky, and fortifying brew. How can we talk about Islamic differences but still recognize the way in which Muslims seem to see each other as connected, as sharing an identity? A minor Indian civil servant, a rural policeman in Alabama, a London train-cleaner – all speak radically different dialects of English, yet they can (sometimes with difficulty) understand each other because all three share much of the basic grammar and morphology of English. Similarly, Muslims from rural Morocco who might revere some local saint and Muslims from rural India who might practice some local propitiation ritual have historically recognized each other as Muslims when by some chance they were brought together. The "parochialist" ("islams") view of Islam can't account for the way Muslims, despite frequently different beliefs and often different practices, recognize each other as Muslim. Nonetheless, the usual alternative – essentialism – cannot be a useful alternative to the parochial islams approach since it, too, much disregards differences of practice and belief among Muslims.

It is important to grasp from the outset that even the "essential" beliefs and practices that essentialists identify as the "core" of Islam frequently function as part of a local dialect. Even the "five pillars," which for so many scholars are the "essence of Islam," differ, for many, in ways we will explore below. In short, the most elemental facts of the phenomenon called Islam are, as Lived Islam, mortared into some particular local realization of it. It is Muslims who live in some particular locale who seek to discern what God wants, and God's law is always enacted in some particular place. If someone suggests that Islam is the religion of the Qur'ān and the Prophet Muḥammad, it has to be borne in mind that neither the Qur'ān nor the Prophet are independent of the context in which they are understood.

Nor can scholars define Islam essentially by reference to its origins in Arabia, between 612 and 632 CE. A historical or genetic understanding *in no way helps* to understand Lived Islam since most Muslims have not lived in the seventh century, in Arabia. The history of Islam too is appropriated and deployed at a particular moment in a particular way that must be interrogated to understand the Lived Qur'ān and Living *Sunnah*, Lived worship, Lived Pilgrimage, etc. It is our starting point that, while the (Arabic) text of the Qur'ān a Chinese Muslim holds in her hand is not different from the Qur'ān that a Turkish Muslim holds in his hand, the *understood* Qur'ān of those two Muslims is likely to be quite different.

We need a new and intellectually rigorous way to think about what it is that Muslims have in common, an interpretative strategy that allows for varieties of understanding and appropriation. Though demonstrably every element of what we call Islam is locally practiced and affirmed, nonetheless the term Islam has not just a particularist referent, but a transnational, transhistorical one as well.

"Koiné Islam"

To describe the one and the many Islam(s), it is useful to continue the language analogy we have used so far and consider the concept of a koiné. What is a koiné? It was originally used to refer to (1) a dialect of Greek that developed primarily from the Attic dialect and became the common language of the Hellenistic world from which later stages of Greek are descended. It also means, however, (2) "A lingua franca."[1] Linguists have for the most part focused on how the Koiné Greek was the *simplification* of Attic Greek – how it was shared in a debased form by provincials,[2] but functioned effectively for the educated and the mercantile classes in the Eastern Mediterranean to communicate. But it is another aspect of Koiné Greek that attracts me as a useful analogue for our study of religion.

[1] Its origin is the Greek "*Koiné (dialektos)*," common (language) from *koinos*, "common." *Random House Dictionary of the English Language*, s.v. "Koiné."

[2] My colleague Lindsay Whaley gave me some guidance on this topic that got me started. See H. H. Hock, *Historical Linguistics*, 485–487; J. A. Holm, *Pidgins and Creoles*, 10; D. Hymes, "Pidginization and Creolization," 133–135; P. Trudgill, "Standard English: What It Isn't," 106–108. Classical Arabic serves as the Koiné for speakers of the so-called Arabic dialects, though in an article that Dr. Linda George called to my attention, Ferguson argued that an Arabic koiné developed alongside Classical Arabic. See C. A. Ferguson, "The Arabic Koine." Dr. George also reminded me of Ferguson's famous article, C. A. Ferguson, "Diglossia."

On the one hand a koiné differs from a language or a dialect in that it is a functional rather than a home language and is shared across language and culture boundaries yet remains intelligible to all. It is, nonetheless, always tinted by the native or "home" language of the speaker. Thus, for example, there are telltales that alert a scholar that the Gospel of Mark's author, who wrote in Greek, was nonetheless a native Aramaic speaker.[3] The Gospel of Mark is written in a koiné intelligible to Christians throughout the Mediterranean, but Biblical scholars are nonetheless able to discern the influence of Mark's Aramaic on his Greek; his Greek would presumably have been different had he been a native Latin or Gothic speaker. I use the term koiné here in the sense of *a language common to all, yet that frequently varies under the influence of the real native language or "home language" of the user.*

English is a koiné in India and is used and shared by speakers whose *home language* is Tamil or Hindi or Malayalam. (Both English and the other language are "native" languages to the speaker who may very well have been *educated* solely in English.) Experienced listeners can tell from the English spoken whether the speaker's home language is Tamil or Hindi; nonetheless that spoken English is intelligible and expressive to both speaker and listener, since the listener and the speaker share a common understanding of much of the basic grammar and morphology of English. Either might, however, use this grammar and morphology to improvise with a Sanskritic or Dravidian word "Englished" by the grammar and morphology of the koiné; likewise, the grammar and morphology of Telegu can "interfere" with the production of English, but this needn't prevent a non-Telegu English-speaker from understanding her Telegu-speaking friend when he speaks English.

[3] *Anchor Bible*, volume "Mark"; E. C. Malony, *Semitic Interference*, 1–3, 243–245. "[This particular passage] does not make proper sense in the existing Greek text, and has consequently puzzled scholars for year. In Aramaic, however, it is an entirely lucid piece. We found it possible to account for the transition from lucid Aramaic to obscure Greek not by a rotten translator or by the obtuse and destructive redactor who stalks the pages of NT scholarship, but precisely by means of a careful and accurate translator. This translator was landed with the translator's nightmare, a passage which, by the very nature of the two languages and the difference between the source and target cultures, simply will not go smoothly from the one language into the other. ... [T]here may be a massive difference between the understanding of a text by a bilingual translator moving from one language and culture towards another, and by monoglot speakers who belong entirely to the target culture." M. Casey, *Aramaic Sources of Mark's Gospel*, 255–256. Susan Ackerman kindly offered advice here.

Cognates

The notion of koiné works well for the description of religious traditions. Despite the particularities of Lived Islams, there are certain symbols, certain religious notions, certain orientations that overlap the various isoglossic boundaries of the various "islams." These shared symbols and practices are what we might call the *cognates* of Koiné Islam. Just as "*association*" means somewhat the same thing in English and in French, just as *gut* and good are mutually comprehensible between German and English, there are concepts that cross the regional or cultural boundaries of Islamdom. There is, as it were, a super-dialect of Islam that makes communication among Muslims possible, though often that communion is partial or illusory, and very often the understanding of the practice or belief at issue is shaped by distinctively local conceptions. As a demonstration, let us consider a few of the cognates common to Muslims in most places, and their relation to each other.

Qurʾān

"Anyone who seeks to understand Islam must have recourse to the Koran. The Koran ... is the basis of the Islamic religion."[4] Certainly one of the building blocks of Koiné Islam is the Qurʾān, whose centrality and importance is surely shared and affirmed by Muslims everywhere. Indeed, as we have seen, Asad defines Islam as "a discursive tradition that includes and relates itself to the founding texts of the Qurʾān and the *ḥadīth*."[5] The Qurʾān is invoked constantly – not only in ritual, but in conversation,[6] in phraseology,[7] in architecture and art, and implicitly in the alphabets in which many Muslims write their vernacular language.

Yet if, on the basis of observation, we ask, "what is the Qurʾān?" we are at once confronted with a plurality of answers. The Qurʾān is a book, "what is between the two covers."[8] It is writing, and many scholars have pointed to the meaningfulness even of indecipherable Qurʾānic phrases written beautifully on stone or paper or metal.[9] The Qurʾān is also a talisman, and sits protectively in the front or rear

[4] G. Endress, *Introduction to Islam*, 23. [5] T. Asad, *Anthropology of Islam*, 14.

[6] "Conversation ... is lubricated with Arabic liturgical expressions." M. Lambek, *Knowledge and Practice*, 134.

[7] M. Piamenta, *Islam in Everyday Arabic Speech.*

[8] A. K. Reinhart, "[The Quran in Islamic] Jurisprudence."

[9] A. Schimmel, *Islamic Calligraphy.*

windows of taxis throughout Islamdom, in little home shrines, or prophylactically around one's neck in an amulet.[10] So efficacious is it that its words, once written on a "prayer board," can be washed off and drunk for medicinal purposes.[11]

Yet to see the Qur'ān as only writing is to miss much. The Qur'ān, as scholars have pointed out, is perhaps, first of all, sound.[12] Wherever one travels among Muslims, the Qur'ān is heard – on the radio, at rituals like *khatmahs* (celebration) and marriages,[13] on car cassettes, and of course in mosques and *kuttābs* (children's Qur'ān schools) the world over. As Bowen points out, "[formal] Qur'ān recitation is an important link among local, national, and world-wide Islamic contexts."[14]

These are sounds that consecrate rather than communicate, however.[15] The Qur'ān's words, as pure sounds, are powerful in themselves,[16] and the correct recitation of them is acknowledged even by those who are not themselves competent in Arabic.[17]

Indeed, Lambek points out that because the Qur'ān is in Classical Arabic, the aural Qur'ān must be acquired by formal study, not by informal acquisition, which "raises its value in a relative sense, but also ... in an absolute one."[18] In Turkey, one of the most prominent signs of a reinvigorated Islamic identity is "Koran *kursu*" sessions where young and old alike learn the rules of Qur'ān recitation and then perform it in graduation recitals for family and friends.

For most Muslims, the Qur'ān is an aural phenomenon and the Qur'ān's *meaning* is acquired through other languages.[19] Even in the Arab world, my sense is that it is not listened to word-by-word, but

[10] C. Hamès, "L'Usage talismanique du Coran"; *Coran et talismans*; A. Regourd, "Usages talismaniques du Coran"; E. A. Rezvan, "The Qur'ān and Its World."

[11] In addition to P. J. Ryan, "*Imale*: Yoruba Participation in the Muslim Tradition," see J. H. Barkow, "Muslims and Maguzawa," 71.

[12] W. A. Graham, *Beyond the Written Word*; C. Nelson, "Religious Experience."

[13] E. W. Lane, *Manners and Customs*. On *khatmahs* see 279–280; on marriage observances 171.

[14] J. R. Bowen, *Muslims Through Discourse*, 95. See also A. M. Gade, *Perfection Makes Practice*.

[15] Two excellent discussions of this use of language in scriptural recitation are H. C. Lester, "Hindusim: Veda and Sacred Texts," 128–131, and J. Boyd, "Zoroastrianism: Avestan Scripture and Rite," especially 114–121.

[16] J. R. Bowen, *Muslims Through Discourse*, especially chapter 4.

[17] M. Lambek, *Knowledge and Practice*, 135: "Islam may be said to have been hegemonic in the sense that the sacred quality of the central texts and the necessity or correctness of reciting them at critical moments were unquestioned."

[18] Ibid., 138.

[19] "It may be that the difficulty of learning Arabic grammar leads some Gayo and other Indonesians to especially appreciate tone and melody." J. R. Bowen, *Muslims Through Discourse*, 298.

rather that one is bathed in its effect, though for Arabs and the Arabic-educated, words and phrases leap out meaningfully or insinuate into consciousness. For most, however, the Qur'ān is sacred sound, a Muslim *mantra*, the Islamic "*om*." The fact is that for the majority of the world's Muslims, the Qur'ān is, in any of these three modes – written, recited, or viewed – incomprehensible as language.[20] This is often true even when it is translated. Turks have told me that the Turkish translation of the Qur'ān is (perhaps necessarily) full of untranslated Arabic origin, and archaic Turkish words, unknown to the average Turkish Muslim. This makes it a difficult text to consult, much less, just "read." Such also appears to be the case for Chinese Qur'ān translations, which "are often quite difficult to understand," and often incorporate "'monastic' terms suggestive of non-Muslim ideas intermingled."[21] Indeed, the Qur'ān is often "misheard" and thus "misreported" in ways that make it incomprehensible to the Arabist. In a conversion myth recorded by DeWeese, the Muslim hero Almabet demands of his father and his people that they recite "the Qur'ānic words, '*kulkuldabet kualdet* …"[22] The text's editor identifies these as words from *sūrah* 112, {*Qul huwa 'llāhu aḥad*}; it is only context that would help us see these "nonsense" words as Arabic, much less as Qur'ānic phrases. The dogma that the Qur'ān is only "the Qur'ān" when it is in Arabic tends to facilitate its koiné-ization, that is, its function as universal, experientially, but locally particular in its understanding.[23]

Nonetheless, when it is invoked, Muslims qua Muslims are obliged to defer to its indisputable supremacy. "The Qur'ān says …" tends to end debates. Most Muslims, however, are not experts in Qur'ān. At most times, it is enough that Qur'ānic scholarship exists, and that the Qur'ān is understood, studied, and interpreted – elsewhere and by others.[24] For the rest, one comes to know the contents of the Qur'ān and other sacred texts by

[20] This is an obvious point, but it seems often to be forgotten. "Not only the Qur'ān, but the vast majority of commentaries, legal texts of reference, and personal prayers are written in classical Arabic, an entirely foreign, quintessentially written language, totally unrelated to the Manding language spoken by the Dyula." R. Launay, *Beyond the Stream*, 77.

[21] J. Yijiu, "Qur'ān in China," 100; see also M. B. Wilson, *Translating the Qur'an*, 237–328.

[22] D. A. DeWeese, *Baba Tükles and Conversion to Islam*, 62.

[23] On the use of the Qur'ān in Persian translation – an early problem in Islamic law – see T. E. Zadeh, *The Vernacular Qur'an*. On the translation of the Qur'ān, the best discussion, as well as a substantial analysis of the late-Ottoman, early Republican Turkish case, is in M. B. Wilson, *Translating the Qur'an*.

[24] M. Lambek, *Knowledge and Practice*, 144–145. Indeed, in Islamic law, the understanding and study of the Qur'ān is a "duty of the sufficiency" (*farḍ al-kifāyah*), that is, a duty for some unspecified group of Muslims, not "a duty of each individual Muslim" (*farḍ al-'ayn*).

hearsay.[25] Consequently, there is an odd sense in which the Qurʾān expands as one moves outside of the Arabophone world, as more and more dicta are said to be "in the Qurʾān" despite their actual absence from the text. Loeffler is told by an Iranian that the Qurʾān says, "no capitalism,"[26] and that the Qurʾān says that "a woman must cover her head in a way that all hair is concealed. This can be done by a scarf or kerchief: it mustn't be a full veil, which hinders work."[27] And of course "everybody knows" (whether oil company "expert" on Islam, or random person in the street – Muslim or non-Muslim) that "the Qurʾān forbids portraits and images." In fact, this is not so.[28]

The Koiné Qurʾān, then, can be said to be without any *determinate* meaning, except that, when invoked persuasively, it provides authority to the point it supports and the one who invokes it. The Qurʾān means authority and truth. Claims about the Qurʾān can, however, in some contexts be authoritatively confirmed or falsified, as we shall see in our discussions below of Standard Islam. Over time, the Qurʾān cannot mean just anything, but at any point in time, it may be said to convey many things, regardless of the actual text. It is not only that the Koiné Qurʾān is enlarged by interpolations but it is also reduced by, as it were, forgetting passages that were once considered important, or are elsewhere considered important to the Qurʾānic message. An obvious example is slavery.

Like all ancient cultures, Muslims (and the Qurʾān) took slavery for granted, and it was important in constructing familial relationships, atonement practices, oaths, and other important social and religious facts.[29] However, in contemporary Muslim scholarship, I find almost no engagement with the issue of slavery and freeing slaves that is found so often in the Qurʾān; and very few of even the most fundamental of fundamentalists believe that the restoration of slavery is part of the instantiation of the Qurʾān as "constitution." Muslim feminists brush aside or forget Qurʾānic texts where women are likened to "tillage"; anti-feminists forget that the restrictions on women's movements are addressed solely to the Prophet's wives, who are "not like others."[30] The several Qurʾānic critiques of the Prophet are lost in the mists of exegesis and hagiography.[31]

[25] Ibid., 139. [26] R. Loeffler, *Islam in Practice*, 230–231. [27] Ibid., 227.

[28] F. B. Flood, "Between Cult and Culture."

[29] See the discussion of "forgetting slavery," in J. Casanova et al., "Religion, Law, and the Politics of Human Rights." The disagreement between al-Naʿim and Asad on the process by which slavery was forgotten in Islamic law is instructive.

[30] Q33:32; 2:223. [31] e.g., Q80:1.

Nonetheless, as ideas and dicta, the *textual* content of the Qurʾān is less important than the *colloquial perception* of its contents, which is always selective,[32] and sometimes fictive.[33] In other words, the Koiné Qurʾān is not, in Lived Islam, finite in content nor, on the other hand, does it contain all that is in the Arabic text called "the Qurʾān." It is in fact the local Dialect that determines which, among all its dicta, are known, used, ignored, or imagined.

An example: for the South African Muslim discussion of liberation "undoubtedly the most significant text" was Q28:4–8.

> {Lo! Pharaoh exalted himself in the earth, and made its people factions. And a group of them he oppressed (*yastaḍʿifu*), slaughtering their children and sparing their women; he was among the corrupt. We wanted to show favor to those who were oppressed (*istaḍʿifū*) on the earth and make them the foremost and the heirs. And to establish them in the earth, and to show Pharaoh and Hāmān and their armies that which they feared. (28:4–6)}
>
> This text was quoted with increasing regularity at the rallies of virtually every Islamist organization – both fundamentalist and progressive – during the South African independence struggles of the 1980s, as well as in their magazines, newspapers, and pamphlets.[34]

Yet to cite this passage from the Qurʾān is a choice. One might, to opposite effect, have quoted Q49:13 {We have created you male and female, made you peoples and tribes that you might know one another}, which has been read as a justification of racial distinction. Even for those who actually know the Qurʾān, Muslims' choice of verses to use in a particular situation, in effect, constructs the Qurʾān. In Gayo Sumatra (and Bowen says, in Pakistan and Egypt as well) "at moments of danger one recites the 'Seven Verses,' a selection of seven verses from different chapters of the Qurʾān each of which celebrates the power of God."[35] Bowen goes on to say that "[m]ost Isak Gayo use and appreciate the Qurʾān for the combination of personal

[32] R. Loeffler, *Islam in Practice*, 85, quoting an Iranian villager: "I accept everything in the Qurʾān that's from God. Only what is not from Him, the man-made stories, I do not accept, like the one that God made man out of dust. This wasn't so," says his Persian informant. But of course, the Qurʾān does say that God made Adam from dust (*turāb*). See, e.g., Q3:59.

[33] As with the insistence that "the Qurʾān forbids images," a prohibition no less effective in governing sentiments and action for being utterly absent from the actual Arabic text of the Qurʾān. Indeed, it seems also to be true that the firmness with which a specious point is affirmed to be in the Qurʾān is directly proportional to the distance of the speaker from the centers of Cosmopolitan Islam (see Chapter 5). This is true not just for Muslims, but for "experts on Islam" as well.

[34] F. Esack, *Qurʾān, Liberation & Pluralism*, 101.

[35] J. R. Bowen, *Muslims Through Discourse*, 96.

reassurance, physical protection, and generation of merit that recitation provides."[36] The Gayan-appropriated Qurʾān may not be the Qurʾān familiar to South African Muslims in times of stress, but both Gayans and South Africans orient themselves toward a Qurʾān that is relevant and efficacious. Choosing, imagining, viewing, drinking, reciting, hearing – the Qurʾān is Muslims' to use in all these ways and in more, no doubt, besides.

In sum, for most Muslims the Qurʾān is an icon of various sorts: visual, aural, tangible. But at the ideational level it is also an icon of final authority and an icon of commitment. It is the representation of knowledge otherwise inaccessible to humans, and of definitive prohibition and permission. Since the Qurʾān is the Word of God, in a more literal sense even than the Bible in the most literalist of Bible-believing communities, to pay allegiance to the Qurʾān is to pay allegiance to God. However, to say, glibly, "Islam is universal, because Muslims all believe in the Qurʾān," is to miss the fact that the Qurʾān is variously understood and appropriated. It is affirmed by all Muslims and that affirmation unites Muslims, but it is also, like South Indian or South Alabaman English, locally inflected. It is perhaps the most important of the cognates shared by Muslims; it helps to constitute the Koiné of Islam.

Sunnah/Ḥadīth *and the Prophet*

Similarly, the large majority of Muslims would affirm the centrality of the Prophet to Islam and of his normative acts (*sunnah*) as found in *ḥadīth* collections.[37] In this, it would seem, Muslims must be united (although a number of Muslims over the past century have argued that "true Islam" is based on the Qurʾān and not the *sunnah*, which is congenitally unreliable).[38] The *sunnah* and the *ḥadīth* that convey them are indeed widely, and nearly universally, found in Lived Islamic religious life, but it is not necessarily the canon of "authentic," prophetic *ḥadīth*, with sound *isnād* (transmission headnote) and scholarly critical apparatus that is used in Lived Islam. Instead, the Koiné *sunnah* is really the notion that despite being outside the Qurʾān itself,

[36] Ibid.

[37] *Sunnah* is an Islamic norm; it is recorded in a *ḥadīth*, meaning, an anecdote related from/of the Prophet Muḥammad. The Prophet's biography, which is in part composed of the anecdotal materials collected in the *ḥadīth*, is generally called *sīrah*.

[38] A. Y. Musa, *Ḥadīth as Scripture*. See especially chapters 4 and 5. See also D. W. Brown, *Rethinking Tradition in Modern Islamic Thought*, and the arguments to which Kecia Ali refers in K. Ali, "Progressive Muslims and Islamic Jurisprudence."

there are some authoritative stories that partake of Scriptural and Prophetic authority.

The *sunnah* has certain features that facilitate its appropriation as Koiné. First, it is not the *ipsissima verba*, the very word of God, and so it may be deployed in vernacular languages. For this reason, one might suggest its sacrality is diminished, leaving Muslims freer to transmit the gist of it, rather than the actual text. Though the texts of the Qur'ān are often "translated," the *ḥadīth* are much more frequently found in translation since it is the *idea* that is embodied in any particular *ḥadīth* that matters most. The technical form of the *ḥadīth*, the form found in the Islamic Arabic canonical works of the genre, is formidable indeed:

> [Headnote:] Muḥammad b. al-Muthanná and Ibn Bashshār related (the wording is Ibn al-Muthaná's), Muḥammad b. Ja'far related, Shu'bah related from Simāk b. Ḥarb from Jābir b. Samurah from Abū Ayyūb al-Anṣārī who said: [Text:] The Messenger of God (upon whom be God's blessings and peace), when food was brought to him, would eat from it and send me the left-overs. One day he sent to me the left-overs from which he had not eaten, because of the garlic [in it]. I asked him, "Is [garlic] forbidden?" He said, "No, but I dislike it because of its smell." [Abū Ayyūb] said, "I dislike what you dislike."[39]

These *ḥadīth* are preserved, as shown in the example above, with a daunting list of the authorities through which it was transmitted (called the headnote; Arabic: *isnād*), and the text recording what the Prophet did. The authoritative critique of these *ḥadīth*, done mostly by assessing the worth of the authorities quoted in the *isnād*, is a daunting technical operation that calls for a massive amount of learning culled from biographical dictionaries, lexicons, commentaries, and anthologies.

The example above, drawn directly from a *ḥadīth* compendium, is not, however, the form in which the *sunnah* of the Prophet is usually conveyed in Lived Islam. Rather, someone says "the Prophet avoided garlic" and it is in *this* form that the information is usually related, not as a technical pericope from the canonical *Six Books of Ḥadīth*. The very expertise required to transmit and study *ḥadīth* makes it likely that a more demotic transmission process would arise to transmit the gist, the interesting or relevant parts of Muḥammad's *sunnah*.

Second, and perhaps most important, the *ḥadīth* of the Prophet, and the *sunnah* derived from it, is preserved in an incomprehensibly large corpus, and this too facilitates its incorporation as Koiné. While the Qur'ān is of

[39] Muslim, *Ṣaḥīḥ Muslim*, 14:9.

modest size – a scripture little larger than the New Testament – the *ḥadīth* is an ocean of indeterminate and indeterminable size. It is nowhere nearly exhausted by the corpus of the *Six Books*, and no one can claim to know all of them.[40] Many *ḥadīth* quoted authoritatively in pietistic, sermonic, Sufi works, and elsewhere, have no documentary *isnād* and are otherwise unknown – but they are no less authoritative in the domains in which they circulate, despite their technical imperfection.[41] Some of the most influential *ḥadīth* in popular discourse such as, "seek knowledge even to China," and "in difference is mercy," are, by the standards of the experts, technically weak or insufficiently attested.[42]

The main text of an Indian-Islamic reform group now found widely throughout Islamdom, the Tablighi Jamaʿat, is an Urdu *ḥadīth*-collection called *Fazāʾil-i aʿmāl*. Because it is in Urdu, Pakistanis and Indians can read it aloud, understand it in diverse ways, and discuss it together to tease out relevant meanings. This text is memorized, for instance, by Pakistanis working in Saudi Arabia (where, by the way, the work is banned by Wahhabi religious authorities).[43] There is a sense, says Barbara Metcalf, in which the *Fazāʾil* functions as a vernacular Qurʾān: the speaker here is the Prophet, not God.[44]

In Indonesia, pious Indonesians guide their lives with a twelfth-century *ḥadīth* collection *Riyāḍ al-ṣāliḥīn* – the work of a thirteenth-century Syrian scholar named al-Nawawī – which is translated into Javanese and cheaply printed.[45] These are "old texts" brought into the present.[46] In the book the

[40] Even great legal experts like al-Shāfiʿī assumed that there were many aspects of *sunnah* that none but an elite might know, and others that no one might recall explicitly – there would remain only an implicit deposit in the consensus of the community. See al-Shāfiʿī, *Risālah*, §961ff. For the Shīʿah, the corpus of relevant *ḥadīth* is even larger; one collection, the *Biḥār al-anwār*, runs to over 300 volumes! "In the time before standardized texts and easily accessible indices, and long before searchable databases, knowing the exact contents of capacious *ḥadīth*-collections like the *Ṣaḥīḥayn* proved impossible to all but the most accomplished scholars. Both among the less masterful of the scholarly class, and less literate segments of society, it was difficult to limit the legitimating authority of the *Ṣaḥīḥayn* to the actual contents of the books." J. Brown, *Canonization of al-Bukhārī and Muslim*, 239.

[41] Indeed, the *ḥadīth* in Lived Islam often derives its authority as much from the teller of the *ḥadīth* in the conversation in which it is deployed, as from the Prophet. See the discussion of Kareem Abdul-Jabbar below.

[42] The Imāmī Shīʿah, the second largest denomination of Muslims, have an even larger corpus of authoritative *ḥadīth*, since they draw not just on the model actions of the Prophet, but also on reports of the twelve Imāms' activities. To repeat: the most capacious authoritative collection, the *Biḥār al-anwār* runs to well over 300 volumes in the printed edition.

[43] B. D. Metcalf, "Living Hadith," 599. [44] Ibid.

[45] M. R. Woodward, "Textual Exegesis," 566. Note that this Javanese version contains only the first 657 *ḥadīth* of the original version. Ibid., 569.

[46] Ibid., 569, quoting Anton Becker.

Arabic text is provided – perhaps to provide iconic authority to the translation and exegesis that follow, since the readers are by definition unlikely to be able to check the original Arabic.

> The Indonesian text ... establish[es] analogies between events in the early history of Islam and contemporary life and emphasize[s] the internal ... as well as external ... meanings of the text.[47]

The *ḥadīth* are turned into "lessons" that can be used for sermons and religious instruction. It is "primarily in these 'lessons' that a soteriological text acquires social and political significance."[48] As Woodward says,

> In one sense [this edition of the *Riyāḍ*] is a translation of and commentary on an Arabic work. In another it is an Indonesian work using Nawawi's name and collection of *ḥadīth* ... to establish the scriptural legitimacy of [one Islamist party's] current theological and political positions.[49]

Of the tens of thousands of collected *ḥadīth* these Indonesian activists "choose" this particular subset and appropriate them to analyze contemporary Indonesian realities. Hence the *ḥadīth* are best understood as authoritative stories ascribed to early or formative Islamic times. In short, they are myths.[50] Each *ḥadīth* is a small but potentially efficacious myth inasmuch as it is primordial and authoritative account of norms established by a formative figure and authoritativeness.[51]

For a newly converted American Muslim, Kareem Abdul-Jabbar, the *ḥadīth* were the means by which authentic, as opposed to inauthentic, Islam was conveyed.

> [T]here were a whole lot of funny-time people involved in [Islam] just then; it was in vogue and many of the new "believers" really weren't schooled in Islam. [...] What was being promoted was often not Islam at all.[52]

47 Ibid., 570. 48 Ibid. 49 M. R. Woodward, "Textual Exegesis," 579.

50 Even if, as seems likely, Ibn Isḥāq's *Sīrah* or Abū Dawūd's *Sunan* contain much that actually happened (in the *wie es eigentlich gewesen* sense).

51 The problem of the relation of the historical, or for that matter the cosmic, Muḥammad to the *sunnah* is complex. It seems to me that the person and historical career of Muḥammad is a matter distinct from the Muḥammad of *sunnah*. Affective relations to Muḥammad, the liturgical celebration of his life, and a sense of his life as a historical (and trans-historical) event mostly show up in Dialect rather than Koiné Islam, particularly in the diverse celebrations of the birthdate (*mawlid*) of the Prophet. See J. R. Bowen, *Muslims Through Discourse*, chapter 10; M. Lambek, *Knowledge and Practice*, 138–160; J. Marcus, *World of Difference*, 125–129; C. Eccel, "Cult of Muhammad"; and M. H. Katz, *The Birth of the Prophet Muhammad*.

52 K. Abdul-Jabbar and P. Knobler, *Giant Steps*, 173.

Abdul-Jabbar found an authoritative Muslim named Hamaas Abdul-Khaalis to be his guide into Islam. Hamaas Abdul-Khaalis was an African-American convert to Islam who had been associated with the Nation of Islam (of Elijah Muhammad) but he was certainly an observant Sunnī Muslim when he met Abdul-Jabbar. It was Hamaas who determined for Abdul-Jabbar what was in the Qur'ān.[53] And it is Hamaas who taught Abdul-Jabbar the details of Muslim praxis. He was taught that the greeting "*as-salāmu 'alaykum*" ("peace be with you"), is for "the ill-informed." Muslims, Hamaas said, are to greet each other "with '*bismillāh ar-raḥmān ar-raḥīm*'" ("In the name of God the merciful the compassionate" – a phrase usually said by Arab and other Muslims at the commencement of an action – and the header for nearly all Qur'ānic *sūrahs*, but not, to my knowledge used by other Muslims as a greeting).[54]

The ablution before prayer, rather than the simple washing customary for most Muslims, was something rather more elaborate: "Hammas would have us scrub up for prayer as if we were on General Hospital."[55] These "local norms" were justified by reference to the *ḥadīth*, which, of course, as a novice Abdul-Jabbar didn't know, or expect to know, since he was not "an Islamic expert."

When, however, Abdul-Jabbar attended Harvard Arabic classes in the summer of 1972, he began reading *ḥadīth* from the canonical collections; he also traveled in Muslim countries. In this way he found that many of the "*ḥadīth*" Hamaas had cited were not anywhere recorded. "These things aren't written for a reason," claimed Hamaas, "they are to be handed down from person to person."[56] Abdul-Jabbar was not satisfied, and this confrontation of one kind of religious knowledge (the locally interpreted Koiné) with another (the written, Cosmopolitan) was the beginning of his estrangement from Hamaas, and his movement toward a more orthoprax religious practice, a different dialect of Islam – one closer to Standard, Cosmopolitan Islam.

In Abdul-Jabbar's account, a vernacular Islam, with its own regional version of the cultus, was produced and justified by the use of extra-Qur'ānic stories attributed to the Prophet. These stories were not written down; they lacked the apparatus of scholarly *ḥadīth* criticism, but they were authoritative nonetheless, and in effect took precedence over even the other "sounder" Scriptural *ḥadīth*. Abdul-Jabbar's teacher, Hamaas, had the self-

[53] His teacher, Hamaas, forbade non-Muslims to be present at Abdul-Jabbar's wedding. "Hamaas hadn't told me this beforehand, but I was not so fully studied in the Qur'ān to know whether it was forbidden to have outsiders at a Muslim wedding." Ibid., 232–233.

[54] Ibid., 175. [55] Ibid., 257–258. [56] Ibid., 258.

claimed authority to determine which *ḥadīth* sources were sound and which were not, and indeed authoritatively to transmit *ḥadīth* that no one else knew.[57] At least so Abdul-Jabbar, and Hamaas's other followers believed, in the period following Abdul-Jabbar's conversion.

My point here is that, at least in the early stages of his membership in the Islamic community, Abdul-Jabbar was instructed by reference to a second Scriptural source of authority – the *ḥadīth* or *sunnah*. Yet like the Qur'ān, its content was locally determined. A local teacher in New York defined the *sunnah* and its meaning in the context of local circumstances, needs, and religious concerns. I do not suggest the process is an insincere one. I am pointing out only that conversion to Islam means commitment to the principle that the Prophet and accounts of his life are authoritative. Saying someone is Muslim may enable us to predict the Muslim's commitment to the example of the Prophet, but what a Muslim actually believes the Prophet did, or required, cannot be predicted from the fact that she or he is a Muslim.

This use of *ḥadīth* that fit the circumstance is not some deviant American Muslim practice. There are many historical examples of the same process. We can see the creative use of *ḥadīth* – and indeed, no doubt, their creation – in the *Qudwá* of Sīdī Maḥmūd (d. c. 1640). When he described his own significance not merely as a Sufi shaykh among shaykhs, but also as an eschatological figure, Sīdī Maḥmūd deployed *ḥadīth* unknown to Standard scholarship. These *ḥadīth* were cited without the *isnād* chains of scholarly authority, but they were effective nonetheless because they were ascribed to the Prophet by Sīdī Maḥmūd: for his devotees in seventeenth-century Algeria he was a charismatic religious figure and that charisma guaranteed the texts.

> Verily [said Sīdi Maḥmūd, the Prophet]—peace be upon him said: "This learned man [who will bring salvation] is one of the offspring of Fāṭima; amongst the signs of this learned man are that he will be a master of an informed knowledge, and of an alert attention, and of military expeditions." [The Prophet] is quoted as having said that: "He who does not believe in this learned man who will go forth at the end of time, Allāh will not accept his repentance nor his ransom." It is reported that [the Prophet] also said ... "[h]e who believes in this learned man, believes likewise in me

[57] This flexibility of interpretation is noticed, but simplistically misconstrued by Hering when he says, "For centuries Koranic scholars (*ulamas*) had interpreted the Koran and *ḥadīth* to achieve certain goals. They interpreted the Koran and *ḥadīth* in the interests of the ruling dynasties of sultans or in the interests of certain religious power-groups ..." B. B. Hering, *Studies on Indonesian Islam*, 38.

> and he who disbelieves in him does not believe in me either. . . . " It is also reported that he said . . . "The ships [which are arks] are two ships, a ship which is perceived through the senses and a ship which is an ideal [of spirituality]. The ship which is an object of sense is the ark of Noah, peace be upon him, which was at the beginning of time, while the ship which is related to the mind and to the spirit is the ship of this learned man who will go forth at the end of time. He who boards it and sails in it will be safe, but he who does not board it, nor sail in it, will drown."
>
> [And still more locally significant, if less historically credible] It is also reported that [the Prophet] said, peace be upon him: "Amongst his signs will be that he will build the castle betwixt the Maghrib and the Sūdān, and he will suspend feuding and the people will follow him after five years into the tenth century of the *ḥijra*."[58]

A remarkably prescient *ḥadīth*, an *ex eventu* prophecy, that perfectly foretold the events of this obscure West African saint! Yet a quick search of the *Concordance of Ḥadīth* does not locate any of these texts, and for these *ḥadīth* no chain of authorities (*isnād*) is cited. We see then that the *ḥadīth* corpus, which nearly everyone acknowledges to be a "universal" or "essential" part of Islam, is nonetheless deployed locally for local reasons in locally inflected ways. As something shared by nearly all Muslims it is a cognate of Koiné Islam. It cannot be said, however, to have an essence, to be stable, or to be used in ways shared universally. The *ḥadīth/sunnah* is an idea, a principle. And each *ḥadīth* is an icon of Prophetic authority to which one owes allegiance. But, as always, the content and application is locally determined.

It is not just the anecdotes of particular moments in Muḥammad's life that inspire emulation, but, as Marilyn Waldman pointed out, the arc of the Prophet's life and career as a whole is a paradigm for Muslims in certain situations. His life as a whole becomes a model, but of course what exactly it models is locally determined.[59]

The Islamic world and Islamic history are filled with groups calling themselves Immigrants and Helpers (the two groups that supported Muḥammad in his struggle), with *hijrahs*, and "*jihāds* in the way of God." Leaders seldom take the title Prophet, but invoke the struggles of the charismatic first generation of Islam, with titles like Leader, Successor (*khalīfah*), and Rightly Guided One (*mahdī*).

Waldman points out that certain key features of the Muḥammad biography were deliberately invoked, for example, by the biographer of the nineteenth-century West African reformer Uthman dan Fodio and by dan

[58] H. T. Norris, *Ṣūfi Mystics of the Niger Desert*, 33–34.

[59] M. R. Waldman, "Prophetic Paradigm."

Fodio himself. Muḥammad's delegation of authority for raids to others, the division of his followers following his *hijrah* into Helpers and Emigrants, and a reforming *jihād* against pagans – all were copied and adapted by dan Fodio in his campaigns in West Africa.[60] When Muḥammad Faraj wrote the ideological manual that inspired Egyptian President Anwar Sadat's assassins, he depicted Muḥammad first and foremost as a *mujāhid* – a reforming warrior – whose task was to make "the idols of this world ... disappear through the power of the sword."[61] Faraj's goal was the establishment of an Islamic state to assist God to "make this religion enter into every house of every inhabitant of the desert, of villages, of towns, of cities ..."[62]

On the other hand, for the South African anti-apartheid intellectual, Farid Esack, the salient biographical fact about the Prophet is that, like "virtually all the prophets, [he] came from [a] peasant or working-class background ..."[63] His was a revolution that identified with the poor (*mustaḍʿafīn*), that "challenged the socio-economic premises of [the aristocracy of Mecca, the] Quraysh." The objective was "an egalitarian social order."[64] Muḥammad's task was not only to summon the religiously indifferent and pagans to become Muslim, but to challenge Jews and Christians to live up to their religious ideals, without necessarily becoming Muslims.[65]

Still more creatively, a seventeenth-century Tamil biography describes Muḥammad as "the light of the four Vedas," by which the author intends, the Torah, Psalms, Gospels, and the Qurʾān.[66] Still, in Tamilnadu the hearer would have heard the claim that Muḥammad as thematically connected to the Hindu Vedas but in the context of seventeenth-century India, the supreme human being would of course be linked to the vernacular representation for transcendent wisdom. If Muḥammad is important, then he is important in Indian terms. In this way he is not merely the Muḥammad of seventh-century Arabian history, but more importantly, he is the universal bearer of the knowledge that brings eternal felicity, and, as such, he is as much Indian as Arabian.

Like the Qurʾān, the life of Muḥammad is described as an authoritative template for Muslims, but on close inspection, it is much more a touchstone of Muslim authenticity. Viewing his life, Muslims acknowledge its claim over them, but what exactly is claimed in the process seems to depend on the perspective from which it is viewed.

[60] Ibid., 111–112. [61] M. A. S. Faraj, *The Neglected Duty*, 161. [62] Ibid., 162.
[63] F. Esack, *Qurʾān, Liberation & Pluralism*, 99. [64] Ibid., 100 and 101. [65] Ibid., 174.
[66] V. Narayanan, "Tamil *Cirappuranam*."

The "Five Pillars"

Every "Introduction to Islam" has a central chapter on "the Five Pillars of Islam." These five practices (bearing witness that God is one and Muḥammad is His messenger, five-times-daily worship, the Ramadan fast, some form of charitable giving, and the hajj to Mecca) are defined as the "bottom line" of membership in the Islamic community – both by contemporary Muslims and by academic scholars. Yet just as it startles Bible-believing Christians to point out that the early Christian community didn't have the New Testament, so too the early Muslim community didn't know the phrase "Five Pillars," and the concept shows signs of a century – at the very least – of evolution.[67] Even as the concept of a set of definitive acts came into being, the question of how many pillars upheld the House of Islam remains unresolved, even in the canonical *ḥadīth* works.[68]

If we take a snapshot of Muslims at any point in history, most, of course, would have recognized the claim of something like the "Five Pillars," that is, a set of "core practices" that defined membership in the community. What these core practices might be, we have already shown, has differed from place to place and time to time.

As for the present, we are faced with the unfortunate fact that, as Chapter 2 demonstrated, there has been very little work done by anthropologists, historians, or others, on local instantiations of the Five Pillars. Regarding the "witnessing," for instance, which is a required component of conversion to Islam, it seems that it is neglected by converts in Nupe, Nigeria. Many convert to Islam by "slipping into it," "just by wearing turbans instead of 'phrygian caps' and by attending worship." Indeed, for these converts, "[t]he five basic duties of Islam . . . are, for most . . . reduced to two" [fasting and daily worship].[69]

The daily worship too is locally inflected, though its basic form remains stable. For instance, the quinate acts of worship have been explained to me as instituted by God (1) as symbols of humility, (2) as a form of discipline by which is constructed social order: the cliché has it that "the mosques are the drill grounds of Islam," (3) as a form of calisthenics to prevent arthritis. "Now that we know about Swedish exercises and the need for physical activity," a young Algerian told me, "*ṣalāh* is optional."[70] Where once going to the mosque was a rare act among Turkish bureaucrats, now it is an important act

[67] A. J. Wensinck, *Muslim Creed*, 17–35.

[68] See *EI2*, "*Rukn.*" Also, *A Handbook of Early Muhammadan Tradition*, s.v. "Islam."

[69] S. F. Nadel, *Nupe Religion*, 235. [70] And see A. F. Nizami, *Namaz, the Yoga of Islam*.

of political party solidarity; in Uzbekistan and in parts of Russia and China, at present, it is an act of political defiance.[71]

The mosque itself should be read not just an architectural form but a localized expression of Islamic identity. In the US, the mosque, considered as a community, is poly-cultural – emigrants from all over Islamdom, various forms of converts, all attend – but outside the Americas and West Europe, it is mostly mono-cultural. Perhaps because of this, in the US all purpose-built mosques seem to have domes – a form that seems somehow to say "mosque," in the American vernacular. By contrast, in the Nupe region of Niger and Nigeria, the worship centers are "Nupe-ized" by building "open-air mosques ... [consisting] of a ring of stones laid out in the open usually under a shady tree. This simple arrangement reflect not only the simple needs of a small congregation, or its rational desire to economize; even a small community could easily build a mud-hut [of the usual type] and call it a mosque."[72] But in the Nupe religio-architectural vernacular, this arrangement of stones, sometimes in conjunction with an arboreal canopy, says "sacred space," and so, of course, for Nupe Muslims these stone arrangements and circling trees say "mosque." No domes here, but nonetheless a Muslim sacred prayer space is created in ways that locals understand.

The third pillar of Islam is the fast during the month of Ramadan. Different anthropologists describe Ramadan as shaped by penumbral customs that locally alter the focus and understanding of Ramadan.[73] Ramadan is understood in Boujad, Morocco, as a test of the will's control over passions.[74] In Egypt, Ramadan was explained to me as an egalitarian moment when poor and rich alike feel the pangs of hunger and the joys of the evening's celebration. The experience of Ramadan is very different if it is part of the collective effervescence of Muslim majority observance as in Egypt, or a counter-cultural observance, as in the United States. It was also for militant laicists in Turkey, a core Muslim practice, that, if discredited and denied, would put religion in its properly subordinate place in society.[75]

71 For a more expansive discussion of the various ways that *ṣalāh* can signify, though only in the Indian Ocean context, see the very illuminating collection, D. J. Parkin and S. C. Headley, *Prayer Across the Indian Ocean*.

72 S. F. Nadel, *Nupe Religion*, 237.

73 M. Buitelaar, *Fasting and Feasting in Morocco*; P. J. L. Frankl, "Ramaḍān in Swahili-land"; K. O. Jacobsen, "*Ramadan* in Morocco."

74 D. F. Eickelman, *Moroccan Islam*, 137–138.

75 B. Sarıcan, *1930'lardan günümüze Bursa'da dinî hayat*, 23–25.

A Particular Example: The Hajj[76]

It is not just in studies by outsiders, but also in indigenous accounts by Muslims themselves that we see important differences in the ideation of the five pillars. This is perhaps most obvious in accounts of Islam's fifth pillar – pilgrimage to the environs of Mecca and the rituals that go with it, the hajj. In the hajj, we can most clearly see the case that despite the predetermined form of the hajj-ritual, Muslims' understandings and experiences are extraordinarily diverse, and, in many important ways, conform to their particular local norms. The hajj is shaped as much by what the pilgrim brings from home as by what she or he encounters in Arabia.

In discussions of what it is that unifies Muslims, commentators frequently point to the pilgrimage to Mecca, the hajj, as a shared experience that brings Muslims together from all over the world and in the process unifies them and their practice. One scholar includes it in "the triad of forms central to Islam in general: Muḥammad, the Qur'ān, and the pilgrimage . . . the holy person, the holy book, and a holy rite."[77]

This assertion of the hajj's importance is surely on the mark.[78] Yet at the same time the hajj constitutes the clearest instance of a practice only *seemingly* shared that actually differs in the participants' experience and understanding. The hajj, through a series of communally practiced rites, nevertheless means, signifies, and is understood, in a variety of ways. This is the reality of Lived Islam's Koiné.[79]

Consider a series of hajj-accounts collected by Matheson and Milner.[80] These Malay descriptions of the hajj span a period from the late fifteenth or early sixteenth century CE to 1979 CE. In the first account, from the *Hikayat Hang Tuah*, the Malay ninth-/fifteenth-century traveler Hang Tuah was on his way to Anatolia and stopped at Jiddah simply to visit Eve's tomb – a site

[76] The hajj is usually accounted the fifth pillar of Islam. The study of Islam's "fourth pillar," *zakāh*, is complicated by the indeterminacy or polyvalence of *zakāh* almost from the beginning. See EI2 "*Zakāt*." Nonetheless, it would be an illuminating project to ask diverse Muslims what they understand by the term "*zakāh*" and how they practice it.

[77] J. L. Peacock, *Purifying the Faith*, 101.

[78] This is the case, even though it must have worked mostly in the imagination, since for most of Islamic history only a tiny minority of the world's Muslims were able to make the arduous journey to Mecca. It is only with the development of modern worldwide transport that mass participation becomes a feature of the hajj.

[79] A number of important hajj-accounts could not be considered here but are invaluable as examples of the utter diversity of hajj interpretations and hajj experiences. See J. Āl-i Aḥmad, *Lost in the Crowd*; A. Hammoudi, *A Season in Mecca*; B. D. Metcalf, "The Pilgrimage Remembered"; M. N. Pearson, *Pilgrimage to Mecca: The Indian Experience, 1500–1800*; M. Wolfe, *One Thousand Roads to Mecca*.

[80] V. Matheson and A. C. Milner, *Perceptions of the Haj*.

of considerable importance to pre-Wahhabi visitors.[81] While there, he was persuaded to go on the hajj,[82] which seemed mostly an opportunity to encounter saints such as al-Khiḍr – the Companion of Alexander alluded to in the Qur'ān – to view the Ka'bah, and visit tombs of Islamic worthies.[83] Indeed, as the compilers suggest, the hajj was understood by the narrator largely as a "search for spiritual power," and the rites of the hajj, judging from the space assigned them and the rhetorical plainness of the account, were of secondary significance. Matheson and Milner suggest that, for this Malay traveler, it was the ritual panoply of the hajj that was important to him, more than any normatively "spiritual" meaning.[84]

The significance of the hajj for the author of *Chatetan Ka-Tanah Suchi*, who wrote after 1960, was quite different. For him, it was first and foremost a journey to the historical center of Islam, "where the Prophet Muḥammad had halted," "where Abraham stood before God," where "the Prophet Adam was lowered from heaven and met Eve."[85] Additionally, according to the authors, he was eager to gain status "within Malay Society by undertaking the haj." He was "preoccupied with the Malays and Malayan matters."[86] In other words, the hajj remained an event grounded in the local Malaysian understanding of the ritual's significance and meaning.

Two other quite diverse hajj-accounts confirm the colloquial particularity of the hajj. Malcolm X provides what is perhaps, in the United States, the best-known account of the hajj. This portion of his *Autobiography* is usually read as an experience that expresses, through the hajj-ritual, the unity of all Muslims, and it functions as a conversion-account for his departure from the race-chauvinism of the Nation of Islam.[87] While this reading is certainly not inaccurate, the account, read for itself, is something else as well. From beginning to end, this account is framed by characteristically American (and particularly African-American) concerns – the discovery that status and prestige could be accorded someone who, in American parlance of that era, was a "Negro," and thus disqualified from "first class treatment."

From his first stop in Europe, Malcolm X was "looked upon as a Muslim and not as a Negro. People seeing you as a Muslim saw you as a human

[81] F. E. Peters, *The Hajj*.

[82] "[W]hy don't you wait for *bulan haji*, the month of the pilgrimage, which is almost here. You should go to Mecca and perform the pilgrimage as you are so close." V. Matheson and A. C. Milner, *Perceptions of the Haj*, 5.

[83] Ibid., 7, 11–12. [84] Ibid., 10–11. [85] Ibid., 26–29. [86] Ibid., 29.

[87] Feener points out that some accounts of the hajj emphasize, to the contrary, the immense differences among Muslims, in dress and ethnicity. See R. M. Feener, *Islam in World Cultures*, 9.

being."[88] In Cairo, he met people who "accepted me like a brother."[89] At the Cairo airport, "strings had been pulled" for Malcolm,[90] and on board the plane, the crew treated him with "the same honor and respect I had received ever since I left America."[91] He was piloted through customs by a Saudi engineer, who was then his host in Arabia. This is not just any Saudi, however: "I was in a car with the brother-in-law of the son of the ruler of Arabia. . . . I had never been so honored in my life."[92] He was put into a "three-room suite [that] had a bathroom that was as big as a double at the New York Hilton."[93] The rest of the hajj was equally affirmative. Malcolm was given a car and driver by the Chief of Protocol for Prince Faisal,[94] and attendants guided him through the rituals of the Pilgrimage.[95] "Prince Faisal, the absolute ruler of Arabia, had made me a guest of the state. Among the courtesies and privileges which this brought to me, especially—shamelessly—I relished the chauffeured car which toured me around in Mecca with the chauffeur-guide pointing out sights of particular significance. . . . My car took me to participate in special prayers at Mt. Arafat, and at Mina."[96]

This is not to minimize the significance of the discovery that "whiteness" was an attitude, not a feature of skin color, but to point out that the trip was for him an affirmation, a realization that status, privilege, and honor could be bestowed upon an African-American; the hajj provides a point of view affirming not merely "the brotherhood of man" but the potential for status and power for this particular African-American leader.

The late twentieth-century Pilgrimage of Ibrāhīm Abdulai of Ghana provides a painful contrast to that of Malcolm X.[97] For him, the hajj was no experience of air-conditioned cars and front-of-the-bus treatment, but it was instead an exercise in perseverance and privation. Fleeced and defrauded, too poor to afford a sacrifice at Mina, his whole hajj experience was one of fortitude. He invoked the Koiné Qur'ān at the beginning to explain why he shared out his property,[98] and then plunged into the

[88] Malcolm X, *Autobiography*, 321. [89] Ibid., 322. [90] Ibid., 323. [91] Ibid., 324.
[92] Ibid., 332. [93] Ibid., 333. [94] Ibid., 336.
[95] The account of the whole of the hajj-rituals takes up only a few paragraphs (on p. 337), while the chapter on the trip to Mecca takes up twenty-four pages.
[96] Malcolm X, *Autobiography*, 343.
[97] J. Chernoff, "Drummer's Testament." I am grateful to Charles Hallisey who called this wonderful text to my attention.
[98] Ibid., 73. "God even says something about it in the Holy Qur'ān that if you are going, you should share all your property. If you come back, it is good; if you don't come back, it is also good." There seems to be no such text in the *muṣḥaf*, though of course there is in Ibrāhīm's Koiné Qur'ān.

maelstrom because "you will face many dangerous problems at Mecca. . . . If you fall, you will not be able to stand up again. There is nobody. They are telling you lies. If you fall in that way, they will perform your funeral."[99] What is the Pilgrimage? It is an occasion "to visit all the places our Holy Prophet visited, and you are going to pray at all the places where he prayed." After completing the rites "then to God you are just like a small child. You have no fault to your fellow friend or to God."[100]

Even the rites themselves are seen through the dialect lens of colloquial Islam: "And the Kaaba too, there is something inside the Kaaba just like a hole and there is something inside the hole, like a breast.[101] You put your hand inside and touch the breast and pray to God, and then put your mouth by your hand and suck from your hand and be praying."[102] According to Ibrāhīm, other West Africans, Yorubas, believe that Mt. ʿArafāt is significant because defecation there brings money.[103] This hajj is very different from Malcolm's. It is a trial that brings purification, not an apotheosis into a larger and more admirable community. Ibrāhīm Abdulai's pilgrimage to Mecca also takes place in Ghana, just as Malcolm's also takes place in segregated America.

There is, in short, no essence of the hajj, and the hajj is not the essence of Islam. Both are experienced through a framework particular to the participant. It should be clear that even the universal, in-gathering, shared ritual of the hajj is understood through the colloquial Islam that each Muslim brings to Islam's center. All Muslims share the Koiné commitment to the Pilgrimage, but the *meaning*, and the *experience* of the hajj is determined by the colloquial, by the Lived Islam of its participants.

The Five Pillars, or some subset of them, are central to what it means to be Muslim and are a third cognate shared among Muslims. These are practices that Muslims share, but even these are inflected by local understandings. They serve, however, as "rallying signs"[104] which, to use the old formula, represent and re-present an Islamic identity to the actor and to others. How the rituals are understood, how they mesh with other structures, however, is all locally determined. It seems likely that if the pillars of Islam are further studied in local context, scholars will certainly find a rich and creative set of vernacular understandings.[105]

99 Ibid. 100 Ibid., 79–80.

101 A reference to the Black Stone imbedded in a silver holder, on one corner of the Kaʿbah. It is recommended that at each circumambulation, the stone be touched or kissed.

102 J. Chernoff, "Drummer's Testament," 81. 103 Ibid., 84.

104 A. Hammoudi, *Master and Disciple*, 41.

105 R. Launay, *Beyond the Stream*, 27, and throughout the first section of the book, makes an excellent case for the importance of ritual over belief as the object of study.

Sharīʿah

A fourth cognate common to most "Islamic dialects" is *sharīʿah* – the notion of a plenary set of rules that impartially guide humankind to right and salvific action. *Sharīʿah* is usually translated instead as "Islamic Law."[106] *Sharīʿah* is instantiated in the huge corpus of *fiqh* texts, many of them ranging to ten volumes or more, and until recently written almost exclusively in Arabic. They cover a scope unimaginable to even the most religious-minded Christian.[107] Oral hygiene, sexual positions, table manners, contracts, judicial procedure, child custody rules: no detail of life, it is often asserted, is without its Islamic specification. Yet on consideration, one feature of the *fiqh* texts stands out: it is rare to find an explanation of *why* one should perform the *sharīʿah*-mandated act. The *why* of a rule is left open. This meagerness of specification is, as we shall see, a virtue, not a problem in Islamic practice; it is, as the computer folk say, a feature, not a bug. It is sufficient here to say that into these voids of prescribed meaning, Muslims have from earliest times added interpretations and understandings that helped to construct the shared part of their Lived Islam.[108]

Yet until quite recently the works prescribing *fiqh* rules appeared only in the language of Islamic scholarship – Arabic – a language that the overwhelming majority of Muslims did not know. They are voluminous and written in a very technical, jargon-ridden Arabic that even an Arabic speaker usually cannot understand. From the earliest writings we have, Muslim scholars have anticipated that the laity wouldn't know all the details of the *sharīʿah*. There is evidence that for early Muslims there was a bottom-line set of practices that made one a Muslim, and other complex matters of theology and practice were not considered essential to membership in the community.[109] Yet the teeming foliage of Islamic law and practice have always remained unknown to most Muslims.

One of the Muslim mantras of the present age is, "Islam is a way of life, not just a religion."[110] While as a statement of comparative religious analysis it is not good, this mantra does tell us something important. Muslims experience *sharīʿah* as the concept of authoritative action, that there is in all cases a right

[106] e.g., F. Denny, *Introduction*. [107] Its scope would not, of course, surprise an Orthodox Jew.

[108] On the way in which rituals "call for interpretation," see A. K. Reinhart, "What to Do with Ritual Texts," and the sources cited there.

[109] On the two-tiered nature of Islamic obligations, see al-Shāfiʿī, *Risālah*, 357–360ff. On early understandings of acts necessary for community membership, see A. K. Reinhart, "Difference Between Heaven and Earth."

[110] F. Denny, *Introduction*, 216.

way to do things Islamically. Yet that right way to live a life at one and the same time shared with other Muslims and inflected locally.

The range of acts that Muslims identify with Islam is far from identical with even the content of *fiqh* works. As one ethnographer reports from Morocco,

> A majority [of townspeople] ordinarily assume that ["the way thing are done"] is based upon, if not identical to, Islamic law (*shra'*)[111] in both its jural and its moral sense ... in its moral sense the Islamic law ... prescribes the obligations of a Muslim ... In scholarly texts there exists a complex set of prescriptions for conduct, many based upon the Prophet's life. Few Moroccans know these in any detail. In its more popular sense as a code of conduct, Islamic law as popularly understood glides imperceptibly into "the way things are done ..." Most [townspeople] ... tacitly assume that Islam is what Muslims do, or should be expected to do ... [The *shra'*] is considered ideologically to be immutable ... [but since the *shra'*] is inaccessible in written form to virtually all [of them], there are ... no effective criteria by which the claim of immutability can be demonstrated. Thus ... the code of conduct is responsive to the shared, constantly renegotiated universe of meaning within which Moroccans live and is amenable to transformation.[112]

Sharī'ah, as it functions in Lived Islam, has three important attributes. (1) It has the form of *rules* for action. Its authority, once invoked, is nearly that of the Qur'ān and *ḥadīth* themselves.

> The *sharī'ah* ... regulates the external life of man ... The *sharī'ah,* [according to observant mystics in Pakistan,] if perfectly obeyed by humans, imposes divine order upon the world of men ... [T]he *sharī'ah* structures [the Islamic] community by prescribing rules for most social and private situations. The *sharī'ah* thus defines the orthodox community of Muslims and regulates worldly activity.[113]

Even under the anti-religious Soviets, in formerly Islamic regions the petty commodity economy was "wholly defined by *sharī'a*[*h*], disguised as 'national traditions' at the family, neighborhood, and village level."[114]

(2) It is both comprehensive and limited: its scope is, in theory, unbounded – though the boundaries of Dialect knowledge define many

[111] The Moroccan dialect version of the word "*sharī'ah.*"

[112] D. F. Eickelman, *Moroccan Islam*, 131–132.

[113] K. Ewing, "*Malangs* of the Punjab," 360.

[114] S. P. Poliakov and M. B. Olcott, *Everyday Islam*, 38.

circumstances, sometimes whole domains of human activity, where an Islamic perspective is unconsidered or unknown.[115]

The combination of (a) the commitment to the idea that all of human behavior has divinely ordained norms, and (b) the limited knowledge of what these norms might be, has historically meant that the authority of the *sharīʿah* has spilled into domains and rules not textually part of Islamic law. Thus the interpenetration of *sharīʿah* and "how things are done" described above by Eickelman. Any given local practice can be and often is justified by reference to "Islam" or the law. Loeffler's informants tell him that, "Our religion has ordered us [to fast, worship, etc.] and we have to obey."[116]

But also,

> of course the religion approves of [calendars which foretell the future].[117] [And,] some [mullahs] don't ride in a car because they consider it forbidden, and others . . . say that inoculations and Western medicine are forbidden. But only illiterate, foolish characters say that. . . . The religion indeed demands the pursuit of science . . .[118]

The Ikhwān, the shock troops of the early twentieth-century Saudi state, rejected electricity, which "brought light without oil or wax," and they broke mirrors because they reflected images – all on the grounds that these were items forbidden by *sharīʿah*.[119] Yet most Muslims use these items daily and would consider absurd the idea that they might be forbidden by the *sharīʿah*. The content of the *sharīʿah*, at least in the *Muslim* public mind, is scarcely fixed or stable.[120]

(3) Most importantly, even the Islamic rules embedded in works of *fiqh* transmitted and studied in Fez, Mecca, Bukhara, Lahore, and Jakarta are in a sense, "hollow." They are authenticated formally by reference to authoritative sources, but they are seldom *explained* textually or in the texts that impose them as obligations.[121] Consequently they are always "filled" – that is, interpreted and explained – in the locality in which they are practiced.

[115] "Few Moroccans know [the complex set of prescriptions for conduct] in any detail." D. F. Eickelman, *Moroccan Islam*, 131.

[116] R. Loeffler, *Islam in Practice*, 197. [117] Ibid., 48. [118] Ibid., 28.

[119] *EI2*, 3:1065A; s.v. "*Ikhwān*."

[120] One might say the same is true for the good people of Oklahoma, among other states, who have voted to "ban the *sharīʿah*," via the "save our state amendment" to the state constitution. "Critics . . . paint Sharia as a cruel, draconic legal system that is antithetical to American values, and fear that it is on the verge of being imposed on Americans." C. Kuruvilla, "5 Things You Need to Know About Sharia Law."

[121] Much of *fiqh* was perhaps once merely local rules and customs, but as rules imbedded in authoritative *fiqh* works, it is *déracineé*, but also supremely authoritative. See A. L. Udovitch, "An Eleventh Century Islamic Treatise on the Law of the Sea."

For example, according to Mālikī-rite law books, the minimum bride-price is specified as "one quarter-dinar" (locally *robon dinari*), a classical Islamic unit of money. No one in West Africa, however, uses dinars, nor do most people know what they are. Yet, for each locality in West Africa, there is an equivalent in a local medium of exchange established, and that medium and value of the *roban dinari* varies entirely almost from place to place.[122] In the *fiqh* book there is only the rule – unadorned, plain, and awaiting meaning and rules for application. That rule requires elaboration and understanding through practice.

To help clarify, here is a *fiqh* rule from a standard *fiqh* text, the *Multaqá l-abḥur* of Burhānaddīn al-Ḥalabī, a standard seventeenth-century Ottoman madrasa text. It contains the rules for fasting Ramadan and the rules for those who must observe the fast.

> [The Ramadan fast] is ceasing to eat and drink and have intercourse from dawn to sunset with a ritual intention, by the "legal subjects." And these are [Muslims who are] sane, purified of menstruation or parturition.[123]

Bare and unadorned by any explanation of the why or meaning of the command. Even the commentary on the text is austere [text in boldface; commentary in roman].

> **[The Ramadan fast] is ceasing to eat** and everything that falls into this category, and this does not exclude also what reaches the brain, for [such things] break the fast also; what is intended in putting something in one's stomach by eating or otherwise. What reaches the brain reaches the belly because between brain and belly there is an effective connection **and drink** by deliberate action **and have intercourse** that is, in order to stop the libido from these acts [which are done] intentionally. This does not include what is done thoughtlessly. The act of one who acts thoughtlessly is not efficacious, legally. [And so on.][124]

There is no "why" here, no fitting into a larger context of meaning. The rule cries out for commentary and explanation, but what explanation there

[122] R. Launay, *Beyond the Stream*, 10–11.

[123] D. Efendī and M. A. S. Shaykhīzādeh, *Majma' al-anhur*, 1:230.

[124] There is, unusually for a *fiqh* book, an evocative introduction to the section saying that "fasting Ramadan is a stilling of the perturbative self and a breaking of its strength, in the excess connected to all the 'limbs,' the eye, the tongue, the ear, the genitals. By means of it, their activities are weakened with regard to their sensations." And so on. But this is unusual and shows the particular Ottoman engagement with Avicennan *falsafah*.

might be is provided outside of the legal text. The hollow rule invites refilling by local understandings of its purpose and effect.[125]

In reality, then, even the observance of *sharīʿah* is less about hegemony and more about improvisation. Its form invites Muslims to apply their own knowledge to local circumstances with authoritative results. So it is that one finds quite various explanations of the "why" of a rule or even the "how" of it, depending on the characteristics of the explainer, while there is quite widespread agreement on the rule.

Surprisingly, then, even the most hegemonic feature of *sharīʿah* – the aspect that makes "Islam a way of life and not just a religion" – namely, the idea that there is a rule for every action, is open to local understanding and augmentation – and in fact demands it. Even the most observant Muslim, in short, is compelled to indigenize Islam.

In this way, we can begin to account for the remarkable fact that Muslims, however widely found, recognize each other as Muslims – they recognize in each other's practice cognate features of their own Islam. On the other hand, bearing in mind the previous discussion of Islamic dialect features, we can also explain the success Islam has had in diverse cultural, economic, and ecological domains – from the arid semi-urban and urban domain of Arabia to the inner cities of North America. Even though systemic coherence is enforced by the Koiné of Islam, a great deal of space is left for the insertion of the local – of rituals of life cycle and rites of passage, for local knowledge and local needs to be expressed and addressed. One cognate remains for our consideration and that is the concept of "Islam" itself.

"Islam" as Cognate

More than fifty years ago, Wilfred Cantwell Smith observed that "of all the world's religious traditions the Islamic would seem to be the one with a built-in name. The word 'Islam' occurs in the Qurʾān itself, and Muslims are insistent on using this term to designate the system of their faith."[126] Perhaps, Smith suggests, this is because, "of all the major religious communities of the world today the Islamic is the only one that has come into historical existence ... when schematized religious systems had evolved ..."[127]

[125] This silence that is replaced by local interpretation is not a deficiency but an advantage. As Bowen says in another context, "It is the unsaid, the under-interpreted, the absence of exegesis at the event itself that permits ritual practitioners to reconstruct community on top of a wide variety of individual opinions about what is ritually proper and practically possible." J. R. Bowen, *Muslims Through Discourse*, 318.

[126] W. C. Smith, *Meaning and End*, 80. [127] Ibid., 108.

"Islam" then, as a word and concept, has historically stood in unique relationship to the faithful; and for Muslims, the fact of being "Muslim," of identifying with "Islam," uniquely signifies not just commitment to a set of salvific beliefs and practices, but to an ideology and identity – an identity chosen and one that must be demonstrated and affirmed.

From another perspective, Islam, as Talal Asad has said, is a discourse about the Qur'ān and *ḥadīth*.[128] Of course it is not the texts of the Qur'ān and *ḥadīth* to which Asad must refer, but the authoritative discourse about those texts and their contents.

Benedict Anderson's notion of "imagined community" is also useful here in understanding the Koiné of Islam. To be a Muslim is to imagine oneself as a part of that community, and a community whose nature may be understood differently from place to place.[129] To begin: Surely how one imagines Islam and Islamdom is shaped by being, among other things, a Muslim in the *dominant majority*, as in Egypt; in an *exclusive majority*, as in Arabia; *in a tenuous majority*, as in Malaysia; in a *minority*, as in India; or in a *tiny minority*, as in the United Kingdom. These and many other "extraneous" factors shape one's experience as a Muslim and the local understanding of the "Islam" which guides one's life. But one is seldom a Muslim in solitude, and it as a member of a community that one's Islam is lived. That community, however, exists by the shared commitment of its members who jointly create, or imagine, that community. In so doing, of course, they cannot help but shape that imagined community in light of their own experiences. That "Islam" is an imagined community is hardly unique to Muslims. Benedict Anderson has drawn our attention to the fact that the most tangible of our contemporary communities, the nation, is itself constructed in the imaginations of its citizens or subjects whose belief and commitment make it a reality.

And for Anderson, the very model of an imagined community is seen in the hajj:

> For our purpose here, the model journey is the pilgrimage. It is not simply that in the minds of Christians, Muslims or Hindus, the cities of Rome, Mecca, or Benares were the centers of sacred geographies, but that their centrality was experienced and "realized" (in the stagecraft sense) by the constant flow of pilgrims moving towards them from the remote and otherwise unrelated localities ... As noted earlier, the strange physical

128 See discussion in Chapter 1.

129 This seems to be what Marranici means when he says that to be a Muslim is to feel oneself to be a Muslim. G. Marranici, *The Anthropology of Islam*, 8.

> juxtaposition of Malays, Persians, Indians, Berbers and Turks in Mecca is something incomprehensible without an idea of their community in some form. The Berber encountering the Malay before the Kaaba must, as it were, ask himself: "Why is this man doing what I am doing, uttering the same words that I am uttering, even though we can not talk to one another?" There is only one answer, once one has learnt it: "Because we ... are Muslims." There was, to be sure, always a double aspect to the choreography of the great religious pilgrimages: a vast horde of illiterate vernacular-speakers provided the dense, physical reality of the ceremonial passage; while a small segment of literate bilingual adepts drawn from each vernacular community performed the unifying rites, interpreting to their respective followings the meanings of their collective motion.[130]

At bottom, then, it is self-ascription that makes one a Muslim: "I am muslim," or more modernly, "I am a Muslim."[131] This is hardly a radical proposition – though it is one that theologians of the academy and scholars of the madrasa might reject. To understand the force of saying "I am a Muslim," however, one needs to see the phrase within the field of Koiné Islam. Like the ideal of the Qur'ān and the *ḥadīth*, like the concept of obligatory rituals, "I am a Muslim" provides a framework – however empirically illusory – of unity, of shared identity and practice. This idea of unity – affirmed, but more importantly, experienced, as truth – functions to discipline Muslim possibilities – in practice but more significantly, in theory. Ethnographies, as well as one's everyday conversations with Muslims about religion, are filled with actions or beliefs justified by reference to Islam: "Islam says," "Islam requires," "because I'm a Muslim ..." The Islam to which they refer is empirically diverse but conceptually unitary. That is part of its nature: the metaphor of unity – of God, of truth, of the authentic community – is of course at the core of Muslim dogma.

What Creates Koiné Islam?

When we try to account for efficacy of Koiné Islam as the "tie that binds" Muslims into a community of mutual recognition, a starting point is the common ritual language shared by Muslims.[132] The Qur'ān as a ritual text and ritual object has always been written and recited in Arabic, a language

[130] B. Anderson, *Imagined Communities*, 53–54.

[131] Wilfred Smith's distinction between being someone who endeavors to submit to God in the manner He ordains (muslim), and someone who is a member of a group designated with the name (Muslim).

[132] With the interesting but demographically insignificant exception mentioned above at note 23.

mostly opaque to the Muslim reciting Qurʾān in her devotions, and – to repeat – opaque in most places and over most of Muslim history. Even when the Qurʾān's texts are incomprehensible or abstruse, its iconic status remains. The devotions' texts themselves are in Arabic, too. *Samiʿa ʾllāh li-man ḥamidahu* ("God hears who praises Him") says every Muslim performing *ṣalāh*; *Labaykallāh, labayka* says every *ḥājjī* on arrival to Mecca for the hajj pilgrimage (usually translated as "at thy service, Lord God"). This linguistic opacity, this elimination of the discursive from the ritual, does not empty the ritual of meaning, as anti-ritualists allege. Rather, it amplifies its meaningfulness. This is not the place for a treatise on ritual, but one feature of ritual is that it is devoid of intrinsic meaning, but at the same time it demands interpretation. The opacity of classical Qurʾānic Arabic – no more than translucency even for most Arabs – enhances the non-discursive quality attached to it: diverse meanings, richly various and particularly potent for exactly that reason. It is no coincidence that the most prominent elements of what we are calling Islamic Koiné are rituals not beliefs – they are practices not discourses. Actions, especially actions learned mimetically, are easily shared with others, even others quite different from you, especially others separated from you by a different language. In addition, Muslims' Koiné rituals are, in their normative form, communal: *ṣalāh* with other Muslims, fasting together during Ramadan, traveling together in the millions through the various rites of the hajj. And the finding of cognitive neuroscience suggests that synchronized activity enhances not just solidarity but empathy. It creates feelings of calm and happiness.[133] For all these reasons, the Koiné rituals of Islam – however diverse Muslims' understanding of them – still create a grammar, as it were, of Islam that allows Muslims to recognize each other, to act ritually together.

More discursive *Koiné* elements – "Islam" and "*sharīʿah*" for instance, or accounts of the Prophet's life – still provide a shared focus of attention, a stable set of questions if not of answers, that has similarly allowed Muslims to see in each other citizens in a commonwealth of shared conversations and aspirations. Whether the Prophet is understood as a Logos, or a Liberation Fighter, his authority as the archetypal Muslim remains – either distant and of a different station from the rest of humankind, or utterly approachable and emulable.

[133] Just as a sample: A. Behrends et al., "Moving in and out of Synchrony"; E. Cohen et al., "Religion, Synchrony, and Cooperation"; E. E. Cohen et al., "Rowers' High: Behavioural Synchrony is Correlated with Elevated Pain Thresholds."

And finally, what has helped created the koiné-ness of Lived Islam has been the absence of a single authority for interpreting Islam – no Vatican, no Islamic Academy Française. Consequently, the process of meaning-making, always revolving around the gravitational mass of the Koiné, has been exuberant though restrained, somewhat confined but vigorously creative, an ongoing effort to find Islam in a way suited to the times and places of its adherents.

Conclusion

There are, observably, objects symbols and practices that Muslims from diverse locales affirm to be central to Islam. The discourse that centers on these is at the heart of Muslim identity and practice. Yet the actual content of the texts, the theology of the rituals and the set of practices, is less important practically than local understandings, the local appropriation, of these texts, rituals, and moral requirements. As Lambek points out, the performance of the Koiné texts and rituals, both Islamicizes the locale he studies, Mayotte, and "Mayottesizes" the Islam that is performed.[134] The very idea of "Islam" and "being Muslim" too is irresistibly (for most) affected by local considerations, expectations, possibilities, and constraints. The list of *sharīʿah,* Qurʾān, *ḥadīth,* and rituals does not exhaust the cognates of Koiné Islam; there are other commonly found Islamic notions that may function as part of the Koiné as well – gender hierarchy, perhaps, or charismatic protégés of God. What is important to note is that the Koiné element is not part of an "essence of Islam" because Islam has no essence, only shared forms. In the abstract, these elements are meaningless, contentless, and never exist apart from the meaning instilled in them by the local Lived Islam. Yet few Muslims will deny their importance, or the centrality of these Koiné elements. They are all, in some form, shared by all who call themselves Muslims.

The commitment to the trans-local Islam too is part of Islam. How then shall we think about the aspects of Islam that are not parochial, but which affect and often re-form the local – texts, perspectives, and persons which gain their force precisely from being trans-local and normative. This *Standard,* this *Cosmopolitan* Islam is the subject of our next chapter.

[134] M. Lambek, "Localising Islamic Performances in Mayotte," 71 and *passim.*

5

Cosmopolitan Islam

The Standard Islam of the Scholars

Introduction

Dialect Islam and Koiné Islam are transmitted mostly in the vernacular language. Even the Koiné Qur'ān, the Koiné rituals, and Koiné *sharī'ah* are taught and explained in some local language. This is so even when they are performed in an Arabic incomprehensible to most Muslims. As we saw in the contrasting accounts of Ibrāhīm Abdulai of Ghana and Malcom X of the United States above, the hajj is explained to Dagbamba folk using Dagbani concepts in the Dagbani language; it is described to American Muslims in American English using American concepts although the liturgies of the hajj are recited in Islamic Arabic.

For a small group of Muslims, however, Classical Islamic Arabic functioned and continues to function as a true lingua franca and they have used it to write, to study, and to dispute. Their specialist Islam is also an elite Islam, and its bearers, the *'ulamā'* (from the root *'-l-m* indicating "to know" or "knowing"), are found throughout Islamdom. They interact with and identify with their equally accomplished fellows – both contemporaries and scholarly forebears. They mediate the Arabic textual traditions to the Islamically less literate. Because this kind of Islam is found everywhere in Islamdom, we will refer to it as the *Cosmopolitan* aspect of Islam. It is borne by the scholars (the *'ulamā'*), manifested in their texts, instantiated in institutions of formal Muslim learning that produce the next generation of scholars and scholarship, and embodied in their persons and in their lives. They seek to circumscribe and safeguard Islamic sacred space, to live in Islam's sacred time, using "the language of the angels," as Arabic is called.

This Cosmopolitan Islam is at home everywhere, precisely because its advocates seek to inscribe everywhere an Islam of no place, of no time, in no one's language, as we shall see below. Throughout Islamic history, though it accommodated differences among its qualified membership, Koiné Islam was, in general, and over time, largely critical of Dialect practice and other aspects of local Lived Islam. These Cosmopolitan scholars were intolerant of the contemporary, the particular, and the local, but to them we have to ascribe the persistent Koiné notion of a single Islam shared globally and practiced harmoniously. And to them also we must ascribe the steady discipline that kept Muslims in conversation with each other. When they curb and excise the extravagances of Dialect practices they make the "single Islam" a conceptual reality for most Muslims. Since this aspect of Islam so often is taken for Islam itself, this chapter is the most extensive – it has to "unteach" what is conventionally assumed and to offer an alternate account of how the Cosmopolitan aspect of Lived Islam actually did its work. In it we hope to recast the Islam of scholars, not as the "real Islam," but as the powerful, mythologizing force it was and is – the Islam of those have so far been astonishingly successful in their creation of an Islam of the mind, transcending time and space.

Islamic Knowledge: *ʿIlm* and Its Culture

It is *ʿilm* (textual knowledge) that defines the Cosmopolitan Muslim, and *ʿilm* is the membership card that admits him or her to the circle of Islamic prestige. I keep the Arabic word because it is not just any sort of knowledge that constitutes Cosmopolitan Islam: it is a special subset of knowledge. *ʿIlm* is the universal and universalizing knowledge of Islam. The word, with the characteristic dynamism of Arabic, means both "knowledge" and "knowing." An Islamic scholar (called an *ʿālim*, "knower" [pl. *ʿulamāʾ*]) has as his[1] task "knowing knowledge," though what counts as knowledge has historically come from a tightly limited group of sources.

For the scholars who transmit Cosmopolitan Islam, knowledge is, above all, the data found in the two canonical Muslim Scriptures: the Arabic Qurʾān, of course, and the Arabic-language corpus of reliably transmitted anecdotes about the Prophet's deeds and sayings (called *ḥadīth*). For the scholars, these texts constitute a more or less finite corpus of real data. From these texts, as they supposed, scholars developed a set of tools with which they believed they could determine God's norms for every human act. And

[1] Throughout the section on scholarship I use the pronoun "he" because – though there were women scholars of some note, particularly in the field of *ḥadīth* transmission – the fact is that scholars until the very most recent times have been men. This is changing at present, and that change will be part of our discussion in Chapter 6.

so, effectively, the scope of *'ilm*'s application – according to Cosmopolitan Muslims – is limitless.

'Ilm, however, includes not merely the data of the texts, but also the authorized *techniques* for interpreting those texts, and the *results* of those interpretations. For Cosmopolitan Muslims, no knowledge or means of interpretation other than this single box of hermeneutic tools and texts counted as *'ilm* – not intuition, vision, numerology, pure logic, mathematics, extra-Arabic linguistics. Other knowledge might be recognized as useful or valuable in its own domain, but it was irrelevant to the business of Muslim scholarship, and so it was peripheral to the real, authentic, universal Islam.[2] This official knowledge, one might call it, was taught from Arabic books in formal institutions. Someone not trained in these schools generally could not participate in Cosmopolitan Islam's formation. "In a quite literal sense [the non-scholars] 'did not speak the language'" and this was even truer as one moved outside the Arab world.[3]

Oddly, it is the very specificity of this *'ilm* – its Arabic language corpus, its specific interpretative tools – that facilitates its universalization. The Arabic used in Cosmopolitan scholarship is not spoken Arabic but Standard, Classical, bookish Islamic Arabic – as far from the vernacular as Latin is from Spanish or Romanian. Consequently the Arab *hoi polloi* (*al-'awāmm*) are as excluded from having legitimate Cosmopolitan Islamic opinions as the Hindustani, Uzbek, or others of the Muslim masses. Yet on the other hand, anyone, anywhere in Islamdom has only to master Islamic Arabic, to study the *'ilm* corpus, and to learn the tools of interpretation and he (and now, she) is on an equal footing with every other Cosmopolitan scholar wherever and whenever he lives.

One of the two sources of *'ilm* was unitary from the start – according to pious history, the Qur'ān, the "Book of God," was codified within thirty years of the Prophet's death and was promulgated throughout all the Islamic diaspora; it was *the* indisputable Scriptural source. According to received Islamic theory, the other source of *'ilm*, the *sunnah* (norms) of the Prophet (preserved in the anecdotes called *ḥadīth*), was dispersed when those who had known the Prophet traveled outward with the Islamic conquests. They

[2] There are exceptions here, when technical knowledge is drawn into *sharī'ah* texts, as when maritime manuals become part of *sharī'ah* texts, A. L. Udovitch, "An Eleventh Century Islamic Treatise on the Law of the Sea," or when builders' knowledge becomes part of the genre of "Books of Walls" in *sharī'ah* works. Simon O'Meara kindly called my attention to this latter genre and taught me a lot on the subject; I can record my gratitude here. See S. O'Meara, *Space and Muslim Urban Life*.

[3] P. Burke, *Popular Culture in Early Modern Europe*, 28.

took their knowledge of Islamic acts and norms with them as they moved to Egypt, Syria, Iraq, and Iran. At first these different data about the Prophet were a kind of regional lore, and scholars speak of Egyptian lines of *ḥadīth* transmission, of Kufan or Syrian, and so on. (There is no doubt, however, that extra-Prophetic local beliefs and understandings passed at this point into the corpus of *ḥadīth* and were Islamicized.) The regional distinctiveness of *ḥadīth* disappeared when scholars of the second, third, and fourth Islamic century developed one of the most remarkable practices of any religious history. This was the culture of Islamic scholarly travel – the *ṭalab al-ʿilm* ("seeking knowledge"). *ʿIlm* fueled Islam, and scholars traveled in search of *ʿilm* as geologists travel today in search of oil.

At first, these scholars merely hunted the *ʿilm* of Prophetic norms, thought they were themselves also carriers of their own and others' scholarly knowledge which they freely shared. In the event, however, they created an expectation that a serious scholar would travel. More importantly, they created an identity – the transnational scholar dealing in the matter of mythic Islamic times and standing apart from any local culture. The hajj, as a duty incumbent on Muslims who could manage it, gave added impetus to the expectation of scholarly wayfaring, and the result was an astonishingly cosmopolitan culture among the intellectual elites.

The copious biographical literature about scholars always lists their travels and the "foreign" scholars with whom they studied. To cite an example: one Cordoban Spanish scholar studied in *Arabia* (at Mecca and Medina); in *Syria* (at Jerusalem, Gaza, Ashkelon, Tiberias, Damascus, Tripoli, Beirut, Caesaria, and Ramla); in *Egypt* (at Farama, Alexandria, and Qulzum) – and this after he had been well-trained already in *Spain*![4] It seems right to observe that Muslim civilization,

> in the fullest sense owed its vibrancy to constant movement. Travel in all its myriad forms ... expanded the mental and physical limits of the Muslim world, and preserved and nourished the various contacts that Muslims perennially maintained with one another.[5]

By the fifth Islamic century (1000s CE), institutions such as hostels had developed to facilitate exchanges of knowledge among traveling scholars, but also between generations of scholars. The madrasa, or "college," sprang up in Eastern and Central Islamdom and then spread wherever there were Muslims, to teach the Islamic "sciences" (*ʿulūm*, literally, "knowledges") to the young. In and around these madrasas, books – original and

[4] S. I. Gellens, "Search for Knowledge," 55. [5] Ibid., 51.

commentarial – were written, copied, published, and collected in libraries. In madrasas, Muslims read aloud from and commented on books they had written or had authoritatively transmitted – to visiting scholars as well as younger scholars. Lectures were given. Debates were held. Scholarly visitors were pressed for information and drew knowledge from local scholars.[6]

Given the astonishing amount of travel and interaction of those premodern Islamic scholars, it is little wonder that the literature they produced was so remarkably homogenous in form. At every stop along the road it was refined, discussed, and molded in the interaction of its author and readers. These texts themselves, however, exerted a compelling discipline of their own. By the time of Mālik b. Anas (d. 796), that is, within less than one hundred and seventy years after the Prophet's death, the categories of Muslim law (*fiqh*), and even their order within the law book, were more or less fixed in the way still used in legal works at present, some twelve hundred years later.[7] These texts, however stable their form, were never perfectly homogenous in content. Within the stipulated configurations there was considerable leeway for difference: "Difference is a mercy," as the *ḥadīth* has it. So the works of the four different Sunnī schools of law were mutually recognized; the seven, ten, or fourteen different Qur'ān readings were all held to be acceptable; the Six Books of *ḥadīth* were regarded as quasi-canonical despite their differences; *sub rosa,* Shī'ī works influenced Sunnī scholars and vice versa; in this and many other ways the principle of divergence within limits was not just tolerated but embraced by these Cosmopolitan Muslims.

Within three hundred years of the Prophet's death, almost all the genres of Islamic scholarship had been formed, and Islamic Arabic texts were produced that could be recognized and read by subsequent scholars – up to and including the present time. It is hard to imagine Yale Law School professors – other than legal historians – reading and commenting on German *wergelt* texts, but Muslim legal scholars still study and apply Mālik's great eighth-century *Muwaṭṭā'* and *Mudawwanah.*[8] The stability of form, and to some extent content, meant that the scholarly masters of the Cosmopolitan culture were quite at home whether they found themselves over the course of their lives in the madrasas and law courts of Spain, India, Ghana, or Central Asia.

[6] The master study of this subject is G. Makdisi, *The Rise of Colleges.*

[7] A. K. Reinhart, "Ritual Action and Practical Action"; see especially pp. 67–69.

[8] Hence Fatima Mernissi, a Moroccan feminist critic of Islamic gender practices, has to begin her argument by taking on with Mālik's classic *ḥadīth* work, the *Muwaṭṭā'*. F. Mernissi, *The Veil and the Male Elite.*

The Mythology of Islamic Scholarship

Cosmopolitan Islamic scholarship is grounded in certain assumptions, certain myths one might say, about the text of Islam and the textual tradition associated with them.[9] Cosmopolitan Islamic texts draw their authority in part from the Koiné Islamic commitment to the Qur'ān and *ḥadīth*. These Scriptural sources, it is believed, have a determinate meaning that can be grasped only through the use of the scholars' hermeneutic. It is a creedal commitment of the Cosmopolitan Muslim that, properly studied, these texts are seldom irresolvably ambiguous or uncertain; in every case their application is *functionally* certain. The certainty of the Scriptural texts, in turn, has a radiance that casts the light of reliable authority and meaningfulness on any text that is in dialogue with Scripture or purports to be derived from it.

The Scriptures and their haloing texts seem to be self-sufficient – there is almost never a need to go outside them for the solution to a problem – and if there is such recourse it is because the scholarly texts themselves call for it. The autonomy of the texts, their imperviousness to time, their dispersion far from where they may originally have been written, all give these texts an aura of detachment from the immediate and the contingent. The seventh-century Arabic Qur'ān of Mecca and Medina is decontextualized when it is studied in Indonesia or Philadelphia. And therefore a *fiqh* text written in Egypt appears to be, with little if any modification, equally applicable to Shāfiʿī Muslims in Indonesia or Philadelphia; Ḥanafīs in Albania use works written in Central Asia without reservation. Shāhwālīallāh, writing in eighteenth-century India, found inspiration in a renewed emphasis on the *Muwaṭṭā'*, composed in eighth-century Arabia. Scholars had what amounted to a faith commitment, and pledged allegiance to the Islam of texts, believing that the real sense (*ḥaqīqah*) of the term "Islam" was to be found in the textual tradition.[10]

Even now, it is a remarkable fact that in the quarter around the Azhar University and mosque in Cairo, in the Sahaflar book bazaar in Istanbul, in Fez and in Muslim Delhi, one finds many of the same books for sale. Most often they are in Arabic; sometimes they are translated. Usually they are premodern. In these diverse places it is the canonical works of *ḥadīth*, al-Ṭabarī's commentary on the Qur'ān, Ibn Taymiyyah's *Siyāsah sharʿiyyah*, al-Jazīrī's synoptic *fiqh* work, and many, many more that one finds, mixed in of

[9] Here and elsewhere "myth" is used not to mean "falsehood" or "mistaken understanding," but to refer to foundational stories, usually about the foundational period, of a religious tradition. These stories explain and normalize sets of ideas and practices.

[10] A fundamental work on this tradition of textual engagement is J. Brown, *Misquoting Muhammad*.

course with local religious textual products. The unofficial canon of supra-Scriptural books of course has local variations, but there is astonishingly little variation in the *form* of the works, depending on their genre, whatever the origin of the authors, whatever their position.[11]

As a result, the Cosmopolitan Islamic scholar – with his command of Scripture's language (Islamic Arabic), with access to those timeless texts, and a mastery of their form – is also himself haloed with textual authority. His training and his position allow him to "recall" what local traditions of Islam have "forgotten" or never knew. He can discern what is indistinct in a text; he can invoke authorized norms of trans-regional practices to resolve ethical uncertainties; he can work to efface local norms and practices that do not fit his understanding of Islam. The universal *'ilm* (textual knowledge) that he controls gives him a powerful authority for the formation and articulation of Lived Islam in his particular place and time.

The Role of the 'Ilm-*Bearer in Temporal Society*

For their part, the temporal authorities of Islamdom – kings, sultans, princes, and commanders – gained prestige by deferring to *'ilm* and honoring its bearers. When scholars visited, rulers paid homage to the idea of trans-local *'ilm* by patronizing those in whom it was embodied. This homage was not pro forma. In some cases it also meant real power and wealth. For instance, when Ibn Baṭṭūṭah arrived in Delhi – far from his home in Morocco – he was given presents, honored, and saluted. Then,

> [o]ne day [the Great King] sent Khudhāwand-Zāda Ghiyāth al-Dīn and Quṭb al-Mulk, the governor of Sind, to us to say, "The Master of the World says to you 'Whoever amongst you is capable of undertaking the function of ... judge or professor or shaikh, I shall appoint to that office.'" ... I replied, "... *qāḍīs* and shaikhs [are] my occupation, and the occupation of my fathers before me." ... Then I went in and found the Sultan on the terrace of the palace with his back leaning on the [royal] couch, the vizier Khwāja Jahān before him, and the "great king" Qabūla standing there upright. When I saluted him the "great king" said to me "Do homage, for the Master of the World has appointed you *qāḍī* of the royal city of [Delhi] and has fixed your stipend at 12,000 dinars a year, and assigned to you villages to that amount, and commanded for you 12,000 dinars in cash, which you shall draw from the treasury tomorrow (if God will), and has given you a horse with its saddle and bridle and has ordered you to be invested with a ... robe of honor," ... I said to him "O Master, I belong to

[11] On the persistence of genre in *fiqh* and *ḥadīth* works, see A. K. Reinhart, "Ritual Action and Practical Action," 66–69.

the [legal] school of Mālik and these people are Ḥanafīs, and I do not know the language." He replied "I have appointed Bahā al-Dīn al-Multānī and Kamāl al-Dīn al-Bijanawrī to be your [deputies]; they will be guided by your advice and you will be the one who signs all the documents."[12]

Despite all the impediments to a Moroccan Mālikī jurist working in Ḥanafī India, the prestige of the outsider-jurist, the Cosmopolitan *ʿilm*-bearer from abroad, compelled the local ruler to appoint Ibn Baṭṭūṭah as judge in his Indian kingdom – to lend the ruler his prestige no doubt, but also in the sincere belief that such a rare commodity as a Moroccan Mālikī *ʿilm*-scholar deserved recognition by those in power.

Methodology: **Naṣīḥah** *(Advice) and "Commanding the Good"*

ʿIlm is not just prestige but also power. *ʿIlm* conveys norms, and the bearers of *ʿilm* have a duty to effect the norms drawn from that knowledge; they draw further power from the expectation that they will police the practices of Muslims and enforce the norms of *ʿilm*, if only by calling the attention of temporal authorities to violations of those norms.[13] The bearers of Cosmopolitan Islam aim to construct an ideal Islam and a Cosmopolitan *ʿilm*-oriented one. The tool for the demolition of deviant Islam, and the construction of proper Islam, is "fraternal criticism" (*naṣīḥah*).

From the origins of their community, Muslims have been enjoined to be self-critical. The Prophet himself is criticized in the Qurʾān,[14] and the Qurʾān is critical of the imperfect commitment of Muslims throughout. After the Prophet's death and the end of Qurʾānic revelation, some Muslims continued to pronounce upon the religious practices of their fellow Muslims from then to the present. Among these moral critics are some of the most hallowed names of Islamic religious history such as the caliph ʿUmar, al-Ḥasan al-Baṣrī, Abū Dharr, Aḥmad b. Ḥanbal, and Ibn al-Jawzī, right on into the eighteenth, nineteenth, and twentieth (Christian) centuries with Muḥammad b. ʿAbdalwahhāb (the ideological founder of the present Saudi state), Aḥmad Sīrhindī, Abūlʿalāʾ Mawdūdī, Ḥasan al-Bannā, and Ruḥallāh Khomeinī. "Fraternal advice-giving" and "commanding the good and forbidding the reprehensible" are themes repeated in the Qurʾān and

[12] Ibn Baṭṭūṭah, *Travels of Ibn Baṭṭūṭah*, 3:745–747.

[13] The definitive account of the theory behind this whistle-blowing, and many historical examples, is M. A. Cook, *Commanding Right*.

[14] Q80:1–2, 5–6 {He frowned and turned away/Because the blind man came unto him. . . . As for him who thinks himself independent, to him you pay regard . . .} This is understood to refer to the Prophet ignoring a blind petitioner in favor of someone of more status. See, e.g., al-Ṭabarī, *Jāmiʿ al-bayān*, 30:50ff.

throughout the history of Islamic moralism. The concept of giving advice, or of commanding the good, is one of the fundamental themes of Islamic moral practice. If there is to be a normative tradition, there must be norm-bearers and norm-enforcers.[15]

We have an almost ethnographic description of how the process of advice-giving worked among the *'ulamā'* in premodern times once more in the accounts of our friend Ibn Baṭṭūṭah. In his *Travels*, Ibn Baṭṭūṭah does not merely observe and record, but judges also; wherever he went, he commanded the good, forbade the reprehensible, and offered normative Islamic correction. When a preacher in Basra gave a sermon full of solecisms, the visitor, Ibn Baṭṭūṭah, complained of it to his acquaintance, the judge.[16] When he saw men dressed immodestly in the steam bath at Munya, Egypt, the Moroccan scholar

> went to the governor and informed him of it. [The governor] told me not to leave and ordered the lessees of [all] the bathhouses to be brought before him. Articles were formally drawn up [then and there] making them subject to penalties if any person should enter the bath without a waist-wrapper, and the governor behaved to them with the greatest severity, after which I took leave of him.[17]

Did the governor have no personal knowledge of local bathhouse customs? Did no one of his entourage ever go to the baths? Did no local judge ever go to the baths? This is hardly likely. Yet when an outsider, this Moroccan scholar, complained, the governor felt compelled to act. Ibn Baṭṭūṭah interceded to change local practice as an outsider and so, in some important sense, as a more efficacious bearer of Islamic norms.

In the Maldives, Ibn Baṭṭūṭah again became *qāḍī* and didn't hesitate to intervene in local practices, as is the obligation and right of the Cosmopolitan Muslim:

> [T]he [king] forced me to take the office of *qāḍī*. The reason for this was that I had reproached the *qāḍī* for his practice of taking a tenth of all estates when he divided them amongst the heirs, saying to him: "You should have nothing but a fee agreed upon between you and the heirs." Besides he never did anything properly. When I was appointed, I strove my utmost to establish the prescriptions of the [*sharī'ah*]. . . .

[15] "Norms must be carried and at times be imposed by some persons over others; they do not simply exist." D. F. Eickelman, *Knowledge and Power*, 12.

[16] Ibn Baṭṭūṭah, *Travels of Ibn Baṭṭūṭah*, 2:277. [17] Ibid., 1:63.

> The first bad custom I changed was the practice of divorced wives staying in the houses of their former husbands, for they all do till they marry another husband.[18] About twenty-five men who had acted thus were brought before me; I had them beaten and paraded in the bazaars, and the women put away from them. Afterwards I gave strict injunctions that [worship was] to be observed, and ordered men to go swiftly to the streets and bazaars after the Friday service; anyone whom they found not having [worshipped] I had beaten and paraded. I compelled the salaried [worship]-leaders and muezzins to be assiduous in their duties and sent letters to all the islands to the same effect.[19]

Whatever had been the local norms of the Maldives, Ibn Baṭṭūṭah felt himself authorized to change them in the name, one might say, of the Cosmopolitan Islam grounded in scholarly *ʿilm*.

In Īdhaj (Izeh, Kuzestan province, Iran), where he stayed in the madrasa, he had an audience with the sultan, Atābek Afrāsiyāb, and he gently reproached him for the sin of drinking wine.

> "You are the son of the sultan Atābek Aḥmad, who was noted for piety and self-restraint, and there is nothing to be laid against you as a ruler but this," and I pointed to the two goblets [of wine]. He was overcome with confusion at what I said and sat silent. . . . [He] said to me, "to meet with men like you is a mercy."[20]

This same sultan, who had just been called to account as an errant Muslim, nonetheless sent Ibn Baṭṭūṭah food, fruit, and money.[21] Neither the sultan nor Ibn Baṭṭūṭah saw the intervention as impertinent. This is what scholars from Elsewhere do – they reprove and reform, they instruct and improve, they bring the Local into line with the Ideal.

Cosmopolitan Islam is grounded in a certain idealist view of texts – texts corrode imperfect reality and at the same time construct idealistic aspirations. By the classical Islamic era, the Qurʾān was understood as a document "outside of time," that is, despite the importance of the Ḥijāz as the historical and cultural homeland of Islam, the Qurʾān ceased to be understood primarily as a seventh-century Ḥijāzī document, but instead as the realization in time and space of the heavenly Qurʾānic prototype, the Preserved Tablet (*lawḥ maḥfūẓ*) mentioned in the Qurʾān (Q85:22).[22] As an uncreated and

[18] Under normative Islamic law, at divorce the husband and wife are once more outside each others' families, and must not be intimate with each other.

[19] Ibn Baṭṭūṭah, *Travels of Ibn Baṭṭūṭah*, 4:840–841. [20] Ibid., 2:293. [21] Ibid., 290.

[22] Though the Qurʾān's language was understood as most accessible through a study of seventh-century Bedouin language norms, these too were understood to be themselves a kind of revelatory event. See B. Weiss, "Medieval Muslim Discussions of the Origin of Language."

transcendent text, it provided a sacramental immanence for an otherwise very transcendent God. Hence, according to some, when the Qur'ān was recited, it was not the reciter speaking, but God; one academic scholar has compared memorizing the Qur'ān to taking communion – by memorizing the Qur'ān God is, in a sense, internalized.[23]

The concept of the transcendental text, only adventitiously revealed in a particular language at a particular time, in turn shaped the understanding of the Prophet's life. Once Muslims came to understand the Prophet's life as a twenty-year-long commentary and elaboration of the Qur'ān, as a realization of the Islamic ideal, the Prophet's life too became deracinated and idealized. Once more the accidents of nationality, temporality, and biography were blurred, and, from this perspective, Muḥammad became only a model Muslim, a beloved intercessor, and his life a Scripture for all Muslims everywhere. The light of these two self-subsistent texts – the Qur'ān and *ḥadīth* – spilled onto texts derived from Qur'ān and *ḥadīth* and lent them likewise a glow of timeless truth and transcendent authority, undimmed by the flux and particularities of the ordinary and the particular.

Because the Qur'ān and *ḥadīth* were uprooted from history, the scholars who were its bearers and interpreters also stood mythically apart from society, to greater or lesser extents, as impartial, authoritative, and to some extent sacramental figures. Eickelman has compared the *'ālim* to Simmel's "Stranger" in that "[h]e is near and far at the same time"; he is the link between the local community and the wider world of Islam.[24] He was also a link between the transcendent and the contingent – however personally clay-footed he might actually be.

Scholars' apartness gave them an authoritative perspective on local life and faith. Not infrequently, as they looked down from their textual Olympus, they saw practices too local, too particular, to be acceptable for Muslims because these practices were not vouched for in the transcendent Islamic texts. Sometimes the *'ulamā'* persuaded the generality (*al-'awāmm*, the

[23] W. C. Smith, "Some Similarities and Differences between Christianity and Islam," 56–58.

[24] D. F. Eickelman, *Knowledge and Power*, 67; citing an edition equivalent to G. Simmel and K. H. Wolff (eds.), *The Sociology of Georg Simmel*, 406–407. It is worth quoting Simmel (402): "The stranger is thus being discussed here, not in the sense often touched upon in the past, as the wanderer who comes today and goes tomorrow, but rather as the person who comes today and stays to morrow. He is, so to speak, the *potential* wanderer: although he has not moved on, he has not quite overcome the freedom of coming and going. He is fixed within a particular spatial group, or within a group whose boundaries are similar to spatial boundaries. But his position in this group is determined, essentially, by the fact that he has not belonged to it from the beginning, that he imports qualities into it, which do not and cannot stem from the group itself." This concept is a fruitful one and worth elaborating.

technical term for all who were not scholars) to look up to them as the Standard of Muslim behavior; often enough, however, they failed to persuade the generality to act normatively, or they themselves became enmeshed in the local. Yet their putative distance from the mundane ensured an ongoing dialectic that constantly corroded Islamic particularity and that endeavored to construct Islamic universality.

This otherness, this distance from the local, was not always merely metaphoric. The history of Islamic reformist movements is the history either of outsiders who come to visit, or of community members who leave for the Cosmopolitan center – whether the nearest big city, the regional center of Islamic scholarship, or the Islamic heartland of Mecca and Medina – and return as virtual outsiders now liberated from the local perspective by exposure to the scholarly ideals of the Cosmopolitan Islamic elite. In early twentieth-century Morocco, after a local boy's return from a study-visit to the big city, Marrakech, he said,

> Until I went to the Yusufiyyah [madrasa], I thought that the Sufi religious brotherhoods were a part of Islam ... I began to realize that even the practices of my father were not part of Islam. By the time I left the Yusufiyyah, I knew that the brotherhoods were an error.[25]

Yet it is not enough to know that scholars reproached faulty (in their view) observance. What was it that they positively advocated as "authorized" Islam?

For this we may turn to the most abidingly influential and brilliant of these Cosmopolitan Islamic critics, Ibn Taymiyyah (d. 1328), a medieval scholar of the Ḥanbalī legal school who spent his life agitating against the local practices of Syria, Egypt, and elsewhere. It may be objected that in choosing such an extreme figure – an Islamic chauvinist largely rejected by his contemporaries – we stack the deck against Islamic urbanity and openness. Nevertheless, our argument is that while Lived Islam as a whole has been urbane and receptive, the very rigor, ardor, and vehemence of Ibn Taymiyyah's polemic reveals, through a magnifying glass as it were, not just norm-setting but a creative effort to create, establish, and perpetuate a single, timeless, utopian Islam, distinct from the imperfect, the local, the contingent.

The Mythic Islam: The Islam of "Nowhere and Never"

Ibn Taymiyyah himself was not a Syrian, but an outsider who had come from Northern Mesopotamia (Ḥarrān) when he was seven, after his family was

[25] D. F. Eickelman, *Knowledge and Power*, 116.

displaced by the Mongol invasions.[26] In Syria and Egypt he positioned himself still further as an outsider by allegiance to the minority Ḥanbalī *madhhab* – indeed he was often at odds even with his own school – but an outsider too by an unrelentingly critical Scripturalist approach to the Lived Islam of his milieu.[27] Throughout his life he campaigned against what he believed to be "un-Islamic" practices, and his repeated and irrepressible criticism ended with his imprisonment and death in Damascus.[28]

Ibn Taymiyyah lived his life agitating for his Cosmopolitan vision of Islam and in fierce attack on local Islam(s). He wrote a long work on just this subject, whose title is *The Book of Setting Apart the Straight Path: In Controversies with the Inhabitants of Hell.*[29] An attentive reading of this will guide us as we attempt to understand further the ideal Islam of the *'ulamā'*.

Ibn Taymiyyah wanted to end the local practices common among fourteenth-century Syrians and Egyptians. His was not merely an academic critique – he actually brought a stone-mason to smash a "sacred rock" in Syria.[30] Practices and faith were linked, he believed, and deviations in practice caused deviation in the faith.[31]

To make his case, the book's first eight chapters (the first 180 pages of the text) establish three categories of practice – pre-Islamic, non-Islamic (Persian, Christian, Jewish), and deviant Islamic practices that are to be distinguished from the practices of the authentic, Scripturally defined

[26] Ibn Taymiyyah is still influential today. Not only are his treatises the ur-texts of Wahhabism in Arabia, but his legal opinions, his treatise on civil regulation (*Risālah fī l-ḥisbah*), his *fatāwá* or legal responsas, above all his *Islamic Moral Policy* (*Siyāsah shar'iyyah*) are widely distributed, sold, and read by conservative and radical reformers throughout Islamdom.

[27] *EI2* 3:952b.

[28] On his life, see *EI2*, s.v. "Ibn Taymiyyah" [H. Laoust]. See also the collection of articles by Y. Rapoport and S. Ahmed, *Ibn Taymiyya and His Times.*

[29] This work is translated by Muhammad Umar Memon as *Ibn Taimīya's Struggle Against Popular Religion*. Memon used, and I have consulted, the 1950 Cairo edition, Ibn Taymiyyah, *Kitāb al-iqtiḍā'*. It is only by reading Memon's translation against the original that one can appreciate the elegance and erudition of his translation. I have drawn from his pellucid translation with minor modifications of transliteration. I have also omitted or inserted transliterated terms and emphases without notice. I have explained any changes of translation in the notes. Citations are to: Memon translation/original Cairo text.

[30] *EI2*, 3:952.

[31] Ibn Taymiyyah, *Ibn Taimīya's Struggle*, 97/11 (tr./text): "The Straight Path is in itself comprised of certain internal and external elements. The former include beliefs (*i'tiqādāt*), intentions, and the like; the latter tenets (*aqwāl*) and deeds. In turn deeds may be acts of worship or also customs, such as pertain to food, dress, marriage, dwelling, congregation, separation, travel, sojourn, riding, etc. These internal and external matters are, inevitably, interrelated, so that the emotion and mood in the heart must, of necessity, [induce] some external phenomena, and the various external acts must, of necessity, generate in the heart certain emotions and moods."

Islam.[32] His argument, in a nutshell, is that *present* time and *local* space intrude transgressively into Islam, which is properly timeless and universal; when the local and the contemporary do intrude, they corrupt proper (Cosmopolitan) Islam.

Ibn Taymiyyah is useful not only because he is an ethnographer of the Lived Islam found in fourteenth-century Syria, but also because when he criticizes, he also imagines, defines, and exemplifies Cosmopolitan Islam, and what his ideal Islam should be. The ideal Islam is sharply defined by *ʿilm* texts; it is definitively set off from what preceded it – the Era of Ignorance – but also from superfluous practices added to it which are called *bidʿah*, meaning blameworthy innovations. These are ritual acts whose origins precede Islam or postdate Islam's mythic origin time – both categories are equally *bidʿah* and equally abhorrent. All Islamic practices may be performed everywhere, except for those practices connected to the hajj, which must be performed only in the cosmic center of the Meccan sanctuary. All prior practices may be performed at any time except those connected to specified times and especially specified seasons. To perform an Islamically specified act at the wrong place is, as we shall see, a transgression. So too it is a transgression to specify a time for pious act that has no *ʿilm*-specified time attached to it.

The Boundaries of Cosmopolitan Islam and Resistance to Blurring Them

The *ʿālim* Ibn Taymiyyah hated Muslim participation in what he saw as non-Muslim festivals, and non-Muslim participation in Muslim festivals. Both of these were common in the Syria and Egypt of Ibn Taymiyyah's time and which are still found to some extent today.[33] Because of the value of his description to the entire argument of the book, quite extensive quotations from his work are provided in this chapter.

Here is Ibn Taymiyyah describing Muslim participation in Christian practices of Holy Week. He is not a sympathetic ethnographer!

[32] The term Scripture here refers to the normative texts of particularly Sunnī, Islam – namely, the Qurʾān and the normative behavior (*sunnah*) of the Prophet as preserved in anecdotes (*ḥadīth*) verified by scholars as authentic.

[33] For later Syrian Islam, see J. Grehan, *Twilight of the Saints*. See also E. W. Lane, *Manners and Customs*, 489ff., and the film "For Those Who Sail to Heaven" for the participation of Coptic Christian clergy in the festival of the Muslim saint Sīdī Abū l-Ḥaggāg. I knew Coptic Christians who fasted somewhat during Ramadan, and listened to the special Qurʾān broadcasts and sermons, and gave other indications that Ramadan is a religiously significant time. See also the citations in Chapter 3 above of Dialect Islam's blurred boundaries between Islam and Other.

> [M]any who claim to be Muslims are seduced by Satan into doing what they do at the termination of the Christian fast—gifts, merry-making, [expenditures], clothing children, and similar other things by which their festival takes on the air of the Muslim festival. This is even more true of areas closer to Christian population whose Muslim dwellers, weak as they are in knowledge (*'ilm*) and faith, allow themselves to be fully dominated by these festivals which appear to them even more appealing than the festival granted by God and His Prophet.[34]
>
> ... [T]he Christians visit tombs and burn incense on them, so also in their homes, not because of its pleasant odor, but because it carries blessing and wards off evil—so they claim. They consider incense-burning as sacrifice, as animal offering. This is accompanied with incantations to the beat of a small copper knocker and with repeating of special formulas. They hang crosses on doors of their houses and do similar other disreputable things. I am not aware of all of their practices and *what I have mentioned here is what I have personally seen many Muslims do and which in its origin derives from these Christians.*[35]

It is clear that the Lived Islam of fourteenth-century Syria was far more complex and diverse than the Islam of textbooks. It included practices grounded not in the Scriptural sources of Islam, but in traditions of local religiosity. However, for Ibn Taymiyyah, to participate in local practices was to remain locked into un-Islamic error.[36] And Ibn Taymiyyah regretfully makes it clear that these practices of "deviant" Dialect Islam were not rare or unusual among Syrian Muslims, but rather that he and his Cosmopolitan Muslim brethren were very much in the minority.

> Except for a very few whom God wishes to guide, all or most common people—and by common people I mean those who do not know the true nature (*ḥaqīqah*[37]) of Islam, (for despite their claim to have religious knowledge and faith[38] many people participate in these practices)—are given the explanation that incanted incense-burning, by virtue of its blessing, neutralizes the effects of the "evil eye", sorcery, ailments, and pests. They [also] draw pictures of snakes and scorpions and paste them in their houses, believing that these pictures—accursed be he who draws them, and

[34] Or, "though it is nearer to knowledge and faith." Ibn Taymiyyah, *Ibn Taimīya's Struggle*, 208/9.

[35] Ibid., 210/11–12, my italics.

[36] "[P]articipation with them in their festivals, wholly or partly, is synonymous with participation with them in unbelief (*kufr*) wholly or partly." Ibid., 206/7.

[37] Memon has "essence" which here, I think, misleads.

[38] Arabic: *fiqh wa-dīn*. Above (Arabic text 208), Ibn Taymiyyah has used *fiqh* in this sense, rather than in the usual technical sense as "Islamic law."

angels do not enter the house where they are found—prevent pests from coming inside.[39]

Here there are two important points to note. First, Ibn Taymiyyah urges Muslims to remain a *distinct* community – distinct from other religious communities, and in some sense distinct from the (Syrian) environment in which they live; he urges them also to participate only in uniquely Islamic practices.

> Holidays of the infidels, whether [Scriptuary] or [pagan], are placed by Islam in the same category . . . [A] Muslim . . . should avoid both equally.[40]
>
> Now if the Jews have a festival and the Christians have a festival, these are then *exclusively* associated with them. We do not participate with them in these festivals just as we do not in their *qiblah* (direction of prayer) and *sharīʿah*. By the same token, we should not call upon them to join us in our festivals.[41]

So it is the blurring of boundaries separating religious traditions that provokes Ibn Taymiyyah's scorn. He demands categorical clarity, and it is ritual that most effectively distinguishes religious communities from each other.[42] "At the root of all these evils lies the facts of 'resemblance' and 'participation,'" he says.[43] To avoid resembling, one must avoid participating. Just as linguistic nationalists try to purge Turkish or Serbian or Hindi or French of "foreign" elements, so too the advocates of Cosmopolitan Islam exclude all that is not part of "pure" Islam from their Islam.

The Myth of Islamic Geography It is not just boundaries between religions that exercises Ibn Taymiyyah. He is also haunted by the notion that the boundaries of Islam's sacred geography might be blurred – even by Muslims acting from pious motives. The idea that any locality – other than the mythological homeland of Islam – can be sacred repels him.

> Religious corruption is of two kinds. One is related to acting (*ʿamal*), the other to the place of acting (*maḥall al-ʿamal*). . . . [The second kind of corruption makes one] a heretic [with regard to[44]] the Sanctuary [at Mecca] (*ḥaram*). The greatest place of worship is

[39] Ibn Taymiyyah, *Ibn Taimīya's Struggle*, 210/12. [40] Ibid., 199/91–92. [41] Ibid., 201/194–195.

[42] "Nay, festivals are that which most particularly serves to differentiate one religious law from another and constitute their most prominent symbols." Ibid., 206/208.

[43] Ibid., 214/215. [44] Instead of "in."

the Sanctuary [at Mecca]; it is a graver offense to defile the sanctity of a location ... than ... a time.[45]

What does he mean by "a heretic with regard to the Sanctuary?" It is to venerate any locality other than the three approved sites of Islamic sacred geography – Jerusalem, Medina, Mecca – and in particular to perform acts proper to the Meccan sanctuary anywhere else in the world. For example, one of the rituals of the hajj-pilgrimage is (*ta'rīf*) "standing at Mt. 'Arafah," a hillock outside Mecca.[46] To imitate elsewhere a practice properly performed in the Meccan *ḥaram* is somehow to defile the *ḥaram* itself.

> A practice about whose forbiddenness I do not think there is disagreement among Muslims is to visit on the Day of 'Arafah the tomb of one held in good esteem, to throng around the tomb, as is done in certain lands of east and west, and [do] *ta'rīf* there, just as one does in 'Arafāt. ... The same is true also of journeying to Jerusalem for *ta'rīf* there—a manifest error. Visiting Jerusalem is both commendable and lawful for prayer and devotional retreat. .... Yet it is wrong to make such visits at the time of the pilgrimage to Mecca. It is tantamount to setting a specific time for visiting Jerusalem; there is no [textual] reason to prefer visiting it at this particular time [and so it amounts to inventing an un-Islamic ritual].[47]

For the Cosmopolitan expert, sacrality arises only with the proper conjunction of time, place, and act. To perform act at an unsanctioned place profanes the ritual by contaminating it with an inappropriate locality. In Dialect of Islam, one sacred place may be the same as another in its sacrality – particularly when the Cosmopolitan-authorized sacred place is, in practical terms, unattainable. Mecca is far away from most of Islamdom, and in premodern times travel there for all but the elites was impractical or impossible. For Ibn Taymiyyah, however, to perform the standing ritual elsewhere than at 'Arafāt, however well-intentioned, is wrong. It adulterates the ritual by mixing illegitimate geography with the ritual act and time relevant only to Meccan worship. The separation between the *ḥaram* of Mecca, with its particular idiosyncratic sacrality, and the rest of the world must be bright and distinct.

[45] "That is why one is forbidden to seek grounds of game and grazing in the *sacred place*, though in the *sacred month* one may search for these (elsewhere)." Ibn Taymiyyah, *Ibn Taimīya's Struggle*, 143–144/76.

[46] *Ta'rīf* is one of the Pilgrimage rituals; it is standing at Mt. 'Arafah on the ninth of the month of Dhū al-Ḥijjah in supplication. The ritual is more commonly called *wuqūf*. See M. R. Qal'ājī, *Lughat al-fuqahā'*, 115.

[47] Ibn Taymiyyah, *Ibn Taimīya's Struggle*, 251/309.

> The visitation is to a *particular area itself* for the purpose of *taʿrīf*, for instance the tomb of a saint or the Aqṣá Mosque, is to equate the place with ʿArafāt.[48]

Similarly, visiting saints' tombs on particular days is not just sacralizing an unauthorized locality, but it also mocks the ordained *calendrical* observances unique to the pilgrimage time.

> Certain graves are thronged around by the [believers in the efficacy of grave veneration] on a certain day of the year, where they come traveling to celebrate a festival [sometimes on recognized Muslim holy days], yet on other occasions, at another time, in such a way that a certain day of the year is marked for visitation to them for congregation, [just] as one visits ʿArafah, Muzdalifah, and Minā on specific days of the year.

Adding sacred times to the times sacralized in the Cosmopolitan sources diminishes the unique sacrality proper to Cosmopolitan Islam. The inevitable consequence of such practices is that rites of local religiosity come to replace recognized Koiné (and Cosmopolitan) rituals.

> ... In the same way, people will proceed to some city at a scheduled or unscheduled time with the intention of [supplicatory prayer] and religious exercise, just as one may go to the Sacred House of God [in Mecca].... That this travel is for religious exercise ... need hardly be doubted; some even go so far as to call it pilgrimage (*ḥajj*), saying, "We intend to go for *ḥajj* to the grave of so-and-so."[49]

All Muslims, Ibn Taymiyyah believes, must share only a *limited* set of authorized places marked off from the rest of the world, and *particular* times defined by the universal Islamic ritual calendar. To act as if other places and other times had religious value, or worse, to translate practices from the Cosmopolitan Islamic sacred geography to local sites at sacred times, is hopelessly to muddle the true and the false, the Islamic and the non-Islamic, or as we would suggest, the Cosmopolitan Islamic and the Dialect. We have seen that "muddling" is, for Ibn Taymiyyah and his ideological kin, the worst of religious errors.[50]

[48] Ibid., 252–253/311, my italics. [49] Ibid., 294–295/375–376.

[50] The technical term of opprobrium for textually unjustified ideas and practices of this sort was *bidʿah*, usually translated as "(blameworthy) innovation." Given the post-eighteenth-century valuation of the new and the creative in Europe, the derogative quality of this translation has suggested to many that Muslims derided creativity and progress. This is an error.

The religious meaning of the term is, in one definition, "a [new] act in religion after perfection/completion (*al-aḥdath fī al-dīn baʿd al-ikmāl*)." Abū l-Baqāʾ, *al-Kulliyāt*, 1:421 (s.v. "*al-bidʿah*," 421–422). It thus translates the German *Aberglauben* (believing beyond; having faith

From his angry text we can see that the fourteenth-century Damascenes had a rich alternative Islamic sacred geography that enriched and supplemented the Cosmopolitan Islamic cosmography of Mecca, Medina, and Jerusalem; we see also that this Dialect supplementary spiritual topography was unacceptable to a Cosmopolitan Muslim like Ibn Taymiyyah.

> Some places may wrongly be considered the tomb or station of a prophet or saint ... Damascus has a number of such places, for instance the *mashhad* [martyrs' tomb] of Ubaiy b. Ka'b, outside the Eastern Gate.
>
> ... Likewise, the spot at the southern wall of [the] Damascus Mosque. The rumor has it that it encloses the grave of the Prophet Hūd. ... Or, take for instance, the *mashhad* outside the Western gate in Damascus. People say that it is the grave of Uways al-Qaranī. ... There is a certain grave [also] said to be of Umm Salmah, a wife of the Prophet.[51] ...
>
> Under this heading [of superstitious local sacred geography] come also places which in popular belief are said to contain a relic of the Prophet, *largely for rivalling Abraham's station at Mecca.*[52] For instance the ignorant claim that the impression of the Prophet's foot is lodged in the Ṣakhrā' [Dome of the Rock[53]], which is at Jerusalem, and, I am even told, that some ignoramuses go so far as to assert that the impression is that of God's own foot![54]
>
> These false *mashāhid* [martyria] have been indeed set up *to rival the houses of God, to sanctify what God has not sanctified,* to encourage [Muslims to have recourse to them] which is neither availing nor harmful [though since it is pointless, it is therefore *ultimately,* harmful], and, finally, to divert mankind from the path of God.[55] ...
>
> It is wholly un-Islamic to venerate in any way these places which popular belief has invested with a special character, whatever it be, because *hallowing a location which the Shar'*[56] *does not venerate is even worse than hallowing a time which the Shar' does not keep holy,* and because the unlawful worship of mortal beings by religious acts, more than an act of venerating a certain time, approaches idol-worship, so that one must really avoid praying at such places, even if one does not intend to venerate them[57] ...

beyond) and the Latin *superstitio* (standing beyond) with allowance for a focus on praxis rather than belief. Practices beyond those stipulated by the *shar'* are, to the likes of Ibn Taymiyyah, merely superstitious accretions, adding finials and crenellation to the classically pure lines of *Dār al-Islām*, the House of Islam. See now the definitive discussion of the term in R. M. Ukeles, "Innovation or Deviation."

[51] Ibn Taymiyyah, *Ibn Taimīya's Struggle*, 255–256/316. [52] My italics.

[53] Precisely, the rock inside the Dome of the Rock in Jerusalem.

[54] Ibn Taymiyyah, *Ibn Taimīya's Struggle*, 257/317–318. [55] Ibid., 258/319.

[56] The norms of Islamic practice derived from the authentic Scriptural sources of Islam.

[57] Ibn Taymiyyah, *Ibn Taimīya's Struggle*, 258/318–319, my italics.

Venerating any place, any relic, any time, not justified by scholarly texts amounts to idols and idolatry. These Dialect practices dilute the sacrality of Cosmopolitan Islamic recurrent festivals (*ʿīd*) and the sacrality of the Cosmopolitan Islamic geography – that is, what is shared by all Muslims wherever they might happen to live.

The Cosmopolitan Islamic aspect has features that are both negative and destructive. Cosmopolitan Muslims often attack as "un-Islamic" practices that seem too divergent from textual authority or Koiné practices. Yet, more positively, it also constructs an ideal that transcends local particularity and in its very unreality is equally appropriate everywhere in the world.

Cosmopolitan Islam theoretically is bounded Islam – it is firmly framed by *ʿilm* and minimally augmented so as to be a plain and unadorned reflection of the imagined seventh-century (CE) Islam of the Prophet and the Companions. The boundedness is an important – really a crucial – component of Cosmopolitan Islam, and to the extent it has prevented the assimilation of Muslims into amorphous local pastiche religion, it is important to Lived Islam as well. Practically speaking, it is Cosmopolitan Islam that has prevented the fissiparation of Islam into separate religions: The *ʿilm*-masters' policing of Lived Islam disciplines the most extravagant, most culturally particular, Local Islamic practices. While the *ʿulamāʾ* and rigorists do not turn every Muslim into a Cosmopolitan scholar, they still press the cognates of Koiné Islam to the fore and help to construct them as definitive of Islam, even when, in fact, for Locally oriented Muslims the five pillars and the like may have been formerly peripheral to their experience of Islam. Yet it is not enough for Cosmopolitans that Muslims everywhere must observe the Koiné. At the extreme, Cosmopolitans believe they should actually detach themselves from the locale in which they live. Ibn Taymiyyah's aspiration is to a utopian Islam – literally an Islam of no particular locality, the literal meaning of the word *utopia*.

Ibn Taymiyyah phantastically asserts, for example, that Muslims, wherever they are, should speak only the Scriptural language of Islam, their own distinct language – namely Islamic Arabic. A Muslim's Turkish, Syriac, Coptic, or Aramaic, and no doubt vernacular Arabic too, must be put aside if one is to be a utopian Muslim.[58]

[58] In at least one private Islamic secondary academy in contemporary Jordan, the girls are encouraged to speak Classical Arabic (no one's spoken language), and the thirteen-year-old girls observed have "a very high level of spoken classical Arabic, above and beyond that found in other Jordanian schools." A. S. Roald, "Tarbiya," 174.

> It is detestable that a man should become habituated to speaking in non-Arabic. Because Arabic language is one of the symbols of Islam and Muslims ... to an extent that this other language becomes a habit of a whole city with its dwellers, of an entire household, of a man and his associates ... this, then, is undoubtedly detestable.[59]

Muslims must resemble no one but themselves in the present time. For Ibn Taymiyyah, time, space, language, and action are to be Islamic and only Islamic. It follows that this is an Islam that is paradoxically of everywhere – as an ideal of an Islam without local inflections – and of nowhere, because as Ibn Taymiyyah so despairingly admits, Islam in Syria *is* in fact Syrian, not Cosmopolitan, and it is not the imagined utopia of his texts. Perhaps by flattening time as myths do, contemporary Muslims may hope to assimilate to primordial Muslims.

Ibn Taymiyyah's Islam, set entirely apart from its cultural environment, was an ideal, of course, and never a reality. Yet it was and remains a potent ideal, for reasons coded into the very structure of nearly all understandings of Islam, as we will see below. Just as Ibn Taymiyyah wants his Syrian-Muslim followers to live in exactly the same manner as Muslims anywhere else should live, so too he wants his contemporary fourteenth-century (CE) Muslims to live, as it were, in an Islamic time, the time of the Prophet and his Companions. For Ibn Taymiyyah, Muslims and Muslim practice are, through history, drawn downward and toward degeneration. This doctrine of "the corruption of the times" (*fasād al-zamān*) is crucial to understanding the detached Islam that scholars like Ibn Taymiyyah professed.[60] In his stance as a Cosmopolitan Muslim, Ibn Taymiyyah confronts practices of a particular temporal moment from an a-temporal, mythic perspective.

However, on closer examination, this formative Islamic time is not the historical seventh and eighth century (CE) of history – particular time is an enemy – it is *illud tempus*, "that time," the founding moment of Islamic mythic history, the time-out-of-time, in Eliade's term, to which Muslims must ever seek return.[61] While the Arabian 600s of real history were wracked with civil war, disagreement, and contest as Muslims vied to understand the implications of Islam itself, Ibn Taymiyyah's seventh century (CE) is a Golden World in which Islam – born fully-fledged, perfected, and as yet uncorrupted – was perfectly performed by those spiritually gifted Arabs of

[59] Ibn Taymiyyah, *Ibn Taimīya's Struggle*, 205–206/3–6.
[60] E. Dickinson, "Ibn al-Ṣalāḥ and the *Isnād*," 486; H. Gerber, *Islamic Law and Culture*, 124–126.
[61] M. Eliade, *Patterns*, 395–397.

Muḥammad's time, the Companions, the "pious forbears" (in Arabic the *salaf*[62]).

> [O]ne who has knowledge of the biographies of early Muslims realizes that the Muslims during the Prophet's time did not use to participate with unbelievers in any of their affairs, nor changed their habits during non-Muslim festivals. Nay, whether for the Prophet or for the rest of the Muslims, non-Muslim festival days were like all other days. They did not mark such a day in any way, unless it be to differ from the unbelievers, such as by fasting on a non-Muslim festival day.[63]

Likewise, a practice that postdates the time of the Prophet and Companions, is an innovation (*bidʿah*).[64]

> All made-up[65] holidays and festivals are disreputable and reprehensible . . . for two reasons: They come under the head innovation (*bidʿah*) and things fabricated[66] . . . The . . . reason why festivals and holidays of recent origin should be reproachable is that they corrupt faith.[67]

Throughout the *Iqtiḍāʾ* Ibn Taymiyyah appeals to the practice of the Prophet and the early community to criticize the norms of his contemporary Muslims.[68] Practices that exist before or after this sacred time are unacceptable.[69] The mere fact that a practice predates Islam and has no subsequent Islamic justification means that it is Islamically unacceptable. These are called practices of the Era of Ignorance (*jāhiliyyah*) – hearkening back to the religiously clueless era from which Muḥammad and the Qurʾān rescued Muslims.

Scriptural speech, unlike other sorts of speech, addresses not merely the actual persons to whom it was directed, but all Muslims throughout

[62] From which we get the term "Salafi," often erroneously translated as "fundamentalist."

[63] Ibn Taymiyyah, *Ibn Taimīya's Struggle*, 202/195–196. [64] Ibid., 231–237/70–80.

[65] Memon has "new fangled," but it is not novelty but arbitrariness that Ibn Taymiyyah dislikes.

[66] Memon has "of recent origin" for *aḥdāth*.

[67] Ibn Taymiyyah, *Ibn Taimīya's Struggle*, 229/267, 238/282.

[68] This is true throughout his work and the work of other Cosmopolitan scholars. For example, in a work urging Muslims to resist the Mongols ("Tatars"), Ibn Taymiyyah repeatedly analogizes from his own time to that of the Prophet and the Companions: "The Muslims were tried in the Battle of al-Khandaq. And likewise in this year the faithful are tried by [the Tatar's] enmity as the Muslims with the Prophet were in the year of al-Khandaq." This identification is made over and over on nearly every page of this treatise. See Ibn Taymiyyah, *Thalāth rasāʾil fī al-jihād*, 69.

[69] Ibn Taymiyyah, *Ibn Taimīya's Struggle*, 93/4: "The Prophet said that there would be in his community imitation on the one hand of the Jews and Christians, . . . and on the other of the Persians and Byzantines. . . . The Prophet was wont to forbid imitation of both the People of the Book and non-Arabs." And of course, new ritual practices, rituals that have arisen after the sanctified era of the *salaf* are *bidʿah*, blameworthy innovations.

time.[70] Consequently, the Muslim who follows the dictates of *'ilm* in the many domains of life it guides, lives mythically in the time of the Scriptures. The scope of the *shar'* extends to a wide set of life practices and effectively ritualizes those aspects of life as well. For the Cosmopolitan textualist, life can, through study and discipline, be lived nearly entirely in *illo tempore* – those mythic times. The goal of Ibn Taymiyyah in all his works, and indeed in his life, was to assimilate his life to life in the "time of the Prophet," of the Companions, and Followers, the Pious Forebears (*aslāf*, sing. *salaf*), an Islam that is everywhere (in theory) because it is not yet or no longer practiced in any particular place, an Islam that is at all times a perfectly a-temporal, ubiquitous Islam that we may well call "Cosmopolitan," whose "home city" is the entire world, because it is both everywhere, and at the same time only in the primordial Islamic Arabian city of Medina. This feature of Cosmopolitanism is not unique to Muslims. Jews return at the Seder to *illud tempus*, the time of *the* Passover in Egypt. The European Christian Reformation was nothing if not an attempt to replace the "blameworthy innovations" of the Roman Church with the idealized (and mostly imaginary) ideas and practices of Jesus and His disciples. What is remarkable about the Cosmopolitan Muslim impulse is its persistence throughout the whole of Islam's history. Already the *ḥadīth* are filled with idealizations of the Companions and Islam's First Generation.

For alienated or critical Muslims, books that are hard to find, written in a language that is at first opaque, become mysterious places filled with surprising discoveries. It is the sense of surprise, of renewed revelation one might say, that explains the power of the scholarly study of Islamic texts. Koiné Islam's focus on ritual means that most Muslims know "how to act Islamically." But when a scholar studies the justifications and origins of a ritual, or the precise points of its practice, a heretofore unknown and exciting world of meaning is opened up. Scholars' "discoveries" in the texts have again and again confronted the vagaries and diffusion of Dialect Islam with the precision and certainty of Cosmopolitan Islam; this confrontation is one of the most powerful dynamics in Islamic religious history. It is not too much to say that the history of Islamic religion can be written as a history of encounters between Vernacular Muslim pragmatists and Cosmopolitan

70 Ibid., 107:226: "[T]he imperative used . . . in . . . Koranic phrases . . . [addresses] not only the generation of the Prophet but also all people down to the Resurrection Day; such is the nature of divine speech, and the Messenger is merely enunciating the divine word."

Muslim idealists. Like Americans who go abroad and suddenly realize that they speak not English but American,[71] many of these reformers have left home as Dialect Muslims and returned as Cosmopolitans. Travels to the realm of Cosmopolitan Islam, as we saw with the Moroccan boy who went to big-city Marrakech, can shock a Muslim out of provincialism and into Cosmopolitanism. When the local returns home, he has the double prestige of being a home-town boy and a learned scholar. So often, in major and minor ways, this process has helped realign Dialect Islam toward more widely shared Islamic understandings and practices.

A Case Study: Hajji Shariatullah – A Cosmopolitan Returns to Nineteenth-Century Bengal

The little-studied history of Hajji Shariatullah, an eighteenth- and nineteenth-century Bengali Cosmopolitan Muslim, is a good case study to see how Cosmopolitan Islam works in historical and social context.

Hajji Shariatullah (Ḥājjī Sharīʿatallāh [1781–1840]) left his native Bengal as a young man and spent eighteen years in Mecca; he then returned home to lead a movement called the Faraizi (*Farāʾiḍī*) movement.[72] The Lived Islam of Bengal had been a rich Dialect version of Islam – with unique Bengali features now celebrated in some literature.[73] Still, it is easy to understand why the Ḥājjī (the term of honor for a person who has made the Pilgrimage to Mecca, the hajj) was compelled to offer a Cosmopolitan critique.

Of course the Qurʾān itself was opaque to the Bengalis who followed Hajji Shariatullah – most of them surely illiterate in any language, nor had they memorized its texts. According to a source "not one in ten . . . could repeat the *kalimah*," the declaration (in Arabic) that there is no god but God and Muḥammad is His messenger, the most elementary creed of Islam.[74] Without a modicum of memorized Qurʾān, the five-times-daily worship service was impossible. It was not just the laity who were Islamically illiterate. Indeed, even "most of the *qāḍī*s of Bengal read the Qurʾān without

[71] Or Britons who discover they don't speak "English" but "British English."

[72] Named after the *farāʾiḍ*, or indispensable, canonical duties of Islam (daily prayer, fasting Ramadan, sacrifice at the Feast of Sacrifice) that Hajji Shariatullah found neglected when he returned to his vernacular Islamic homeland. The definitive work on him seems to be M. A. Khan, *History of the Faraʾidi Movement*. See also *EI2*, s.v. "Sharīʿatallāh," and M. Abdul Bari, "Reform Movement in Bengal," 544–549. I follow Khan on any points in dispute.

[73] A. Roy, *Islamic Syncretistic Tradition in Bengal*.

[74] M. Khan, *History of the Faraʾidi Movement*, 63, quoting W. W. Hunter, *England's Work in India* [Madras, 1888], 47ff.

understanding Arabic"[75] – even the Islamic judges were unqualified for the Cosmopolitan role required of them. They had no direct access to Cosmopolitan sources and so must have been restricted to Dialect and Koiné features of their Lived Islam.

As a true Cosmopolitan Muslim by contrast, Hajji Shariatullah could read all the Cosmopolitan sources, choose among them, and emphasize what he believed needed to be emphasized. His authority was, in effect, the authority of the texts to which most Dialect Muslims were religiously committed, but of which they were utterly uninformed. Based on his reflected prestige, Haji Shariatullah began his effort to delocalize, to Cosmopolitanize Bengali Islam.

His Faraizi program had five elements.[76] The *first* was *tawbah*, or repentance for one's past (mostly ritual) transgressions and a resolve to reform. The *second* was observance of the *farā'iḍ*, that is, the Koiné five pillars of Islam. At the Feast of Sacrifice, Hajji Shariatullah also urged his followers to slaughter cows since cows were more cheaply obtained than sheep or goats and the expense of sheep for sacrifice prevented Muslims from observing the duty to sacrifice an animal in commemoration of the hajj and Ibrāhīm's near-sacrifice of his son.[77] (Their often British-appointed Hindu tax-collectors did not approve.)

The *third* element, shared with other reformist groups, in Bengal and elsewhere, was an emphasis on the significance of *tawḥīd*, or the exclusivity of God's transcendent action. This meant, first and foremost, a disdain for the cult of saints and a contempt for belief in their intercession. The Faraizis prohibited the inappropriate veneration of saints,[78] by force if necessary. In India, the line between "saints" and indigenous or Hindu gods and goddesses was blurred – as we have seen – and many Muslims by choice or coercion participated in the veneration of Durga and other deities. By banning the veneration of saints, Hajji Shariatullah sharpened communal lines and heightened Bengali perceptions of themselves as virtuous, universal Muslims.

The *fourth* element of the Faraizi program, and perhaps the shibboleth of the movement, was, counterintuitively, the prohibition of the community Friday noon prayer and the communal prayers of the two feast days. Hajji

[75] M. Abdul Bari, "Fara'idi Movement," 199, quoting a source identified only as Martin, *Eastern India*, 1:134, 2:431–432, 446, 724, and 3:512, evidently summarizing the findings of a "Dr. Buchanon."

[76] This discussion is drawn from M. Khan, *History of the Fara'idi Movement*, chapter 6.

[77] Ibid., 17.

[78] Included in his condemnation of pagan-like practices was the distinctively Islamic, though textually unattested, observance of the Prophet's birthday, *mawlid al-nabī*.

Shariatullah asserted that the conditions necessary for these collective prayers were not met by the circumstances of Bengal according to the Ḥanafī *madhhab* rules on prayer in provincial lands.[79] The effect of this drastic ban on communal worship was to sharpen Muslims' view of themselves as a threatened minority in a Hindu-British world, a minority whose existence was threatened if they continued to be unable to perform the distinctive practices that defined Muslims everywhere.

The *fifth* aspect of the Faraizi movement was the "denunciation of popular rites and ceremonies," by which the Faraizis referred to nonstandard Islamic practices, whether of Hindu origin or any other. As we would expect from a Cosmopolitan reformer, practices purged included life cycle rituals such as birth rites, marriage rites, and funeral rites that had augmented the "thin" Koiné Islamic ritual lexicon with more elaborate, indigenized observances. The Ḥājjī also condemned Shīʿī observances of the death of al-Ḥusayn at the Islamic month of Muḥarram (which were often performed not just by Shīʿīs but also Sunnīs and Hindus). The Faraizis intervened also in matters of dress and urged their members to wear either *pajama* or *lungi*, but if they had to wear the customary *dhoti*, it had to conform to *sharīʿah* requirements and cover the thighs, and not be tucked between the legs – since that would have led to indecent exposure, especially during prayer. While these changes separated Faraizis from imperfect Muslims, and particularly from Hindus, it also joined them – in the Bengali Muslim *imaginaire* – with all "good" Muslims, whether past or present.

Hajji Shariatullah is remembered now as a proto-Pakistani nationalist and an early resistor of British colonialism. In his own time, however, he was understood to be "a profound scholar in Islamic sciences, and one who had the privilege of being associated for a considerable time with the birth-place and center of Islamic culture [Mecca] . . ."[80] A contemporary observed that,

[79] Khan's discussion (pp. 67–80) of this subject is particularly thorough. He uses important original sources to assert that the reason for the ban was that none of the towns of East Bengal met the requisite condition of being *miṣr jāmiʿ*, that it be, essentially, large enough to legitimate observance of the congregational prayers according to Ḥanafī *fiqh* standards. Khan rejects the other reason often adduced, that it was due to British-ruled India being the Abode of the Enemy (*dār al-ḥarb*) rather than the Abode of Islam (*dār al-islām*); he says this is unattested by Farāʾiḍī sources. Yet Khan elsewhere shows that this view of occupied India was very much in the air during the period before 1860, and the Farāʾiḍī sources he uses all date from after 1857. It seems reasonable to speculate that in the climate of Muslim fear following suppression of the Revolt of 1857, Farāʾiḍīs might have preferred to justify their practice in terms that the British, ever vigilant against "pan-Islamic subversion," would find unthreatening. Yet even if the issue was indeed the more technical Ḥanafī reasoning, the effect was similar – to induce the feeling of Muslims as a beset minority in a sea of more powerful Hindus and Christians.

[80] M. Khan, *History of the Faraʾidi Movement*, 9.

like Hajji Shariatullah, the Faraizis "profess to adhere to the strict letter of the Koran, and reject all ceremonies that are not sanctioned by it."[81] Hajji Shariatullah is an exemplary case of a scholar doing what Cosmopolitan Muslims do: "a (re)ordering of knowledge that governs the 'correct' form of Islamic practices."[82] It was the religious commitment to the idea, the myth, of an Islam properly unaffected by anything other than the universal Qur'ān that motivated Bengalis' Muslim reform. For Cosmopolitan Muslims, the Islam of the Qur'ān is not merely an Islam for Bengal in the nineteenth century, but it is an Islam of the Prophet's time and all times, an Islam both Arabian and utopian. Hajji Shariatullah and his followers sought to practice an Islam for eternity.

Since the texts – not just Scriptural texts but also the guides to action derived from them – were shared across Islamdom uninflected for place or time, throughout Muslim history the scholars' imperative was to constantly discipline Lived Islam, measured against the Cosmopolitan ideal. Over time, this effort effectively prevented the Dialects from separating and becoming distinct languages – that is, a Local Islam as permanently irreconcilable with other Muslims' Islam as German Lutheranism is with the Christianity of Italy. The absence of regional Islamic denominations that were institutionally separate from the Islam of some other place attests to the structural power of Cosmopolitan Islam in the disciplined construction of Lived Islam throughout Islamdom. It also facilitated the development of the notion of the *ummah* as a transnational state-like entity in the modern world when enhanced travel and communication made the visualization of such an entity possible, and its cosmopolitan contrast to the nation-state attractive.

Standard Language

Cosmopolitan Islam has the prestige of texts, but also the effective socializing force of institutions like madrasas. It also has the ability to coerce, since it was Cosmopolitans who staffed the courts, which were in constant cooperation with the state. This cooperation sometimes turned to competition as the state sought to usurp the institutions of Cosmopolitan Islam.[83]

So far we have argued that Islam has Dialect-like features, as well as a Koiné, whose cognates are shared among most Muslims. The analogue of Cosmopolitan Islam and the way it has worked throughout most of Islam's

[81] M. Abdul Bari, "Fara'idi Movement," 201, citing Taylor in *Journal of the Asiatic Society of Bengal*, vol. 68, pp. 48–51.

[82] T. Asad, *Genealogies of Religion*, 210.

[83] J. E. Baldwin, *Islamic Law and Empire*, 99ff.

history is the concept of what sociolinguists call "Standard English." "Standard English" is a controversial concept because it has usually gone hand in hand with *prescriptive* rather than *descriptive* understandings of English. Standard English is "correct" English. It is the right way to speak and write. Speakers of "nonstandard" English mark themselves – and are marked – mostly in negative ways (though in local sub-communities to speak the dialect may be prestigious since it marks the speaker as "one of us"). From the perspectives of power and wealth, however, deviations from Standard English stigmatize the speaker as uneducated, provincial, lower-class, coarse, and often poor.[84]

The etymology of the term "Standard English" is splendidly descriptive. When coined, it referred to the "standard," as on a ship's mast, to which all could turn for guidance. Of course it was no accident that, to see this standard, one looked up – up toward the upper-classes, and toward the aristocracy; a telling synonym for Standard English is "the King's/Queen's English." It became a myth of English speakers – one believed, taught, and enforced – that there was a set of speech habits (pronunciation, vocabulary, stress patterns, inflection) that, taken together, constituted "correct" English.

Yet linguists know that Standard English is no one's native tongue.[85] At the prestigious English "public" (meaning private) school, Winchester, for example, considerable pressure is exerted on newly arrived students with regional speech to assimilate to the Standard English of the British "public" school. Lessons are given by other students; norms are enforced; deviants are shamed.[86] The norms now have a life of their own, and even the royal family themselves can be mocked for their pronunciation and usage of when it deviates from what used to be called "the King's English" and is now referred to as RP (Received Pronunciation).[87]

Standard English is not an organic dialect; it is only an *abstraction* derived from an informal corpus that represents "how the better sort of person writes and speaks." Particularly these days that means "the better sort of newspaper," and the media of radio and television.[88] The opposite of Standard

[84] See, e.g., P. Trudgill, "Standard English: What It Isn't."

[85] R. W. Bailey, *Images of English*, 3–12. [86] *The Story of English*, first episode.

[87] "Kings and Queens have rarely been honored as exemplars of English in Britain . . . the sovereign, the Queen Mother, and the heir to the throne all speak a variant of RP which is not the most widely admired or imitated accent—indeed in the mouths of other speakers it is actually ridiculed—nor is it anywhere taught. . . . The Duchess of York takes 'miwlk' rather than milk in her tea, while the Princess of Wales believes she was married in a place called 'St. Paw's' Cathedral . . ." R. W. Bailey, *Images of English*, 3.

[88] "The standard language in the United States and Britain is the prestige variety of the language used by those regarded as educated. Standardization is manifested mostly in grammar and

English is regional, or lower-class, Scouse, Brummie, Aussie, Valley Girl, Alabaman, or whatever – all terms that mark a linguistic performance as particular rather than universal.

So Standard English is both the norm and at the same time an artificial ideal. It is a form of English one aspires to speak and write, while it is understood and tacitly accepted that almost no one does.[89] It functions as a point of reference rather than a practice, but very importantly *it is this form of English that we teach to non-English speakers.*[90] It is no locality's native dialect – that is the whole point.[91] Deviance is defined as precisely any speech marking or reflecting one's class or place of origin. Yet what may be seen as tyranny or oppression of one class by another can also be a crucial instrument for social mobility – knowing and manipulating the rules of Standard English makes one's origins opaque. Humble origins are concealed if one's speech is correct, classy, posh. Also, precisely because no one natively speaks it, Standard English does, through enforcement of its norms, create the boundaries and bonds that keep English from morphing from different dialects into different languages in the way that Latin dissolved into Spanish, Romanian, Italian, and French.

Standard Islam

Cosmopolitan Islam should also be understood as a kind of "Standard Islam." It is taught (and where possible, enforced) by scholars and professionals. It is the more prestigious form of Islam, but it is no one's Lived Islam.

vocabulary (though there may also be some standard regional variations) and in spelling and punctuation. ... It comes closest to uniformity in the neutral and formal styles of written English."

"... The development of the standard language in Britain and the United States was ... not planned. It emerged from a consensus (in which there remains room for some diversity) of what educated speakers and writers accepted as correct. This consensus was shaped, however, by codifications that generally focused on the written language: dictionaries, grammars, and guides to usage.... The standard language is maintained by the education system, where it is required at least in writing. It is preserved in printed English by editors who do not hesitate to query (or to correct silently) the language of their authors ..." Ibid., 17–18.

89 P. Trudgill and J. Hannah, *International English*, 2. "RP ['Received Pronunciation'] is used by perhaps only 3 per cent to 5 per cent of the population of England."

90 Ibid., 1.

91 Ibid., 9. RP "is now a genuinely regionless accent within Britain, i.e., if speakers have an RP accent—you cannot tell which area of Britain they come from." [Of a Tory candidate for Parliament]: "She has Blue Lagoon eyes, a serious manner, and one of those unplaceable accents that mark out a specific quintile of the upper-lower-upper class." www.independent.co.uk/opinion/commentators/simon-carr/simon-carr-nancy-mogg-no-its-annunziata-reesmogg-actually-1957284.html.

We teach Arabs or Japanese "English" and not "British" or "American" (although, mostly silently, dialect choices are made nonetheless); we do not teach "rural Alabaman" to a German who wants to learn English. So too *Standard Islam is what Muslims teach to each other and to would-be converts.*[92] Like Standard English, Standard Islam has privileged access to the media, and now in the Islamic fifteenth century it attempts to drive Dialect Islam to the margins (though as we shall see in Chapter 6, the matter is more complex). The vision of a "Standard Islam" (in contrast to the sociological reality of Cosmopolitan Islam) becomes prominent in the later nineteenth and twentieth centuries and most widespread with the rise of nationalism and the national media.[93]

No serious ethnographer of English would dream of describing Standard English as "real English" or "true English" nor would she confuse the "English of books and media" with "English." Yet that is exactly what essentialists and parochialists alike do with Standard Islam. The essentialists fail to recognize the full scope and significance of Dialect Islam; the parochialists are deaf to Lived Islam because they attend only to the Dialect and suppose that Standard Islam is just another dialect among many. The parochialists must grasp that Lived Islam is never only Dialect Islam; in the twenty-first century everyone's Lived Islam is in constant dialogue with the powerful Standard version. And just as with Standard English, media presentations of Islam – not to mention Islam classes in high school – privilege the Standard, that is, the Cosmopolitan, variety. As Francis Robinson said,

> increasing contact with [non-Indian Muslim] cultures which are thought to represent more fully the pattern of perfection ... often seems to draw [Indian Muslims] toward *higher* Islamic standards.[94]

This complex relationship between Dialect and Cosmopolitan Islam (now presenting itself as Standard Islam) is an ever-present feature of Lived Islam. The relationship is in no way so unilinear – from vulgar to sophisticated – as Robinson suggests, nor is it as much a top-down imposition as anthropologists seem to believe.[95] The fact is that, properly regarded, Egyptian *ʿulamāʾ* are both *ʿulamāʾ* and Egyptian, just as prescriptive grammarians are both

[92] Oddly, academics, even non-Muslims who theoretically have no stake in which Islam is "true" or "real" Islam, collaborate by also teaching Standard Islam as "Islam" in their university courses.

[93] For the Ottoman world, see S. Deringil, *Well-Protected Domains*, 75–84 and chapter 4.

[94] F. Robinson, "Islam and Muslim Society in South Asia," 92–93, my italics.

[95] As, for example, Antoun seems to believe. R. T. Antoun, *Muslim Preacher*.

advocates of the Standard English and speakers of American at the same time.

What Standard Islam's professionals have that practitioners of the Dialects do not is both their Cosmopolitanism in the literal sense – travel does much to convince Muslims that Standard Islam is what Muslims share and is therefore of the essence – and their prestige as *ʿilm*-bearers. Because of the Koiné commitment to, for example, the Qurʾān, those who can quote it and apply it authoritatively can inspire commitment and change from those to whom Cosmopolitan Islam is, as it were, foreign, however prestigious. Moreover, the Cosmopolitans' privileged access to authoritative texts means that it is their Islam that becomes Standard Islam because it is taught in institutions that produce scholars, madrasas, and also those that now increasingly teach all Muslims about their religion – schools, television and radio, and more broadly, the state. In short, the myths of an unchanged, non-spacial Cosmopolitan Islam are now no longer grounded merely in the prestige of *ʿilm* and the *ʿilm*-bearers, but also in the power and resources of the modern state. This alters the dynamics of the Dialect–Koiné–Cosmopolitan forms of Islam but not always in ways that are predictable, as we will see in Chapter 6.

The Limits of Cosmopolitan Islam

The fact is that, to return to our case study of Hajji Shariatullah and the Faraizis, even as they broke free from Local practices, the Islam of the Faraizis remained locally inflected nonetheless – distinctively Bengali. An Egyptian or Syrian wearing a *dhoti* – however wrapped – as a sign of his conformity to Cosmopolitan Islamic norms is inconceivable. Similarly, to insist that it is an Islamic requirement to slaughter a cow at the Feast of Sacrifice would baffle Muslims in Arabia, Anatolia, or Morocco who take it for granted that in most cases it is a sheep that must be sacrificed. The reality is that Cosmopolitans never succeeded in creating the ideal world they sought. The Lived Islam in Bengal, as elsewhere, remained a composite of the Dialect enrichment of Koiné observances, leavened with prestige and reform Cosmopolitan interventions – and so it remains today.

What was true in the past is true in the present – that Cosmopolitan scholars never dwell completely removed from Lived Islam, floating above their locale like balloons. In fact, most *ʿulamāʾ*, like the commonality of Muslims, were deeply imbedded in their particular time and place. Cosmopolitans' Lived Islam was a critique of those who most comfortably blurred categories and who unreflectively lived their religious life embedded in only the Dialect features of their local Islam. Yet few scholars could maintain the corrosive a-temporalism of an Ibn Taymiyyah – and if more had done so, the world would no doubt contain fewer Muslims. Ibn Taymiyyah is useful because he is a maximal case, a pure idealist of a sort seldom seen again before the eighteenth century (CE). Yet he is exceptional, and for that reason perhaps he is enormously influential across the Islamic world, and increasingly so from his time to the present.

Schoolmasters, however refined their pronunciation and grammar, are still recognizably British, American, or Indian. Just so, Ibn Taymiyyah's opponents and prosecutors were also Cosmopolitan *ʿulamāʾ*,[96] who in good faith believed and practiced in good faith an Islam that was particular to their locale. Those same practices would in the nineteenth and twentieth centuries would be regarded as hopelessly provincial, ignorant, and inauthentic by that time's Cosmopolitan Islamic reformers. It was, in reality, just this open-texturedness on the part of the Cosmopolitans that allowed Islam to take root and flourish while the rigors of other Cosmopolitans disciplined Islam and connected it to the shared Islamic discourse.

Indeed, the cosmopolite with whom we began our chapter, Ibn Baṭṭūṭah, failed to reach the idealist bar set by Ibn Taymiyyah, despite his madrasa training and his willingness to offer fraternal correction. He visited Syria just after Ibn Taymiyyah's arrest and famously asserted that Ibn Taymiyyah had a "kink in his brain."[97] Ibn Baṭṭūṭah, rigorist critic of practices he believed fell short of scholars' Islam, nonetheless participated enthusiastically, even wallowed, in local Syrian Islam and the piety of particular places. He took for granted that the tombs at which Ibn Taymiyyah scoffed were genuine, and he found sacrality at the putative tomb of Uways that Ibn Taymiyyah had scorned.[98] He likewise believed that the Prophet Hūd *was* buried in the Great Mosque of Damascus.[99] Not only did Ibn Baṭṭūṭah believe that Moses' footprints were to be found in the "Mosque of the Footprints," but he participated in a special Damascene Dialect ritual involving fasting, nights of prayer, then barefoot procession to the Mosque of the Footprints accompanied by

> "the Jews . . . with their book of the Law and the Christians with their Gospel, their women and children with them; the whole concourse of them

[96] H. Q. Murad, "Ibn Taymiya on Trial," 3, 7ff.; see also D. P. Little, "Did Ibn Taymiyya Have a Screw Loose," 96; S. A. J. Jackson, "Ibn Taymiyyah On Trial in Damascus"; D. P. Little, "The Detention of Ibn Taymiyya."

[97] Ibn Baṭṭūṭah, *Travels of Ibn Baṭṭūṭah*, 1:135. [98] Ibid., 139. [99] Ibid., 128.

in tears and humble supplications, imploring the favor of God through His Books and His Prophets," for relief from the plague.[100]

The seemingly rigorist Ibn Baṭṭūṭah deeply believed that this intercommunal ritual, this noncanonical ritual innovation, was Islamically efficacious. Indeed the same displaced observances of hajj season that so inflamed Ibn Taymiyyah were recorded by Ibn Baṭṭūṭah as among of the virtuous practices of the Damascenes. By contrast to Ibn Taymiyyah, Ibn Baṭṭūṭah describes Syrian Dialect practices not to excoriate, but to praise them.

> It is a custom of the people of Damascus and all the other cities of that region to go out [of the covered part of the mosques] after the mid-afternoon prayer *on the day of ʿArafah*, and to stand in the courtyard of the mosques, such as the Sanctuary of Jerusalem, the Umayyad congregational mosque [at Damascus], etc. Their imāms stand with them bare-headed, their bodies humbly bowed in prayer, with lowly voice and downcast eyes, entreating the blessing of God. Observing thus the hour in which the *homagers of God Most High and pilgrims to His House stand at ʿArafāt*, they continue in humble reverence and prayer and earnest supplication, imploring the favor of God Most High through the Pilgrims to His House, until the sun sets, when they hurriedly disperse, *in imitation of the rush of the pilgrims*, weeping that it has been denied them to join in that illustrious station at ʿArafāt, and praying God Most High that He may bring them thither and not withhold from them the blessing of His acceptance of that which they have done [on this day].[101]

The famous rigorist scholar ʿAbdalqādir al-Jilānī (d. 1166) commended the textually dubious Raghāʾib prayers,[102] and the authoritative al-Ghazālī (d. 1111) supported this same innovative ritual because he saw the people of Jerusalem performing it, and he admired it.[103] It is clear that even the *ʿulamāʾ*, some no doubt more than others, some at one time and not in another, have lived also in the colloquial Islam of particular places and times, that their Lived Islam always contained a Dialect component.

If we look at Europe, especially in the premodern period, we can find useful analogues to the situation we describe. There, too, was "great regional variation in popular culture."[104] Peter Burke observes that religious ideas descended from elites to *hoi polloi* but also ascended from the masses to

[100] Ibid., 144. [101] Ibid., 152–153, my italics.

[102] Which Ukeles describes thus: "*ṣalāh al-raghāʾib* (the prayers of desirable gifts), a special [performance of *ṣalāh*] recited on the first Thursday evening of the [Islamic] month of Rajab and sometimes on the evening prior to the fifteenth of the month of Shaʿbān." R. M. Ukeles, "Innovation or Deviation," 239.

[103] Ibid., 246. [104] P. Burke, *Popular Culture in Early Modern Europe*, 56.

"their betters," and that these ideas changed as they sank to the masses or rose to the elites.[105] Burke says that "popular culture" is a misnomer, if by that we mean something that excludes elites of class and education, because, as in Ibn Baṭṭūṭah's Damascus, and in sixteenth-century Spain, quite "different social groups often walked [together] in [these Dialect] processions, or lined the streets to watch the others."[106] "[In Spain] the upper class participated in popular culture, and on the other hand, the life of rural notables and parish priests [and likewise provincial rulers and rural *'ulamā'* in Islamdom] was not so different from that of the peasants around them."[107] The difference between the clergy in Christendom (as in Islamdom), and the masses was a difference "between the majority, for whom popular culture was the only culture, and the minority, who had access to the great tradition but participated in the little tradition as a second culture. [The clergy] were amphibious, bi-cultural, and also bi-lingual."[108]

Dialect tradition "was 'popular' only in the sense that it was predominantly lay." But most of the clergy "fully participated in it as well."[109]

In Islamdom this meant that the most localized, uneducated member of the laity was susceptible to the prestigious Cosmopolitan call – as in Bengal. Yet even Hajji Shariatullah's call to reform was framed by Local assumptions – about dress, observance, and language. In Damascus, with its unusually heavy Ḥanbalī-rigorist presence, scholars may not have

> "fought [with the laity] for a scrap of the shrouds of their shaykh over his open grave or scurried to dip their clothes in the water that had purified his body," but they too sought blessing-filled objects (although, as members of the elite) "they could acquire them in more respectable ways, or receive them as presents."[110]

The blessing or intercession the scholars hoped for may have differed conceptually from that of the non-scholarly, but it may not have differed as much as textbooks suggest it ought to have. A Damascus school for teaching *ḥadīth* of Muḥammad – surely a Cosmopolitan institution – was constructed nonetheless around a purported sandal of the Prophet.[111] Equally "popularly," a scholar's visions were adduced as proof to justify the cult of al-Ḥusayn's head in Cairo.[112] And as we have seen, the *'ulamā'* in Egypt

[105] Ibid., 59–63. [106] Ibid.

[107] Ibid., 24, 28; for the Muslim case in nineteenth-century Syria, see J. Grehan, *Twilight of the Saints*.

[108] P. Burke, *Popular Culture in Early Modern Europe*, 28.

[109] W. A. Christian, *Local Religion in Sixteenth-Century Spain*, 148.

[110] D. Talmon-Heller, *Islamic Piety in Medieval Syria*, 224. [111] Ibid., 208.

[112] E. W. Lane, *Manners and Customs*, 213–216.

collaborated to reconceive the dating of *Shamm al-nasīm* to preserve a popular Egyptian holiday by speciously supplying it with a date disconnected from to the Christian religious calendar.

Moreover, a popular religious holiday that is for most of Islamdom an important Islamic event – the Prophet's birthday – has trickled up from the masses and has been justified by scholars, despite the objections of hardcore Scripturalists. Ethnographic reports of the *mawlid* celebrations suggest enthusiastic scholarly participation and support.[113] The Cosmopolitans, then, aspire to an Islamic utopia, an *illud tempus*, but are, in hundreds of ways, major and minor, imbricated in the Lived Islam in which they find themselves. They may have a more elevated form of Islamic discourse but, if they are relevant, most will know the local Vernacular Islam and will, willy-nilly, be affected by it.

The relationships among Dialect, Cosmopolitan, and Koiné Islam have shifted over time and according to place but they remain the constituents of Lived Islam. The twentieth and twenty-first centuries have realigned these three features of Islam in what may at first seem to be a predictable privileging of the institutional forms of Islam since those institutions are now often allied with the power of the modern nation-state. Yet the full story is more interesting than that, and seeing Islam as constituted by these three aspects helps us partially to understand Modern Islam in its continuity with the past and its distinctive modern form.

[113] N. J. G. Kaptein, *Muḥammad's Birthday Festival*; M. H. Katz, *The Birth of the Prophet Muhammad*; R. M. Ukeles, "Innovation or Deviation."

6

Modern Islam

Introduction

Modernity is the "great disrupter."[1] Like the agrarianate revolution of the fourth millennium BCE, the collection of forces, factors, and practices we call "modernity" has altered the world utterly. In the modern world, just as during the agrarianate revolution, the organization of society, commerce and learning, the way we make things, the sources of our status and power, our gender and social roles, are now being profoundly reshaped and remade. Yet many cultural legacies of the premodern world have survived into the contemporary world. Perhaps the most prominent of these "souvenirs" are the major religious traditions. Most of the "world religions" (both "religion" and "world religions" are modern concepts[2]) were products of the agrarianate civilizations that arose when agricultural surpluses enabled the development of urban centers. Most "world religions" are rooted in the so-called axial age[3] – roughly 500 BCE to 700 CE – yet to the consternation of sociologists, secularists, and theoreticians of modernity, despite their great antiquity, the "great

[1] J. O. Appleby, *The Relentless Revolution*; M. G. S. Hodgson, *Rethinking World History*; K. Polanyi, *The Great Transformation*.

[2] T. Masuzawa, *The Invention of World Religions*; J. Z. Smith, "Religion, Religions, Religious"; W. C. Smith, *Meaning and End*; G. G. Stroumsa, *A New Science*. This is not to suggest that there is no religious life aside from the world religions, but religions that have arisen in the modern period – like Tenrikyo or Mormonism, or more ephemerally, Ghost Dance Religion, or the Taiping Rebellion – nonetheless draw heavily on premodern models for their authority. Good discussions of this phenomenon are found in M. Dressler, *Writing Religion*; M. Dressler and A. S. Mandair, *Secularism and Religion-Making*. On "world religions," see T. Masuzawa, *The Invention of World Religions*.

[3] R. N. Bellah, *Religion in Human Evolution*; R. N. Bellah and H. Joas, *The Axial Age and Its Consequences*. See the literature cited therein.

religions" are still very much present in the modern and postmodern world.[4]

Islam too comes to us from premodernity. Many of the examples we have used for understanding Lived Islam have come from the premodern period. Ibn Baṭṭūṭah was a great fourteenth-century traveler; Ibn Taymiyyah was a great, if marginal, fourteenth-century scholar. How can their lives and their perspectives be relevant to a world utterly discontinuous with the religious environment, as well as to the social, economic, and cultural environment in which they lived?

The Lived Islam argument is anti-essentialist. Koiné, Dialect, and Cosmopolitan Islam are not essences but notional aspects, facets, characteristics, traits, forms, registers, or features of the phenomenon we identify as "Islam." They are aspects of Islam in the medieval period and in our own times, just as morphemes, dialects, and syntax are aspects of English in Chaucer's time and in our own. However, to focus a chapter exclusively on "Modern Islam" will further clarify the concepts at the heart of the book's argument, and allow us more precisely to describe the relationships among them. Focusing on the Lived Islam of the modern period particularly helps us also to understand some distinctive features of Modern Islam.

Lived Islam in the modern world draws particular attention to the notion of "place." Analytically, as we will see, place and locale are no longer synonymous. We live in both the modern world, and, nascently, in the postmodern world. In the modern world there are ways in which particular places have been sanctified and linked to power and control. In the postmodern world, the apparatus of the state may still discipline residents of a place, but at the same time "place" and "physical locale" have been decoupled in a way that is historically unprecedented, yet that fits particularly smoothly with the internationalist and cosmopolitan history of Islamic thought and practice. Hyper-localization – the heightened emphasis on place – is due to the development of the nation-state, while hypo-localization – the disengagement from physical place in the formation of culture – gives to some forms of postmodern Lived Islam a quality as distinct as formative period Lived Islam was from Lived middle period Islam.[5]

[4] I will for most of this chapter use the term "modern" to include both modern and postmodern periods. Nonetheless, I do believe that the emergence of the knowledge economy in the 1980s has truly created another major disruption that deserves the term "postmodern," or "post-industrial." On the cultural concept of postmodernity, see P. Anderson, *The Origins of Postmodernity*; on the material-culture features of it, see D. Bell, *The Coming of Post-Industrial Society*.

[5] On the characteristics of these periods, see M. G. S. Hodgson, *Venture of Islam*, especially p. 96.

The Triumph of Standard Islam?

Modernity is the age of standardization and homogenization. Mass education, mass media, and mass culture erode particularity and difference. It stands to reason that the Islam of Everywhere (and Nowhere) would become more prominent and dominate local religious idiosyncrasy. After all, just as Standard English is the English we teach in classrooms, Standard Islam is the Islam we teach in Intro to Islam courses – whether in the university, the parochial school, or the mosque. And many more Muslims learn their Islam in school than was ever the case in the past.

Three features in particular press Muslims toward a hegemonic Standard Islam that erodes differences and promotes homogeneity. These are literacy, travel, and the rise of media.

The Religion of the Book

Islam is the religion of the book par excellence. Islam's sacrament, its Incarnation, is the Qurʾān. The Qurʾān reflects and creates a prestige for the Book that modernity's mass literacy only amplifies. Like the Gutenberg Bible, the printing of the Qurʾān has allowed every home to have God's *ipsissima verba* on the bookshelf. Moreover, the Qurʾān has now been translated into virtually every language on the planet so that the vast majority of Muslims who cannot read the Qurʾānic Arabic can now study its imagery and meanings.[6] More people than ever before know what's "really" in the Qurʾān.

More important than the availability of the Scriptural text, however, is the existence of a mass Muslim reading public. For many Muslims – educated, reading, reflective Muslims – the relationship of Muslims to texts in general has been profoundly altered in the modern world.

Scripturalism and Modern Religion

The new focus on Scripture and other texts diminishes the role of Local Islam, and would seem to enhance the Standard Islam, the Cosmopolitan Islam of scholars. Following Geertz, we may call this new emphasis on Islam's Scripture to the exclusion of other aspects of Islam "Scripturalism."[7] In the modern world more Muslims are literate – in general

[6] M. B. Wilson, *Translating the Qurʾan*. See also now B. B. Lawrence, *The Koran in English*.

[7] C. Geertz, *Islam Observed*. I am more significantly influenced in this discussion by H. Soloveitchik, "The New Role of Texts"; "Rupture and Reconstruction." I am indebted to my colleague Susannah Heschel who first called my attention to "Rupture and Reconstruction."

and also in the sacred language of Islam – but it is not merely this fact that has altered Islam's texture. In addition, as a consequence of this literacy, the place of the text and textual tradition has been radically transformed.[8]

To paraphrase Soloveitchik, in the premodern world, a religious tradition was primarily conveyed mimetically. One's [Islam] was "a way of life, not learned but rather absorbed. [It was] imbibed from parents and friends and patterned on conduct regularly observed in home and street, [mosque] and school."[9] Each of these domains "had its own keepers and custodians, who, in authoritative accents, informed men and women what their duties were and how they should go about performing them."[10]

These distributed religious domains nourished a diverse set of religious practices and customs, local practices, and distinctive religious dialects. Diverse religious institutions – not just madrasa and mosque, but also Sufi convent, home, and market, with their diffuse loci of religious authority and instruction – were the laboratories and classrooms of the protean Lived Islam of the premodern period. There were always those, such as the Ḥanbalīs of fourteenth-century Damascus, or the Kadızadeler of the seventeenth-century Ottoman world, who aspired to live solely by Scripture. They were only transiently important, however, because most Muslims found this textual Islam thin gruel compared to the richness of a more diverse, more fecund Lived Islam.

Modernity creates self-consciousness about, among other things, religion. In the modern world the previous wholeness of the religious world is broken by disharmonious and, from a religious viewpoint, competing domains of authority – the state, the state school, science, and the media – and suddenly the hegemony of religion is gone.[11] More importantly, the authority of custom is diluted, and in religion, as in the rest of society, textbooks and rulebooks, experts and rationalized procedures become uniquely authoritative and normative. Consequently, in the religious imagination, God as benevolent King is replaced by God as Bureaucrat and Legislator.[12] Moreover, the place of Islam in this competing chorus of authority has been cast into doubt, as nonreligious figures assert authority over religious authorities. Doubt, as Geertz noted, for Scripturalists is less about the existence of God than of one's own allegiance to Islam itself, and to

[8] The following section is partly drawn from my article "Fundamentalism and the Transparency of the Arabic Qur'ān." I am also heavily influenced by conversations with Ibrahim Moosa and especially and repeatedly Bruce Lawrence and miriam cooke.

[9] H. Soloveitchik, "The New Role of Texts," 197. [10] Ibid., 219.

[11] C. Geertz, *Islam Observed*; C. Taylor, *A Secular Age*.

[12] H. Soloveitchik, "The New Role of Texts," 213–216.

preserving a significant place for it in one's life.[13] For the religiously committed, the result is not an increase in medieval piety, but in what Geertz calls modern "religious mindedness."[14] An obvious manifestation of this religious mindedness is clear to anyone who regularly talks with Muslims, and is encapsulated in W. C. Smith's observation that,

> in the Qurʾān, the word "God" appears 2,697 times; the word *islām*, eight times. (In a good deal of modern Muslim writing this ratio is perhaps, roughly, reversed.)[15]

For many Modern Muslims, Islam itself becomes the object of allegiance, and the question becomes not "what is true?" but "what is true Islam?"

The means to answer this question is mostly, in Muslim discourse, a reference to a textual Islam. "The Qurʾān is our constitution," say Islamic activists, harking back to a mythic time of seamless piety and virtue, power and efficacy. Yet whatever the Qurʾān was to the first Muslims, it was certainly not a constitution – the concept of a consensual legislative compact defining the state's interaction with citizens had not, of course, yet been invented. Nonetheless, the Qurʾān is now read as a constitution, and also as a textbook of economics, of social science, even of physics. "All the discoveries of modern science are already found in the Qurʾān," one is frequently informed.[16] Following the commitment to reading the Qurʾān as the masterwork of each of these genres, it is approached and understood as if it were just such a thing.

Of course, this procrustean reading is difficult and to effect it thousands of handbooks, manuals, and other secondary literature have been produced recasting Scripture as data, text as textbook. To take but one example, between 1990 and 2018, the University of California library system acquired at least 306 books with titles that using Arabic, Persian, English, Turkish, or Indonesia equivalents of "Islam and Economics," or "Islamic economics"[17] a concept apparently unthought before 1947,[18] and

[13] C. Geertz, *Islam Observed*, 61. The Christian focus on belief in God's existence as the locus of doubt and the distinctive feature of the modern view of transcendence reflects Christianity's obsession with creeds, and their commitments to precisely defined metaphysical ontologies.

[14] Ibid. [15] W. C. Smith, *Meaning and End*, 111. See also J. Smith, *Study of the Term Islam*.

[16] Bucaille is the foremost of these scientistic Muslims, though the movement goes back at least to Abduh. See M. Bucaille, *La Bible, le Coran et la science*.

[17] These are a fraction of what must have been produced throughout Islamdom, especially considering all the books on Islam and Finance, Islam and Banking, that do not use these particular key words, and of course all the other languages besides English in which such works have been produced.

[18] Search of the University of California library catalog, May 2018. Terms: "Islam" and "economics" (English) or "Islamic economics" 130, "Iqtiṣād" and "Islām" (Arabic and Persian) 34, "Islam"

unimaginable to Ibn Taymiyyah – not only because "Islamic economics" uses such utterly modern concepts but because the mode of discourse is completely discontinuous with inherited Islamic thought, and connects instead with the discourse of contemporary economics.[19] Justification for the purported Scripturally derived economic precepts of the Qur'ān is provided by recourse to economic theory and sociology, not to strictly religious arguments. The concepts of *maṣlaḥah* (welfare) and *ribā* (usury) are stretched and extended to create this novelty, Islamic Economics.

I do not mean to suggest it is an illegitimate enterprise. Only that it is a novel one whose goal and purport was previously unknown to Muslims, despite the claims of the authors that this enterprise is restorative, that it brings back the economic justice of formative Islam. These works' authors labor to create a Modern Islam grounded entirely in texts because in the modern world texts provide not just authority, but certainty. The matter produced in contemporary books of this sort is offered not as a version of Islam but as what *the* Islam, "true Islam," requires. This "true Islam" is a version of Standard Islam, but extended into new domains. Nonetheless, the premodern authoritative claims of Standard Islam are, if anything, enhanced and made more stridently, and its utopian vision is fully retained and expanded. This utopian vision subordinates local specificity. The claim is that Islam is one thing, universally true for all, and like the laws of Marxist history, Free Market economics, or Newtonian physics, it applies everywhere. Islamic economics, therefore, is not just for Pakistanis – for these Scripturalists it is mandatory for all Muslims.

Scripturalism, the reduction of a complex tradition to its founding documents, is a characteristic move of moderns. The Protestant Reformation, the Jewish neo-Orthodoxy that Soloveitchik discusses, perhaps even the neo-neo-Confucianism of contemporary China, are evidence of a desire for certainty, found in indubitable sources procured directly from the mythic time of origins. In this respect too, the modern period would seem conducive to a heightening of the place of Standard Islam in the mix with Koiné and Dialect Islam. Other forces too press Muslims in a similar direction.

and "Ekonomi" ((Indonesian) 134, Islam* and Ekon* or İktisat (Turkish) 8. Earliest use of the term in book title: M. Ahmad, *Economics of Islam*, published in 1947.

[19] See H. Soloveitchik, "The New Role of Texts," 210–211. On medieval Muslim understandings of the market, see A. A. al-Maqrīzī and A. Allouche, *Mamluk Economics*.

Travel as a Standardizing Force

Local particularity is subverted also by mobility. Where once travel was the domain of some merchants and of Cosmopolitan scholars, now many more ordinary Muslims from all walks of life can and do travel – for work, for recreation, and for religious learning and observance. Because of travel, many more Muslims are, in the literal sense, and to some extent in our special terminology, Cosmopolitan Muslims – for the term applies not only to those who read texts from all over Islamdom. "Cosmopolitan Muslims" now include the many who have traveled throughout Islamdom. Where once the number of hajjis was in the tens of thousands, now it is in the millions – and on these travels Muslims from one place talk to Muslims from elsewhere; on their return they discuss what they have seen and heard with their local Muslim friends and family. While performing the hajj they are also susceptible to Official accounts of what constitutes "real" Islamic behavior – whether from their own state (in most countries in Islamdom, the hajj is organized by an office of the government) or by the Saudi state with its own sectarian commitments.

The ability to travel, and the mixing that results, shapes also the Muslim religious "laity" and the transmission of religious ideas to large communities; these communities are unlike any seen before in Islamdom. Now in places like the Azhar and al-Madinah International University but also in the United States and particularly in Europe, ethnically and ideologically diverse groups of Muslims share mosques, Ramadan celebrations, and social functions.[20] It is hard to remain unaffected by this dislocation. As a result, Malay students are Arabized at al-Azhar in Egypt, but Malay students are also Americanized at engineering schools in the US. Algerians are (further) Francified at the Sorbonne; Turks are Teutonized in Berlin. More interestingly, South Asians may be African-Americanized at a mosque in the US, where they will also find Arabs, Afghans, and various sorts of converts mingling and creating a truly, not metaphorically, Cosmopolitan Islam.

Consequently, many Muslims are no longer "local" in the way they once were. When Muslims are in constant contact with other Muslims around the

[20] For the fast-breaking prayers one year, the Houston Muslim community rented the "Albert Thomas Exhibition Hall in downtown Houston[;] people begin to file in. Pakistanis, Arabs, and Indians [wore] the clothes of their traditional cultures, intentionally flaunting their ethnicities." M. M. J. Fischer and M. Abedi, *Debating Muslims*, 312. "Under superficial expressions of Islamic brotherhood, there was intense competition, wariness, and mutual proselytization." There are "widespread existential dilemmas, personal and social, which activists with their eyes on their countries of origin and, differently, immigrants with their eyes on America are seeking to identify and resolve." Ibid., 288.

globe, and to the extent that they conceive of themselves as part of a larger Muslim whole, they often resist practices that mark them as distinct or provincial, just as a village student going to Eton or a Texan going to Dartmouth filters out the regionalisms in her speech so as not to stand out. Dialect customs – "superstitions" to the unsympathetic – are vanishing at a rate that makes De Tassy's *Muslim Festivals* in India or Westermarck's *Ritual and Belief in Morocco* as exotic to an Indian or Moroccan Muslim as to a suburban American. Just as folk Catholicism is fading in Italy, or the colorful rural British customs that undergird Frazer's *Golden Bough* are going the way of outdoor plumbing or hedgerows in the English countryside, so too the healing practices of Dialect Islam and many of its rites of passage and seasonal observances are fading in the obscurity of elders' memories and colonial ethnographies.

Citizens of the Ummah

The new textualism, together with travel and many other forces, have together led to a shift in Muslims' understanding of Islam, but also to a shift in Muslim self-understandings as well. In the construction of modern identities, complex and multiple as they are, the Muslim part has not been left out. It may, in fact, be amplified and moved to the center by a new sense of shared self-description and purpose. Muslims construct themselves also as Muslims, locating themselves on a map of Dār al-Islām (the Abode of Islam) so that they imagine bonds with other Muslims alongside and sometimes superseding nationality and language. Adeeb Khalid has pointed out that, already in the nineteenth century, reformists published journals with titles like "The World of Islam" (*Islam dunyası*) or "Introducing Muslims" (*Tearüf-i Müslimin*). He adds that

> [t]here was substantial novelty in this view of the Muslim world. The concept of the universal *ummah*/*ümmet* might have existed as long as Islam, but the *ümmet* had never been imagined as a political or geographic entity as such until the late nineteenth century, when such a move became possible, thanks largely to print. The circulation of newspapers and magazines, the availability of printed maps, and new technological developments led to the creation of new networks of information through which Muslim elites acquired what might be called a "global consciousness." It now became possible to imagine a worldwide community of Muslims in new ways. It was a community that existed together on a single planet with other communities, but one which also faced a common threat from an expansionist Europe. *İttihad-ı İslâm* [Islamic unity] was the strategy to mobilize

this newfound community for political purposes, but it presupposed this new vision of the world.[21]

We see the results now in Muslim countries' television news programs. The gruesome and outraged Turkish media coverage of the slaughter of Muslims in Bosnia went far beyond coverage of the horrendous massacres in Rwanda. Muslims being ethnically cleansed in Burma seldom appears on US television. They appear often on Al Jazeera. The coverage of the Palestinian–Israeli conflict in most Muslim countries shows scenes of Israeli violence that would never appear on American television. (Americans have their own imagined bonds of identity of course.) In addition to the images of Muslim suffering, the media in Muslim countries cover transnational Muslim organizations such as the Organization of Islamic Cooperation, or transnational Muslim charities, such as Islamic Relief that aid the Muslim (and other) poor and victims around the world.

Moreover, Islamic texts are translated into various languages; the Indo-Pakistani Mawdudi into Arabic in the 1950s;[22] the Egyptian Muslim Brother Sayyid Qutb into Turkish in the 1980s;[23] the Iranian progressivist Sorush was translated from Persian into Arabic early in this century;[24] the Syrian modernist Shahrur into English in the 1990s.[25] (English translation is aimed not just at British, Australians, Americans, and the like; it is a second language for millions of Muslims, including most of those trained in engineering and the natural sciences.) Something called "the Islamic world" lives in English, Arabic, Turkish, Persian, and Urdu, and conceptually it is taken for granted as a concept in the *geographie imaginaire* of many Muslims.

The notion of a world comprised of all Muslims also evokes for some an imagined norm – whether at present or in the future. This ideal is of a world unified by a single set of beliefs, practices, and rules. When these utopias confront the real diversity of Islamdom, they imagine not merely that those who differ are wrong but – drawing on the sentiment created by nineteenth-century anti-imperialists like Ali Su'avī and Jamaladdīn al-Afghānī – they are made anxious: Difference is no longer a mercy, but something that weakens Islam and makes Muslims vulnerable. Difference itself is a threat to the fabric of Islam. As a result, Dialect Islamic practices that are not part of everyone's Islam are seen as not merely heretical, but injurious. These

[21] A. Khalid, "Ottoman Islamism," 202. For a survey of this concept see now, C. Aydin, *The Idea of the Muslim World*. Aydin dates the "achieving full flower" of the term to the 1870s.

[22] A. A. Mawdūdī, *Naḥwá al-dustūr al-Islāmī*. [23] K. Çayır, "Islamic Novels," 193, 216.

[24] A. Soroosh, "The Evolution and Devolution of Religious Knowledge"; *Reason, Freedom and Democracy in Islam*.

[25] M. Shahrur, *The Qur'an, Morality and Critical Reason*.

sentiments promote Standard Islam and justify the repression or at least the denigration of local particularities.

Nothing is more effective at creating the notion of shared identity and sometimes shared grievances than the new media. Many Muslims have embraced cassettes, CDs, and DVDs, but particularly the new media – the internet, social media, websites, blogs, streaming media, and of course email and Skype – with exuberance. In addition to written texts, now sermons and seminars, advice and religious courses, and other forms of speechifying have become a central experience in twenty-first-century Lived Islam. Religious rhetoric of all kinds is amplified through the religious media. Walk the streets of Fez, take a taxi in Yemen, go into a religious bookstore in Turkey, or past an Islamic association in Syria, and you hear the high voices and artificial diction of Arabic and Turkish sermons, or calm, New Agey monologues on "realizing your religious potential" or on fighting temptation.[26] Religious TV, DVDs, and CDs are filled with wild-eyed, hellfire-and-brimstone threatening, pulpit-thumping preachers, and smooth, soothing, TV personalities in natty suits and beautifully barbed beards.[27]

Television and radio are as much the domain of the Islamic religious in Islamdom as of the evangelical religious in Texas. Websites, by definition, are the tools of the literate and – as the implications of the worldwide web have been realized – these are the tools of Cosmopolitan Muslims. This privileges textual Islam, and handicaps experiential and Dialect Islam: because Sufism is concerned with spiritual discipline and experiential knowledge, there are websites *about* Sufism but you cannot *do* Sufism on the web. In contrast, Islamic legal prescriptions and debate, fatwas, ruminations on Islamic economics – all these things comprise the very performance of Standard Islam and fit perfectly into the "cooler" media, in Marshal McLuhan's taxonomy.[28] There are radio muftis dispensing religious advice in Yemen and dial-a-muftis throughout Islamdom.[29] One can get immediate guidance from www.fatwa-online.com or search fatwa archives at www.islam-online.net/fatwa/english/searchFatwa.asp. The widely viewed Al Jazeera television network has regular appearances by the renowned Azhar-trained shaykh Yusūf al-Qaraḍāwī, who also sponsors the influential website Islamonline.com.[30] There is Islamic

[26] C. Hirschkind, *Ethical Soundscape*; D. E. Schulz, "Evoking Moral Community."

[27] J. B. White, *Islamist Mobilization in Turkey*; E. Mariani, "Cyber-Fatwas, Sermons, and Media Campaigns."

[28] M. McLuhan, *Understanding Media*.

[29] B. Messick, "The Mufti, the Text and the World"; B. Schott, "Dial-a-Fatawa."

[30] B. Gräf and J. Skovgaard-Petersen, *Global Mufti*. On Islamonline.com, see M. El-Nawawy and S. Khamis, *Islam Dot Com*, 11–13.

investment advice at Muslim-investor.com, and marriage opportunities at www.islam.tc/ads. All these resources, and thousands more besides, create a sort of global consciousness among Muslims, and eventually press Muslims toward a textualist orthodoxy, a literate homogeneity, and a Standard Islam that is the "true" Islam.

The mass media and communications technology also facilitate transnational reform organizations like the Muslim World League – a Saudi religious arm – and the Tabligh-i Jamiat – an Indian quietist revival organization – all of which deplore localism and exhort Muslims to the universal Islam of texts.[31] Accredited Muslims teach Egyptians, Saudis, Turks, and Omanis the Standard Islam in much the same way that Moroccan or Algerian Arabic is being "standardized" by Lebanese television series in Standard Arabic, by universal Arabic textbooks, and government-sponsored campaigns to Arabize. Religious novels, religious soap operas and dramas, and movies like *The Messenger* – all sand away religious eccentricity and particularity.[32] And of course radical Wahhabi groups like al-Qāʿidah and ISIS incite and organize campaigns to bomb or otherwise destroy Shīʿī and Sufi shrines alike, as well as to kill Shīʿī and Sufi leaders for their religious deviance. This is a Standard Islam with teeth.

In the world of mass culture, mass media, and the global village, Standard Islam would seem to have an advantage it has not enjoyed since Islam's inception. Since the eighteenth century, Muslims have had some variant of "reform" as a slogan. Whether it be Ibn ʿAbdalwahhāb in Arabia, Hajji Shariatullah in India, ʿUmar Tal or ʿUthmān dan Fodio in West Africa, there has been an Islamic leadership that summoned Muslims to alter Lived Islam in the direction of Standard Islam. This call for reform is now shared among conservative rigorists, radical Islamists, but also liberal reinterpreters such as Aḥmad Khān, Muhammad Shahrūr, and "Progressive Muslims." In Indonesia and Malaysia too the reformist "*ulamak*" are "mostly educated in Mecca and the al-Azhar University in Egypt." There the call for "a perfection of Islam [implicitly criticizes] the rural Islamic scholars involved in syncretistic practices. Their campaign [is] a reflection of Middle Eastern reformed ideas ..."[33] Standard Islam, Cosmopolitan Islam, the Islam of Everywhere, seems set to become *the* Islam, eliminating dialects and differences, and producing a universal, a Standard Islam. This is all the more so when we take into account the role of nation-states in the propagation of religion.

[31] J. Esposito, *The Oxford Encyclopedia of the Modern Islamic World [Online]*, s.v. "Muslim World League"; B. D. Metcalf, "Living Hadith."

[32] K. Çayır, "Islamic Novels"; M. Huq, "Reading the Qurʾan in Bangladesh."

[33] A. S. Roald, "Tarbiya."

The State

The modern state is categorically different from the premodern kingdom, principality, territory, or sultanate. A vast literature has mapped the discontinuities between rule and power now, and rulership and power in the premodern period. In particular, the unmediated relationship between citizen and state differs utterly from the complex, variously mediated relationship between subject and ruling elite in the premodern period.[34]

Official Islam and the State

The power of the state varies, of course, from country to country, and the ways the state interacts with persons and institutions are diverse. Yet in Islamdom, and also in countries with Muslim minorities such as France and Germany, the state plays a major role in defining the Islam of citizens. At first glance, it is obvious that states tend to enforce a Standard Islam, very much as they enforce a Standard language. Above all, mass education and mass literacy create the national language-speaking citizen, and it is also through mass education and mass literature that the citizen Muslim is created.[35] Just as states have enforced Standard versions of the national language, altering by fiat the language's grammar and lexicon, or indeed to a large extent inventing the language, so too modern nation-states play a crucial role in defining the religion to which citizens adhere.[36]

There is also a collaboration between the state and the Standardization process described above. In many places reform-minded Muslims have taken control of new institutions – institutions of the central nation-state – to convey their message, and more importantly, to enforce it. Those reforms are almost always in the direction of Standard Islam. In most Muslim-majority states there are ministries or directorates that determine the form and content of acceptable Islam. These disciplining organizations historically have had no place for Dialect Islam. They discourage, suppress, or at least constrain Sufi and other nonstandard forms of Islamic practice and culture (but they also repress radical Islamist critiques of the state). In self-proclaimed Islamic states such as Saudi Arabia and Iran, liberal

[34] Classic works on citizenship are those of Tilly and Marshall. See T. H. Marshall, *Class, Citizenship, and Social Development*; C. Tilly, *Citizenship, Identity and Social History*; *Identities, Boundaries, and Social Ties*.

[35] Bruce Lawrence's concept of "Citizen Ahmed" was helpful to my thinking here. See B. B. Lawrence, "Citizen Ahmed among the Believers," especially pp. 289–290.

[36] On the radical transformation of Turkish, see G. Lewis, *Catastrophic Success*; on Modern Hebrew in Israel, see the no doubt provocative article G. a. Zuckermann, "A New Vision for 'Israeli Hebrew.'"

interpretations of Islam are restricted too by the enforcers of the Standard Islam. With a more literate population and new media, the reformers use newspapers and state media to bring their message to a mass audience that shares the Cosmopolitan Muslims' literacy, and so, also, their values.

Television and radio, for most of the twentieth century, and in many places in Islamdom into the twenty-first century, emanate from the center. Nowhere that I am aware of are the features of Dialect Islam featured in these media. Sufism may be displayed on TV, but except as folklore it is almost never exemplified. There are no real *dhikr*s on Egyptian television, no healings, no religious dancing. Instead, the viewer sees conservatives and conservative reformers teaching Standard Islam with incessant honorifics when the Prophet is mentioned, citations from Scriptures, references to the shared rituals of the Koiné. This is all the more so as satellite networks – overwhelmingly from conservative Gulf states – transmit throughout the Arab world and Islamdom. In this way someone like Shaykh al-Qaraḍāwī, mufti of the Al Jazeera network, can profoundly affect Muslims' self-understanding throughout the Arab world and beyond.[37]

For a host of reasons, states prefer a predictable, unobjectionable, tractable, mostly private Islam. Since in most Muslim-dominant states the media are mostly controlled from the center – by the government and state – the message promulgated in most Muslim-majority states is that of conservative "reform," which means textual, state-approved Islam. Muslim ritual effervescence, deviant practice and belief, devotion to charismatic leaders – other than of course the president, king, or generalissimo – are either suppressed or allowed to shrivel. All sources of leadership – political but also religious – are formally or informally vetted by the state and its organs of support and control. Islam becomes an instrument of state discipline.[38] Islam helps to define what it means to be Egyptian, Omani, or Moroccan, or even "secular" Turk,[39] as much as flag, monarch, or anthem. There are a few examples – Morocco comes to mind – where distinctive local forms of Islam are used to mark the prestige of the leader, though even in Morocco, the Higher Council of Religious Scholars campaigns to tamp down *moulids*, *līlah*s, *mousims*, and other popular devotionals that traditionally were part of Moroccan Islam. Many country shrines wither into neglect as the countryside empties and notables cease to patronize them. The colorful Moroccan puberty ceremonies connected to circumcision, for example, are being replaced by clinical

[37] B. Gräf and J. Skovgaard-Petersen, *Global Mufti*.
[38] See the interesting remarks in D. D. Hall (ed.), *Lived Religion*, 15.
[39] J. B. White, *Muslim Nationalism and the New Turks*, especially pp. 35–38.

circumcision in a hospital just after the child is born.[40] So extensive is state intervention that it is worth asking whether, for the most part, in Islamdom we see state repression of everything that is not defined as Standard Islam.

Religion is taught and enforced in state schools. The result is an Islamic literacy, a commitment to a specific form of Islam, akin to Standard Islam, inculcated through mass public education. In nearly every Muslim country we see analogous developments. In laicist Turkey the Religion Directorate controls education, sends out sermons to be read at Friday prayers, controls state-sanctioned religious literature. Even, in putatively secular countries like France and Germany, state-defined Standard Islam is the basis of the religious curriculum taught in parochial schools, in faculties of theology, training programs for religious functionaries, and other institutions. The degree of control is all the higher in places like Malaysia, Saudi Arabia, and Egypt.

This process of state control has been studied for Egypt by Gregory Starrett in his excellent *Putting Islam to Work*, which can be read, in part, as an ethnography of this new mass Standard Islam. He describes the centrally supervised production of children's Islamic storybooks, school textbooks, and a curriculum. Pupils are provided with

> Islamic religious information appropriate to their ages, springing forth from the Glorious Qur'ān and the noble Traditions of the Prophet. . . . By the end of the fifth grade, the industrious Egyptian school child will have read hundreds of pages about Islam in her textbooks, memorizing most of them for repetition on year end examinations.[41]

Textbook Islam is, to some extent, lowest-common denominator Islam; it emphasizes the Koiné practices and symbols, and, in the interests of creating a unified citizenry, ignores the controversial, the particular, the idiosyncratic. Rite (*madhhab*) differences are played down, and alternative commentarial and explicative traditions are ignored. Sufism in particular is, for the most part, delegitimated in the state-school curriculum, or derided as un-Islamic. Consequently, a specific state-sponsored Islamic subjectivity is produced. In Egypt, by the time these students of state-sponsored Standard Islam reach university, they are

> overwhelmingly hostile to Sufi orders . . . [which they view as] low class, popular, primitive, and fundamentally mistaken about the requirements of *true Islam*. Although almost 85 percent of the students expressed ignorance

[40] Following the research of my student Luke Murphy in Fez, 2007.

[41] G. Starrett, *Putting Islam to Work*, 133.

about the goals of Sufism, they felt that [nonstandard Islamic perspectives, like those of] Sufi orders were unnecessary (66 percent) . . .[42]

These Egyptian Muslim students have been convinced by the Standard Islamic texts they have studied, that Sufism – a major vehicle, as we have seen, for the indigenization of Islam and a lens through which perhaps the majority of Muslims once understood the meaning of their practices and commitments – is *prima facie* un-Islamic.[43]

Along the way, non-textual Islam – which is often the Dialect form, the distinctive local practices and understandings – is neglected or actively suppressed. Radical or fundamentalist or political Islam has also been marked as deviant non-Standard Islam, even by Islamist states like Saudi Arabia and Iran. Since the 1990s most state schools have segregated "Islam and politics" from each other in the Official Islam taught in schools. Political Islam is officially said to be linked to violence. While enforcing a conservative Islamic morality, the state has generally excluded Islamic (or putatively Islamic) notions of legitimacy, authority, or community from political discourse.[44]

Recovering Difference

Nonetheless, the forces that seem to cooperate to produce a single Standard Islam paradoxically also produce its opposite. Travel is a good example. More Muslims travel than ever before – within Islamdom and outside of it. Muslims meeting other Muslims, as we have seen, can create a self-consciousness that may abrade differences, but, as it turns out, the encounters can also create a friction that hones disagreements and reframes difference as part of a distinctive identity worth preserving.

Mehdi Abedi, in the course of his youth, went from traditional rural Iran, to modernizing Yazd, and then to Lawrence, Kansas (and eventually to Houston, Texas), in the United States. His auto-ethnography shows that travel and interaction among Muslims does not always produce a shared Islam or a homogenous whole; his own travels led instead to confrontations that sharpened his sense of belonging to a distinctive local Islam. He discovered, when he "speaks Islam," that others not only have other dialects, but

[42] Ibid., 172, my italics. [43] J. Heyworth-Dunne, *History of Education*, 10.

[44] The effectiveness of this pedagogy can be seen in the way in which inept governance by the Muslim Brethren in Egypt following the Arab Spring has been so easily depicted as an illegitimate mixing of religion, politics, and even terrorism when the military returned to its role as de facto rulers of Egypt.

they may despise his personal local Islam, in this case the Iranian Shīʿī Islam of his homeland.

At university (in Kansas), Abedi joined the Muslim Students Association where Muslims from across the world met, worshiped, and discussed Islam. Among them, students from Saudi Arabia. Abedi describes what happened when he shared an apartment with some of his Muslim brethren, Saudis, whose dialect of Islam rejects his Islam, Shīʿism, categorically.

> After the first term ... I moved in with some Saudis. ... One night, I was saying my prayers behind closed doors in my room, while a party was in progress. I had just finished when the door opened, and Ibrahim [a Saudi] came in. He sat on the bed and began asking questions about my religion. "I am a Muslim, just like you," I said. "No, you are from the party of Ali." "So, what do you mean?" "You are a *rāfiḍī*.[45] You prostrate on the dust of Karbala: that is idolatry." "No, it is not." "Yes, it is." "But I do not drink, gamble, or smoke grass [as the Saudi students did]." "That is irrelevant. Wrong is wrong." "But you do not say your prayers. This is the only way I have learned to worship my God." "Your way of worshipping is wrong."
>
> Soon others took his side. I never understood this contradictory fanaticism. But it was an important lesson: one did not have to be a practicing Muslim to be a Muslim zealot.[46]

That Saudi Arabian zealotry reflected differences between the Wahhabi Islam of Arabia and the Twelver-Shīʿīsm of Iran. Neither Mehdi nor Ibrahim would have had this kind of conversation had they remained in their home countries, nor would they have been likely to have had such conversations in the premodern period when a Shīʿī might have concealed his identity outside of Iran.[47] The result of this dialogue was not irenic fellowship but a sharper understanding of difference and, it seems, a firmer commitment by both Abedi and his Saudi roommate to their own understanding of their Islam. Both end up with a stronger allegiance to their local religious vision: "Wrong is wrong." Abedi's commentary: "Much of [his] zealotry [was] based on ignorance." Travel not only harmonizes, it also confronts; meeting other Muslims builds solidarity, but it also leads to fractiousness.

[45] A "rejecter"; a pejorative Sunnī term for Shīʿīs.

[46] M. M. J. Fischer and M. Abedi, *Debating Muslims*, 88–89.

[47] D. J. Stewart et al., *Law and Society in Islam*, on al-Shahīd al-Thānī, a Twelver-Shīʿī who studied in Sunnī Cairo.

The Nation-State and National Islams

The nation-state is certainly a force for Standardization. At the same time it is also a force that cuts against it. In Islamdom, the twenty-first century is not like the fourteenth, in which the weak, fragmentary, Islamicate states necessarily left cultural and social space to be filled with nearly independent religious institutions – madrasas, courts, and Sufi convents.[48] The definition of Standard Islam in the contemporary world is very much framed by the organs of the self-regarding nation-state.[49]

In most of Islamdom, the professional religious are trained in state institutions. As we have seen, there are ministries of Islamic affairs which approve or disapprove books about Islam and the Islam curricula taught in state schools and madrasas, among other things. There are Islamic councils that provide authoritative guidance on Islamic matters through state-sanctioned, and sometimes state-enforced, fatwas. Mosque imams are state employees, and often their sermons have to be approved by the state.[50] In all of these interventions, it is local state interpretations and perspectives that are privileged – the state makes its own particular Islam.

Mass Education and the State as a Force for Localization

Consider once more the case of Standard Islam in Egypt, as Gregory Starrett presents it in his book on Islamic education. The Egyptian state, like most Muslim-dominant states, controls every aspect of education – very much a model they took from the French. Its curriculum is designed to produce the kind of Egyptian citizens the state desires and so, of course, in addition to arithmetic, Arabic, and social studies, the state teaches Islam. While it is true that Sufism and overtly Dialect forms of Islam have no place in that curriculum, it does not follow that the Islam taught is devoid of local content. If we consider not just the teaching of Islam, but the Islam that is taught, we can see a clear localist tendency in Egyptian Islamic instruction.

Egyptian primary Islamic education is shaped by the goal to provide "true religious education which fortifies [students] against surges of extremism and epidemic intellectual trends,"[51] very much a concern of the Egyptian, but not, say, the Iranian or Afghan Taliban government. As Starrett points out,

48 M. G. S. Hodgson, *Venture of Islam*, book 4.

49 One useful discussion of this process – one strong on theory – is E. Webb, "'Church' of Bourguiba."

50 See any of the recent State Department reports on religious freedom (www.state.gov/j/drl/rls/irf/), e.g., United Arab Emirates, Egypt, Jordan, Bahrain.

51 From a newspaper article quoted in G. Starrett, *Putting Islam to Work*, 105.

> [t]his reinterpretation constructs readings of history that legitimate the authority of [Egyptian government] policy makers . . . [and] harnesses divine intention to public policy itself, helping to bring religious instruction into the conscious service of independent social and political ends.[52]

As an illustration he reads the account of Joseph that school children are required to learn.

> The story of Joseph in the fifth grade textbook is a ten-page paraphrase of the 111-verse *sūrah* 12, (Yūsuf), in the Qur'ān. Aside from shuttling introductory and concluding exhortations off into another section, the schoolbook version is a straightforward paraphrase of the Qur'ānic story, with a simplified grammar and vocabulary. Because of his power as an interpreter of dreams and the favor he found with Pharaoh, Joseph was made minister of Egypt and saved the country from famine; even after being reunited with his father (Jacob/Israel) and brothers, he retained his mighty position in the country and instead of returning to Canaan invited his family to settle with him in Memphis. But at the end of the life story of Joseph in the Egyptian fifth grade book, the authors of the text have appended a short patriotic paragraph.
>
> "And thus Egypt has always been, and still is, a refuge for the prophets and the illustrious and outstanding people from the Arab nation and the Islamic world, who have been delighted to experience it, always sure of its welcome, and living within its family as beloved brothers."

Starrett points out what is by design implicit in the school text.

> [In the account, while] Joseph was not an Arab, he was a Muslim, both as a prophet of God in his own right and as the great-grandson of Abraham, builder of the *ka'bah* in Mecca (*sūrah* 12:101). With this brief paragraph, the text's authors have effectively Islamized Egypt twenty-three centuries before Muḥammad.[53]

In this way, state-school Islam becomes an overtly Egyptian Islam: Egypt is placed at the center of Islamic history and salvation history for Egyptian students in a way that would not be the case for state-school students in Pakistan, Yemen, or Morocco. The result is a view of Islam unique to Egyptians and apart from that of, say, Tunisians or Malaysians. Each nation-state in Islamdom, to a greater or lesser degree, creates a National Islam.[54]

[52] Ibid., 138. [53] Ibid.

[54] The National Islam expresses itself in the market as well as in the school, producing uniquely local Islamic commodities, but also determining which among the commodities available to many Muslims are of use or interest. Anyone who has traveled in Islamdom has seen the bumper stickers, the key rings, the velour-covered Qur'āns, and other religious chochkas for

In Palestine, by contrast, the Ministry of Education-mandated textbook communicates the idea that "religion, family, school, and nation [be] portrayed as mutually reinforcing authorities . . ."[55] "The Islam in the textbooks . . . is represented as though no sectarian differences exist . . ." The version of Islam included in Palestinian textbooks is friendly to non-Muslims (*ahl al-dhimmah*).[56] "*Jihād* is discussed in the context of national resistance to colonialization."[57] In Saudi Arabia the schoolbooks too "proclaim the message that there is only one Islam for all Muslims, [but assert] the Arabian peninsula has a special place in Islam, preserved and defended by God's grace and the ruling family."[58] In Saudi Islamic texts it is Muḥammad b. ʿAbdalwahhāb – the ideologue of Saudi Islam – and Muḥammad b. Saʿūd – founder of the Saudi dynasty – who are the Islamic heroes.[59] However, in Iranian textbooks "school children are told that as Muslims they are responsible for . . . defending the regime and their Islamic country [Iran]."[60] Young Iranians learn that when the Twelfth *Imām* (who will come again at the end of time as the Mahdi) vanished, the struggle against tyranny continued under the leadership of the *ulama* (learned ones) and the deputies (*nayeban*) of the last Imām. "The battle continued until our time when it succeeded in the hands of our deceased leader—the deputy of the Imam—Grand Ayatollah Khomeini."[61] In Jordan, Islamic textbooks stress the importance of the family: "The Prophet determined that the

sale by vendors in stores, on little tables in the streets, on ferries and buses. Cassettes of sermons, or Qurʾān recitation, are not just ideas on tape, but they are also commodities, and Starrett has pointed out the many ways in which these shape and reflect Egyptian Islam. G. Starrett, "Political Economy of Religious Commodities." In Egypt, for instance, hand-painted Qurʾān verses are sold as pious decorative objects. They are, however, painted onto papyrus or "fired in blue ceramic to resemble the ancient faience found in pharaonic tombs." More significant than these curiosa, each Muslim state constitutes a discrete Islamic market that shapes and is shaped by local events. One vendor of religious books observed to Starrett that as a response to the religious-inspired violence of the 1980s and early 1990s, "the current wave of terrorism is helping business, too. People . . . they come in here asking for trustworthy books, wanting to know *what Islam really says about these things.*" The Egyptian government itself became a producer, upping its production of religious materials by 400 percent. For Egyptians, "Islam" is decisively shaped by features of the local, national, cultural economy. Ibid., 53–56. See also his argument on pp. 64–65 which asserts, in essence, that Islam itself is shaped by complexities of Egyptian culture and cultural life. (I owe this reference to David McMurray. David's keen criticism years ago of my position in what became the first half of this chapter became the basis for the second half. I am grateful for his reading of a much earlier version of this argument.)

55 N. Brown, "Genesis of a New Curriculum," 132.

56 S. Naʿ Na, "Conflict of Historical Narratives," 142. 57 Ibid., 144.

58 E. A. Doumato, "From 'Wahhabi' Roots," 155. 59 Ibid., 157.

60 G. Mechran, "Shi'ite Curriculum," 60. On the diminution of Islam as a source of actual policy in Iran after the revolution, see O. Roy, *Globalized Islam*, 83–88.

61 G. Mechran, "Shi'ite Curriculum," 62–63.

most important of the benefits of Muslim religious life, after the power of God Almighty, is the righteous marriage." This is part of the Jordanian state view that the Hashemite king is "the father of the Jordanian family, the shaikhs of the Jordanian tribe [and the father of all Jordanians]."[62]

It is clear that the state, while teaching a Standard Islam, is not teaching a truly Cosmopolitan Islam. Instead, the national states have produced and promulgated a National Islam. This National Islam suppresses or displaces Local Islams, but it also domesticates and often eviscerates the Cosmopolitan Islam of scholars. Scholars and their institutions become employees and arms of the state, and express – in part – a nationalist religious ideology that mingles with religion and shapes it. The way that National Islam elbows its way to the center of Islamic discourse can be seen most clearly in Turkey with what is known as the Turkish-Islam Synthesis.

Case Study: Islam in Turkey and the "Türk-İslâm sentezi" (TİS)

Turkey, often, and mistakenly, described as "secular," is a particularly interesting case in the production of National Islam. From the creation of the Republic in 1923, Islam (and Christianity and Judaism) have been under the control of the Directorate of Religious Affairs.[63] This organ of the state existed to create an Islam compatible with laicism – the displacement of religion from the effective public sphere – and nationalism – the notion that Turks are a distinct nation defined by culture and ethnicity. These are two of the foundational principles of the Turkish state, the six arrows enshrined in the constitution.[64] This laic, privatized, and increasingly Turkish Islam was of course unique to Turkey. For fifty years, Islam as a discourse was mostly excluded from the public sphere. To be sure, mosques were built and religious experts were produced – in Imām-Hatip Trade Schools and Divinity Schools – and required Islam courses were taught in public schools after Atatürk's death. Nonetheless, the whole effort of the state was directed toward making Islam as Turkish as it could be: by translating the Qur'ān into Turkish; by producing Turkish-language, regime-approved textbooks and catechisms; even requiring for thirty years that the faithful be summoned to prayer from minarets only in Turkish. By fitting Islam

[62] B. Anderson, "Prescription for Obedience," 75.

[63] For a series of articles on the role of the Diyanet Başkanı in Turkish Islam, see the special issue of *The Muslim World* on the topic. G. Erdem (ed.), "Diyanet."

[64] Six Arrows (*altı ok*): Republicanism (*cühüriyyetçilik*), Populism (halkçılık), Nationalism (*milliyetçilik*), Laicism (*laiklik*), Statism (*devletçilik*), Reformism (*devrimçilik*).

into the New Turkey, the state aimed to facilitate an enlightened as well as enlightening Islam.[65]

Then, in the mid-1980s, mainstream Turkish newspapers were suddenly filled with references to a previously obscure concept, the Turkish-Islam Synthesis (*Türk-Islâm Sentezi – TİS*). And then, equally suddenly it seemed, in 1986 the ruling military junta promulgated precisely this Turk-Islam Synthesis as part of their recalibration of Turkish state ideology.

As the name suggests, the central notion of the TİS is that Islam is inseparable from Turkishness, and belongs at the center of the state's "public cult." Islam is understood not as a private devotional but as part of the essence of being Turkish. The military embraced the TİS not because of any religious conviction on their part, of course. Rather, it was a shocking about-face for the military that had previously subscribed to the ideology of Mustafa Kemal Atatürk; their "Kemalism" had been militantly laicist and directed toward restricting religion to the domain of the private and the ineffectual. But now, the junta reasoned, TİS could solve Turkey's ideological divisions between a Trotskyite left and a Francoist right that had created the near civil war in of the 1960s and 1970s, a civil war that the military had intervened to bring to a close.[66]

For the political middle and the left, as well as for staunch Kemalists, this change was fearfully seen as the beginning of a Turkish spiral into religious fundamentalism.[67] Religion, they supposed, was taking over Turkey, after Atatürk had liberated them from Islamic obscurantism. But, in fact, the belief in a *Türk-İslâm sentezi* comes not from Islamist circles, but from rightist, nationalist, circles, and it was first taken up by Alparslan Türkeş's right-wing nationalist National Action Party (in

[65] An excellent account of this attitude is found in M. B. Wilson, *Translating the Qur'an*. See especially chapters 5 and 6. See also A. Bein, *Ottoman Ulema, Turkish Republic*.

[66] I know of no thorough English-language overview of the "Türk-İslâm sentezi" both in its political function and its ideation, though it deserves study. In Turkish, the standard text is B. Güvenç, *Türk-İslam sentezi*. (The 1994 edition is most often cited; the pagination differs but the text is the same.) P. J. Magnarella, *Human Materialism*, 101–107, provides a short discussion. A brief account is s.v. "Turkish-Islamic Synthesis" in J. Esposito, *Encyclopedia of the Modern Islamic World*. More valuable is B. Toprak, "Religion as State Ideology," and G. Cetinsaya, "Rethinking Nationalism and Islam." White also discusses the TİS as a general orientation, rather than a specific political movement: J. B. White, *Muslim Nationalism and the New Turks*, 35, 127–128. I have learned much of what I know of Islam in contemporary Turkey and Turkish political thought from Haldun Gülalp. I am grateful to him for his many enlightening conversations. I also had a fruitful set of email exchanges with Fethi Açıkel, whose thesis, F. Açıkel, "Twilight of 'the Holy Articulation,'" has an interesting, if very rarified, history of the background of the "Türk-İslâm sentezi" (199ff.), going back to the nationalism of Türkeş but insightfully including the populist leftism of Ecevit. An indispensable source.

[67] B. Toprak, "Religion as State Ideology," 10.

Turkish, MHP) in the late 1970s.[68] The concept seems to have originated with the right-wing nationalist "Intellectuals' Hearth" group in the late 1960s.[69] It is associated particularly with a scholar named İbrahim Kafesoğlu, who in 1985 wrote what might be considered the public manifesto of the movement.[70]

There the argument of TİS is laid out in clear language with cascades of footnotes and allusion to other scholarship. The book begins with a survey of Turkish history, as Kafesoğlu sees it. In the style of classic Turkish nationalism narratives, throughout all of Turks' history, the (Rum) Seljuks (of Anatolia) were key actors. Just as in high school *Turkish Culture* textbooks used since the 1930s, the book elides the particularities of the Mughuls of India, the Mamluks of Egypt, the ancient Turks of Central Asia, the Great Seljuks, and the Seljuks of Rum into "Turkish history." However, his discussion of the Turkish language emphasizes not the intrusion of Persian and Arabic vocabulary and grammatical features – as secularists' textbooks asserted – but the autonomy, efficacy, and dominance of Turkish wherever Turks ruled.[71]

Read carefully, the books that propound the *Türk-İslâm sentezi* are standard Turkish nationalist roughage. They slide imprecisely from India to Central Asia to Anatolia, from the fourth to sixteenth centuries, and are not so much history as ethnic hagiography. They quote admiring European travelers as authorities, and refute nineteenth-century European chauvinists whom no one else reads any more. Like many nationalist works, they argue for a timeless and unchanging ethnic essence, here called "culture," which is imbedded in a fluid "civilization," a term that really means no more than technology and science in the most superficial sense.[72] Most of Kafesoğlu's work as well as the others I have read in the genre could have been written for the most part in the 1950s. What is new is only that the unchanging Turkish essence is constructed in part from Islam, rather than, as the old nationalists would have had it, having been corrupted by Arab Islam.

[68] F. Açıkel, "Twilight of 'the Holy Articulation'"; J. M. Landau, *Radical Politics in Modern Turkey*.

[69] The concept originated in discussions and only later in print. It is worthwhile noting that in book titles, previously the preferred locution was in general "Türk ve İslâm." "İslâm-Türk" appears in a 1940s reference work titled İ. H. İzmirli, *İslâm-Türk ansiklopedisi*, where, however, it seems to be a translation of an Arabic (or Ottoman?) title. In the 1960s, aside from some literary anthologies, the phrase first appears in what appears to be a right-wing polemical work (M. Abdurrahman, *Papa'ların tarih boyunca İslâm-Türk düşmanlığı*) and then, in the sense that interests us, in Y. Boyunağa, *Dost ve düşman gözü ile Türk-İslâm sentezi*. "Türk-İslâm" appears in book titles eleven times in the 1980s, and is common thereafter.

[70] İ. Kafesoğlu, *Türk İslâm sentezi*. [71] Ibid., 201–203.

[72] See B. Toprak, "Religion as State Ideology," 12–13. Her account is very good on this.

Most importantly, Kafesoğlu and his ilk offer an essentialist argument asserting that, before their migration into the Islamicate world, Central Asian Turks, ancestors of the Modern Turks, had a culture uniquely receptive to Islamic (and Islamicate) culture, since it was already monotheistic, valued justice, and had communal values.[73] Indeed, Kafesoğlu claims that the ur-Turks were innately better Muslims than the Arabs, because they had more equal relations between men and women, and a more central place for justice than the Arab originators of Islam.[74] Nonetheless, the Turkish destiny was fulfilled only when Turks actually became Muslims.[75] At that point Turkish natural character was united with the divinely revealed metaphysics and practice of Islam.

In short, the concept of the *Türk-İslâm sentezi* is that Islam is indissolubly a part of Turkish culture. To ignore or repress Islam is to cripple Turkish culture and its citizens, depriving them of their native source of ethics and shared feeling. The laicists who sought to separate Turks from Islam in the name of Turkish nationalism were in reality mutilating the integrity of the Turkish identity. Islam, for the TİS proponents, is necessary to produce the emotional and interiorist solidarity that will bind Turks to Turkish society and state. "Religion is the essence of culture."[76] *This* Islam is particular, however, to *Turkish* culture. It meshes uniquely with essential Turkish features present from the time of the ur-Turks in Central Asia. It is not Islam, the global religion, or an essential Islam shared by all Muslims, but rather, a uniquely Turkish appropriation of Islam that, in synthesis, created two great historical civilizations, and, once reintegrated into Turkish life, will lead Turkey once more to resuming her rightful place in the world.[77]

It might seem that Kafesoğlu and his ilk aimed merely to create a place for Islam in the post-anarchy culture being deliberately constructed by the military rulers and their apparatchiks in the decade of the 1980s.[78] But in reality they were offering a creative synthesis combining a nostalgic vision of

[73] İ. Kafesoğlu, *Türk İslâm sentezi*, 99, 166.

[74] See also Y. Boyunağa, *Dost ve düşman gözü ile Türk-İslâm sentezi*, 293.

[75] İ. Kafesoğlu, *Türk İslâm sentezi*, 160. [76] B. Toprak, "Religion as State Ideology," 12–13.

[77] G. Cetinsaya, "Rethinking Nationalism and Islam." It is noteworthy that some Islamists in fact rejected the *Türk-İslâm sentezi*, saying that Islam and nationalism are incompatible. See ibid., 375. See also the interpretative article P. Dorroll, "The Turkish Understanding of Religion." I'm grateful to Joshua Ralston who called my attention to this very important article.

[78] A. N. Ölçen, *Karanlığın başlangıcı*, 131. A good overview, though one clearly leftist in origin, is V. Timuroğlu, *12 Eylül'ün eğitim ve kültür politikası*. Kafesoğlu's book is remarkably similar in the form of its argument (though Kafesoğlu's book has much more verve and scholarly gloss) to a book published as *Türk-İslâm sentezi*. (Y. Boyunağa, *Dost ve düşman gözü ile Türk-İslâm sentezi*) which was first printed in 1970.

grandfathers' Islam with the Turko-centric worldview that all Turkish citizens had been bathed in for fifty years. In a way, the TİS enriched a Kemalist historical mythology that seemed to have become old-fashioned and affectively bankrupt.

The TİS is both distinctively modern and – more to the point – distinctively Turkish. It is, after all, hard to imagine an Arab agreeing that Islam found its fulfillment only when Turks joined the *ummah*, or that Turks alone were "natural Muslims." This is a view of a National Islam written to appropriate universal Islamic history into a national project. There is also the faint spore of something else, and that is the argument that *this* Islam is different from *other* forms of Islam. The suggestion is that, whatever the critiques of other forms of Islam, including later Ottoman Islam, this critique does not apply to the *true*, the *real*, Islam, the Islam of the Turks. In other words, Islam is subordinated to culture and to the state that defines it; Islam is justified by reference to accepted Truths (accepted in nationalist circles, of course) about Turks. The *Türk-Islâm sentezi* is really about Turkey, more than it is about Islam. It is "the islamicization of nationalism."[79] For proponents of the *Türk-İslâm sentezi*, it is Turkey and the Turks that define Islam, not an essential Islam that defines the Turks.

The *Türk-İslâm sentezi* shows clearly that the nation-state is a kind of gravitational field that pulls "Islam" into its orbit. Islam can be a rhetorical term and set of practices that serve to deepen commitment to the state – but that commitment is foremost and actually an allegiance to the values of the *particular* state. Consequently, it is a mistake to see the *Türk-İslâm sentezi* as Islamic ideation, part of a universal upwelling of Islamic movements.[80] Reflection on the *Türk-İslâm sentezi* points to one of the most characteristic features of modern religion in general – its loss of the power of independent discourse. In this case, Islam is in fact justified by reference to the (*Turkish* canonical) truths of *Turkish* nationalist history. The Turks, Kafesoğlu argues, in effect were already "anonymous Muslims" before they became a formal part of the Islamic *ummah*.[81] Consequently, Islam deserves a seat at the table of the Turkish nationalist state; it is not that Turks need to re-become Muslims. They always, at their essence, *were* Muslims, and in fact, the best of Muslims.

[79] F. Açıkel, "Twilight of 'the Holy Articulation'," 195, citing B. Güvenç, *Türk-İslam sentezi*, 33–58.

[80] B. Toprak, "Religion as State Ideology," 10 and n. 1.

[81] İ. Kafesoğlu, *Türk İslâm sentezi*, 160: "For what reason did Turkish religious history manifest itself thus? The explanation is utterly simple: the former Turkish religious beliefs' bases found a correspondence with Islamic beliefs to an astonishing extent."

The apparatus of the national state produces, through its institutions of promotion and discipline, a National Islam, one distinctively shaped by the national ideological environment from which it arose. On the face of it, this may appear to be the Islam of Cosmopolitans, emphasizing authority and authoritatively disdaining emotion and miracles, masters and shrines. In reality, however, National Islam is more akin to a modern Dialect version of Islam, albeit a dialect with an army and a gendarmerie.

Literacy and Protestantization

Paradoxically, the imposition of mass Islamic literacy – which often creates a state-friendly understanding of what it means to be a Muslim – also provides the means to dissolve any consensus, including one promulgated by the state, on matters Islamic. As more Muslims are able to read about Islam in not classical, but vernacular languages, as well as in contemporary Arabic, individual Muslims are able to sidestep the hegemony of Official and National Islam if they want, and to appropriate Islam in a way particular to themselves. This possibility of autonomy creates what I think of as a protestantization of Muslim text-reading.[82]

In general, protestantization is the result of decoupling religion from social authority. For these new Protestant Muslims, scholasticism of pre-modern religious scholarly commentary and theory is often derided as pedantry that obscures the true and simple message of Islam. Increasingly the vernacular-language Qurʾān creates the belief that the Qurʾān's meaning is transparent, simple, single, and accessible to Muslims without need for the artifice of scholarly technique. Throughout Islamdom, the Qurʾān is now studied in the local language (except in the Arab world), though it is still recited, often artfully, in Arabic wherever there are Muslims.[83] And when it is read – again, almost entirely in translation – by individuals on their own or in groups, those Muslims are given a sense of ownership and authority that allows them to apply and appropriate the Qurʾān. And, as was once the case with Protestant Christianity, there are unintended consequences.

One consequence is that Muslims around the world debate about everything imaginable – from whether green really is the Islamic color (and if so, what shade), to whether to have a Christmas tree, to whether condoms

[82] F. Robinson, "Islam and the Impact of Print." I have written at greater length on protestantization in ways only summarized here. A. K. Reinhart, "Legitimacy and Authority in Islamic Discussions of 'Martyrdom Operations/Suicide Bombings'"; "Fundamentalism and the Transparency of the Arabic Qurʾān."

[83] A. M. Gade, *Perfection Makes Practice*; K. Nelson, *The Art of Reciting the Qurʾan*.

obviate the need for ablutions after intercourse, to whether terrorism can possibly be justified. As ever, most Muslims affirm Islam's Koiné, but their appropriation of it is more various than at any time, perhaps, since Islam's first centuries. The relatively stable set of interpretations of Standard Islam agreed to by Cosmopolitans is undercut by the expansive range of now-legitimate opinions produced by *hoi polloi* when every man, and more subversively, every woman, has access to the authoritative texts. Scriptural knowledge is no longer a monopoly of a hegemonic guild but is possessed by everyone, not just those socialized in the Cosmopolitan madrasa. It is also a product of modern literacy and modern consumerism.[84]

It is not the case, however, that individuals are entirely free agents reading a text naively. Our point from the first has been that Muslims live within specific communities; they are created by these communities. And in modern times, these communities, as Anderson has pointed out, have been those of the national state. But now, in the postmodern world, the communities of Islamic interpretation are more and more freed from the locale where Muslims find themselves living. The Islam of a given locale is more and more diverse, but paradoxically the *ummah* – the transnational conceptual community of Muslims – plays an ever larger part in Muslim self-understanding. Muslims are still Muslims, but increasingly they choose to affiliate with like-minded fellow Muslims. They are Muslims in the company of those Muslims they find congenial, and together these voluntarily affiliated Muslims create a new kind of Lived Islam – Volitional Islam.

Volitional Islam

Now, at the beginning of postmodernity, it is clear that "places" are coming to exist also in virtuality. The proximate fit between *location* as a territorial fact and *place* as a position in the geography of the imagination, as a situation of subjectivity, has to some extent dissolved. That dissolution will continue far into the future, despite the efforts of authoritarian or liberal states to shape the virtual as they have shaped the territorial since the Lived Islamic world is no longer defined exclusively or even primarily by the accident of physical locale.[85]

The variable of "place" in Lived Islam is no longer only about geography. Contemporary Lived Islam is shaped by local consensus but also, for example, by increasingly separated educational and professional identities. It is shaped also by how a Muslim chooses to define herself – revivalist,

[84] O. Roy, *Globalized Islam*, 148. [85] Ibid., 104, on the de-territorialization of diasporas.

progressive, mystical, New Age, feminist, conservative, or a bricolage of any and all of these – and then by the theological and practical norms of the sub-communities to which she affiliates herself.

Religious identities have always been shaped to some extent by class, profession, ethnicity, gender, and other factors. Identities have differed also according to whether Muslims were culturally and demographically superior, as in Egypt by 1500, merely culturally superior as in North India in the 1500s, or demographically and culturally subordinate and isolated – like the Muslims of the coastal trading towns of Southeast Asia in the 1500s. The reader, the listener, the aspirant Muslim has always tuned her or his perception of the Qurʾān, of the life of the Prophet, and other Islamic lore, in ways distinctively fitted to the surrounding lived world and to his or her own life. The solidarity of the premodern world, where rich and poor lived together, where most social contact was face-to-face, where social relations were defined by patronage and clientage, has been dissolved in the modern world. For our purposes, in the modern world three factors have shaped the new environment of Volitional Islam: (1) the specialization of labor, (2) the consumerist mentality, and – too little grasped – (3) the effect of diaspora on all Muslims – not just the emigrants.

As Durkheim recognized a century ago, in "organic," that is, modern societies, increasingly distinct responsibilities and specialization separate person from person. Professional identity (and therefore educational formation) is the way we define ourselves to others. In the US, at least, the first substantial question people ask on meeting each other is not, "who is your family?" or, "where are you from?" It is, "what do you do," meaning, "what kind of job do you have?" The jargon of professions shapes our speech and attitudes, and, around the world, Lived Islam too is shaped by education and profession. In the postmodern world, professional identities more and more constitute distinctive sub-cultures that correlate with, and arguably condition, many things – housing, recreation, voting behaviors, and religion.[86] I was struck when I met with the Muslim Students' Association representatives at a Midwestern university that every male was a member of the faculty of engineering; every female was in the life sciences. Their religiosity was precise, monochromatic, and energetic, as you'd expect from high achievers, good test-takers, and precise lab workers. These were the Muslims who chose to be active in, and who governed, the Muslim Students Association at a school of over 50,000 students. It is no surprise, on reflection, that applied

[86] Mary Douglas in *Natural Symbols* has a smart discussion of how/why professions correlate with things like clothing (think academic tweeds and jeans). M. Douglas, *Natural Symbols*.

technology fields such as engineering and medicine produce the cadres of fundamentalist and Scripturalist, even jihadist, organizations in Islamdom, just as anesthesiology, pathology, and engineering tend to produce political conservatives in the US.[87] For these professionals, the professionally appropriate distaste for ambiguity and the need for precision correlate with a religious identity similarly constructed of true-false, certainty-oriented, Scripture-as-algorithm approaches to religion.

The same of course is true in reverse: tweedy humanities academics and media professionals for the most part are professionally liberal, whether in Euro-America or in Islamdom. Predictably, theirs is religion-lite, "religion-as-if," liberal religion, or disdain for religion altogether.[88] At that same Midwestern university, there were doubtless thousands of Muslim literature, history, psychology, and music majors who spurned the binary-oriented Muslim Student Association. If this university's Muslim community was typical, some of the students marginal to the "Muslim student establishment" would come to Friday prayers – especially the newly-arrived; more would attend Festival (ʿĪd) prayers. Yet, by and large, the thousands of Muslims who found the MSA uncongenial would attend local mosques, or affiliate with like-minded Muslims for worship, or would put their religious lives on hold as they attended to their studies and acculturation.

Professional formation and self-selection create distinctive modes of thought. Across the Muslim world Muslim engineers, doctors, businessmen and women, biologists, find valuable a whole range of books, some obscure, some well-known, some medieval, many contemporary. Through these works they attempt to understand, within what they experience as their meaningful environment, what Islam offers and requires. In my experience, with of course many exceptions (that, after all, is the point of this chapter!) – engineers favor books that de-problematize religion. These are not reflective books but affirmations, often programmatic views of Islam. Their websites and books point to past scholarship *in general* as part of what is wrong with contemporary Islam. Scholasticism and "division" are mocked and the subtle findings of jurists and theologians are seen as *taqlid* – defined as thoughtless emulation – and *bidʿah* – superfluous, even superstitious appendages to the pristine, unadorned Islam of yore. Yet oddly, past scholarship *in the particular* – a work of al-Ghazālī, or Ibn Qudāmah, or Ibn Taymiyyah – is revered as the profound intellectual achievement that it is, and as a product

[87] D. Berreby, "Engineering Terror"; E. Frank et al., "Political Self-Characterization of U.S. Medical Students"; D. Gambetta and S. Hertog, "Engineers of Jihad."

[88] The ways these correspondences work is brilliantly discussed in M. Douglas, *Natural Symbols.*

of the age of faith when Muslims were truly Muslim. There is a nostalgia but also a resolve to personally incarnate Islamic norms in their lives through self-scrutiny, discipline, constant discussion with like-minded Muslims, and fraternal correction.

Other communities of interpretation – more congenial to literature majors, psychologists, and educators, in my experience – see their allegiance to Islam and Muslimness as central to their identity, yet the way in which Islam is appropriated is more ambivalent. The books they read are aspirational, but also more about Sufism or its Euro-Muslim cousin, Perennialism.[89] They also read the Qur'ān itself, looking for verses that are not rules but principles, that are less about observance than ethical disposition. Above all, Islam for the Language Arts type is less a foundation than a challenge, a problematic. If the engineer asks, "how can I be a better Muslim?" the education major asks, "how Muslim can I be?" For these knowledge-economy types, the Islamic past is a challenge but it is also a vast edifice now reduced to rubble, by colonialism and modernity, but also by Muslims themselves. Where structures still stand, they are likely to be oppressive obstacles to living with faith in a world aware of plurality, woman's equality, and the need for political and economic transformation. One scrounges the ruins for bits of progressive foresight – on women's right to keep identity and property and to sexual gratification; for the relative tolerance of Islamdom in the premodern period as opposed to European fanaticism and intolerance; for the rich spirituality of Sufism, but also the ritual transformation of life through interiorist observance of Islamic practices, and they frequently turn to Sufis to use their imaginative techniques for understanding texts and rituals.

The array of possible ways to be Muslim in this world are as varied as the range of professions and vocations in the modern world. This is not to say that the engineer or the historian are, again in my experience, relativistic – "Hey! You be Muslim in the way you wish, and I'll be Muslim in the way I want." Both types (and in reality, most Muslims) arrive at whatever variety of Islam that they come to as a result of searching for the truth of Islam, the real Islam. Both share a commitment to being faithfully Muslim. To be indifferent to misapprehensions about Islam would require one to be religiously indifferent, and they are not.

To the observer, the result of differences in professional formation and affiliation is a set of different Islamic dialects, even among the relatively small set of Muslims at Austin, Texas, at Madison, Wisconsin, in Cairo, Egypt, or

[89] M. Sedgwick, *Against the Modern World.*

Istanbul, Turkey. The educator and the biologist each find congenial books and articles, but more importantly, they both find like-minded conversations and affiliates through their choices of blogs, websites, books, discussion sites, and streaming media. There may be only two other sympathetic gay Muslims in Dubuque or Tanta, but there are thousands more online. It is choice, decision, and volition that creates these dialects, not mere geographical locality. The modern world gives Muslims many choices – among them, which Islam to embrace and how to embrace the Islam they choose. These choices, thanks to high degrees of literacy, to the internet, and new media, are no longer confined by the possibilities of place of residence.

It is not just profession that governs one's Lived Islam. These Volitional Islamic dialects arise also from a feature peculiar to the modern, and especially postmodern world: the belief that an individual's world is largely constructed by choices made – how to dress, what signifying behaviors to perform, what beliefs are chosen to constitute both the self and self-presentation. It is the consumerist understanding of society, of government, of life itself, that crucially shapes Modern Islam (along, of course, with every other religious tradition) in the twenty-first century.

Like members of other religious traditions, Muslims have replaced mimetic learning with book learning. Yet, despite the official Islamic attempts to make one set of texts legitimate and others irrelevant, there are always new books, new cassettes of sermons, new youth groups, new gurus, shaykhs, masters, and mullahs who offer scholarships, dorm space, and fellowship of the like-minded. It is not that Muslims *may* choose, but that they *must* choose which Islam is their Islam. The singular Egyptian Islamic dialect has been replaced with a marketplace of liberal, conservative, Salafi, progressive, jihadist, quietist, feminist, gender-fluid, and patriarchal understandings of Islam.[90] These understandings can be excerpted and assembled almost at will – often, to the outsider, incoherently. A Muslim may assert (and many men and women do) the categorical equality of Muslim men and women, but at the same time, aver that women are by their constitution unfitted to interpret the religion authoritatively. Many assert that violence is un-Islamic but violent resistance is a duty. The websites where Protestant Muslims debate every conceivable issue testify not only to volitional solidarity but to consumerist persuasion. These debates are often not Fox News/MSNBC-type rants but earnest, rational efforts that use logic and evidence to persuade readers to join their Progressive/Salafi/Iranian/Wahhabi

[90] In Mahmood's *Politics*, we see the replacement of the traditional *ʿālim* as a figure of authority by the woman *dāʿiyyah*, a self-motivated, and self-trained religious expert.

understanding of what it means to say, "I am Muslim." To use academese, the assumption of agency by Muslims means that they consume Islam; they do not merely assume it.

We pointed out above that travel heightens self-awareness by confronting the traveler with difference. Different versions of Islam may not only help bind Muslims through the Koiné when they find themselves in a non-Muslim world (and to realize that, "despite our differences we are all one *ummah*!"), but the encounter with Muslim difference can accent disagreements by challenging positions which are then held more dearly. Yet in the modern world everyone, or at least every non-Euro-American, shares the immigrants' culture shock in a world that differs from the world to which he or she was born, and that imposes itself on her, willy-nilly.

Imagine a family in Turkey when the father goes to Belgium to work in a factory. He may hate Belgium, he may admire it; he may be homesick for the charms of his homeland, he may be utterly delighted to flee his homeland's provincialism and restraints. Yet he writes letters, makes phone calls, Skypes and emails his family, and through his reports of another way of living, another way to be a Turk, and a Muslim, the entire family becomes, to some degree, virtual immigrants to Belgium along with the father. Or consider a Malaysian woman who goes to the US to become a biology researcher. She finds a job and marries – probably another Malaysian, possibly another Muslim from elsewhere, conceivably a non-Muslim – and she settles in Boston. Her family stays in touch with her, perhaps visits occasionally. The stay-at-home family are transposed virtually just as their daughter/sister is physically.

The result of this diaspora is alienation, it is sophistication, it is cosmopolitanism of a sort even for those who stay behind. Across Islamdom, in small towns and big cities in Morocco, Yemen, Turkey, and Indonesia, I've seen mothers and sisters, brothers and fathers, shouting at video screens in garish internet cafes. Where I knew the language, the questions were all similar – what is it like, do they like you, who are your friends, how is the job? All questions that allow the caller back home to imagine himself/herself abroad. It is not just to Europe or to the Americas that these intrepid scholars and workers go, but also to the Gulf states, to Africa, to Russia, and to Southeast Asia. The traveler may confront a world in which the scope of Islam is expansive – as in Arabia for instance, or Iran – or one in which Islam is privatized and has little public scope – in Germany or Argentina for example. And because of this new environment these travelers are changed, and so too are their relatives and friends who do not, themselves, travel.

The diaspora of Islam is much larger than the set of actual travelers. In nearly every country where there are Muslims, Muslims are frequently abroad, in reality and virtually. The experience of Muslims outside of Islamdom is important, but the experience of Muslims at home, confronting a different part of Islamdom, is also important. In all cases, the inner world of Islamic life and the meaning of one's Islam is altered.[91] This kind of travel amplifies the travel experience described at the beginning of this chapter and diffuses it throughout the world of Islam. Taken together, these three factors – the rise of discrete professional identities, the consumerist view of life, and the experience of real and virtual emigration – have made choice the precondition of religious life. But the world of virtuality means that one is no longer restricted in one's choices to particular forms of Islam common to where a particular Muslim lives.

The thrust of consumer society is to compartmentalize us into groups – jazz aficionados, sports fans, fountain pen collectors, heavy metal listeners – and these groups reflect and display our chosen identities and aspirations.[92] This is true also for religious life. A great deal of scholarly and even more not-so-scholarly writing has been dedicated to describing "radicalization," particularly of young men. The troubled youth – a convert, or a second-generation emigrant, or an aspirant middle-class boy from a Muslim country, is "led astray" by a recruiter or a friend, or a website. Thus mobilized he joins al-Qāʿidah or ISIS, she moves to Syria or Afghanistan or Somalia, or he is persuaded by an online cleric to commit an act of terror in some country.[93] This is a trope in the popular press. Yet the furor about this radical and miniscule fringe of Muslim life deprives us of the context in which this "radicalization" takes place. When I asked a friend, a Muslim educator and a *ṭālib al-ʿilm* himself, who is the most influential intellectual for Muslim youth where he taught, he instantly and wryly said, "Shaykh Google." As well as becoming hip-hop fans, dreamy viewers of Spanish interior furnishings, and fanatical followers of Barsa and Juventus, young Muslim men and very much so, young Muslim women, everywhere and of every background, log on and develop Islamically in their chosen virtual Islamdom. They find the Official Islam and the Islam of their parents cramped, compromised, or indifferent to their needs.[94] And so they get on the internet, read, listen, travel in their imaginations, and become their own kind of Muslims, often a very different kind of Muslim from many of those around them.

[91] G. Kepel, *Allah in the West*; O. Roy, *Globalized Islam*. [92] P. Bourdieu, *Distinction*.

[93] S. Atran, *Talking to the Enemy*; S. Atran et al., "Devoted Actors," and many other works in both the scholarly and popular press.

[94] "An Appeal to the Ulama in Morocco – A Man's Outcry and Speech."

Conclusion

This discussion on Modern Islam has pulled this way and that. On one hand, the modern world facilitates the homogenization of Islam into the Standard Islam of the Cosmopolitans. On the other hand, the same states that seem to impose Standard Islam are actually creating a local Official Islam. Muslims travel, meet other Muslims, and share more than ever before a concrete sense of a single Islamic *ummah*, a world of Muslims connected by allegiance to the Koiné and commitment to being Muslim. On the other hand, these travels confront Muslims with the fact of Muslim difference that may harden into a willed provincialism and solidify differences into antagonisms.

Literacy and travel – virtual and actual – are the material substrata for Modern Islam, in contrast to the premodern version. Literacy diminishes the hegemony and authority of the professional Muslim whose prestigious voice had shaped Islam in most localities for a millennium. It was they who spun the web of Cosmopolitan doctrines, practices, and values that kept Islam and Muslims from shattering into autonomous local sects and churches, as Christians did. Yet literacy also enables Muslims to drink without adulteration from the source of their faith – to read (mostly in translation of course) the Qur'ān, the stories of the Prophet, and the works of Cosmopolitan Islamic geniuses who guided law, interpretation, and public conduct for 1,400 years.

Now the state, whether in Muslim-majority countries or in Muslim-minority states like France and Germany, presses public Islam toward Standard norms. This religious bureaucracy confines shrine worship, bans unauthorized sermonizers, defunds festivals, and in its state-approved textbooks and classes heaps scorn on healers, spiritual guides, and wonder-workers. The particularities and needs of the nation-state, however, mold the Standard Islam of a given country. The linkage of Islam to the state is irresistible for bureaucrats and ideologues alike. Consequently the state's Standard Islam is in many ways a Dialect Islam with an army and a police force.

Nonetheless the model of dialects located in particular geographic locales has its limitations in the twenty-first century. The literacy and consumer mentality of many modern Muslims has led to many different dialects created less by geography than by profession and individual temperament. Many perspectives on Islam that would once have been confined to a handful of religious eccentrics now acquire a public presence through new-media-forged solidarity and communication. In the 2013 Gezi Park, Istanbul demonstrations against the ruling AK Party, Turkey's Anti-Kapitalist

Muslims were quite important despite their limited numbers. Even now, they have a local web page, a vibrant Twitter presence, and a Turkish Facebook page, but also a frequently viewed English-language Facebook page accessible to any Muslim around the world who has learned English for professional or academic reasons – engineers, pilots, movie viewers, tourist guides, and *lumpen* intellectuals alike. The few anti-capitalist Muslims in Zagazig, Egypt, form a virtual locality with their own dialect version of Islam strengthened by their cohort in Turkey, the US, Norway, and elsewhere.

In short, Lived Islam is no more the Islam of textbooks than it ever was, even while more and more Muslims are in fact learning about Islam from textbooks. The ease of travel and the ubiquity of the internet have diminished both the physical separation of Muslim from each other, and the dominance of a single set of local or Cosmopolitan perspectives on Muslims' religious lives. Despite the standardizing forces of the Muslim world, there remains no "essence of Islam." We should not fail to recognize that Anti-Kapitalist Muslims, gay Muslims, ISIS-oriented Muslims, libertarian Muslims, feminists and hyper-patriarchal Wahhabis all acknowledge the Qur'ān as authority, the Prophet as model, and the Islamic cultus as a lifelong discipline, even as they interpret those symbols and practices in radically different ways. To speak of Islams, then, the way we speak of modernities, or socialisms, is to mislead. It is to Islam (and through it, sometimes, to God) – *conceived of* as a *single* set of symbols, principles, and practices – that Muslims commit and they identity – if only to dispute – with other Muslims. They imagine those other Muslims of whatever stripe as religious kin of a single family in a way that a Christian or a Hindu is not and cannot ever be.

Conclusion

AND NOW THE TEST. HAVE WE SOLVED THE PROBLEM WE POSED AT the very beginning of the book? How do we account for two contradictory realities of Lived Islam: (1) The confounding multiplicity of practices and beliefs that, over time and from place to place, constructed Muslims' experience of Islam. (2) The fact that despite this diversity, Muslims across the globe recognize and have recognized each other and believed that *their* spiritual enterprise was a shared one. Without church councils, an established hierarchy of authority, not to mention an officially recognized head of church – Islam did not (like Christianity, for instance) hive off into multiple churches, denominations, or religions.

Many Muslims in conversation around the world have tried to account for this phenomenon with this argument: there is "Islam," and there is "culture." In my experience, the argument is to assert, not necessarily unkindly, that "culture" is those things that Muslims do, in the name of Islam, that some particular Muslim does not believe to be religiously correct, or at any rate, not to be at the core of "Islam." Then there is the "real" Islam, which is usually Koiné practices, some Standard notions, and other ideas that this same Muslim believes to be a good, and therefore essential, part of Islam. I have been unable to find a scholarly article either arguing for this distinction, or documenting its use among Muslims. But the demotic world of the blogosphere is full of assertions to this effect.

> As an American Muslim, when I see the issues and events about Islam that get treated as "news" in the mainstream media, it bothers me that so many are portrayed as "problems with Islam," the religion, when they are in reality problems of culture, traditions, politics, superstitions, and tribal or ethnic codes of conduct of some Muslim-majority region. I think most Americans would agree with me that it would be unfair to judge a religion

(whether Islam, Christianity, or any other religion) by the practices it does not condone.

The religion of Islam does not condone – and it actually condemns – practices such as dishonorable "honor killings," racism or tribalism, oppression of women, banning women from obtaining an education, and many other un-Islamic practices that make their way to the sensationalized news. If a Muslim, or a Muslim-majority region, practices these despicable acts, it is not because of Islam, but despite Islam.

... As a young boy growing up in Afghanistan, like many people in Afghanistan, I wrongly presumed many of these cultural practices to be "Islamic." At certain times of the year we cooked certain types of food and distributed them among the poor. On certain days, many visited the graveyards and the shrines, and prayed for the deceased, and some asked the "spirits of the deceased" to pray to God for them. These practices are performed by Muslims and are given an Islamic dimension, for instance by the reading of a passage from the Holy Quran, etc. Yet these practices are not Islamic practices.

So then, what is an Islamic practice? Islamic practices and beliefs are those that have roots in the Quran (which Muslims believe to be the last and unchanged revelation from God) and the Sunnah (traditions) of Prophet Muhammad (peace be upon him). Any belief or practice, even if common among some Muslim-majority country, which does not go back to the Quran or the Sunnah, is not an Islamic belief or practice.[1]

Readers of the book so far will recognize that the author's argument is essentialist. For him, there is a "real" Islam and there are practices "falsely" attributed to Islam. He admits that as a child he experienced these "pseudo-Islamic" practices as part of Islam. But later he came to believe these practices were not "Islamic" because they have no roots in the Qurʾān or the *Sunnah*. His set of authentic Islamic practices is essentially what we have called the Koiné Islam, together with a Cosmopolitan perspective that privileges the *ʿilm*-texts. The author's perspective is of course a legitimate Muslim perspective on Islam. It is just not a persuasive descriptive account of Lived Islam in the world.

Throughout this book we have asserted that, like a language, the thing we point to when we talk about Islam has distinctive, locally determined, Dialect features (those boyhood practices – meals, shrine visits, distributing food to the poor, seeking intercession – that were intrinsically part of his Lived Islam at the time). It also includes Koiné features that most Muslims acknowledge as central even while appropriating them in diverse ways (the five pillars, the

[1] T. Saidi, "Islam and Culture: Don't Mix Them Up."

concept of *sunnah*, the concept of "Islam"). And finally there are the ideal and (theoretically) non-local aspects of Islam – Cosmopolitan features – ideals, literatures, and roles. These ideals function like Standard language, and are strongest when institutions that impose and maintain these standards are strong; when education (including religious education) is widespread; when the Cosmopolitan (because somewhat deracinated) authorities are respected and their opinions enforced; and when demotic media discussions of Islam are constrained.

We want to argue that this particular kind of conceptual unity, set in a context of diversity, arises from a kind of deeper logic, a set of relations first arising during the formative period of Islam which itself arose in a profoundly diverse religious world. Muslims are, I believe, mostly unknowingly but still deeply, shaped by and committed to these structural forms and relations and these have given rise to the Lived Islam we see both in past and present-day Islam. The resultant flexibility and diversity of Islam's practices and beliefs arises from a number of structural commitments, including (1) Muslims' insistence on a single sacred language, and a single sacred text – both of which paradoxically are mostly incomprehensible to most Muslims. As we pointed out above, the overwhelming majority of the world's Muslims are not speakers of Arabic nor are they schooled in the distinctive Arabic of the Qur'ān. This is not to say that most Muslims "don't understand the Qur'ān." It is to say that they lack immediate and direct access to the text, while remaining committed to its radiant sacrality and definitive authority. This combination of commitment and deferred access produces a flexible and creative engagement with Qur'ānic doctrine. In this way the Qur'ān, as it were, flexes, expands, and contracts, as circumstances seem to require. Muslims' oblique immersion in the Qur'ān intensifies its numinousness and, unlike commitments to vernacular sacred texts, creates an expansive interpretative space for those engaged with the text as an object of devotion.

(2) Islam is formed not merely by Qur'ānic ordinances, ethics, imagery, doctrine. It is also, in everyday life, a compact set of near universally recognized rituals. The limited number of Koiné rituals – especially of season and life cycle – once again leaves a space for new rituals that, while novel, still rest upon and reinforce the general framework of Qur'ānic and *sharī'ah* practice. Perhaps even the emphasis on ritual, combined with the paucity of ur-Islamic rituals, actually helps to generate these new, local, and immediately relevant practices of Dialect Islam. These two factors – the constraints and openness of the sacred text and the centrality and paucity of Islamic rituals – allow and even demand originality and plurality and, as a result, adaptability.

Ritual in particular has a distinctive aspect that is not immediately apparent to those who either disdain ritual or take it for granted. A ritual has bodily significations, but it does not by itself mean, in a discursive sense.[2] *Ṣalāh*, for example, is not a symbol or representation of something; it is that thing itself, in this case, a performance of humility and subordination. But while the ritual is not discursive, it is the particular feature of ritual that rituals evoke an intense need to explain, to interpret, to generate a discursive account of those same ritual actions and logics.[3] The ritual itself is stable, unchanging, and as a result, immediately apprehensible to everyone as a shared part of being Muslim. The ritual allows Muslims to recognize each other. But the *accounts* of the ritual have always been, even in a contemporary world with all its forces of homogenization and control, necessarily diverse. The very same rituals found across Islamdom have produced distinct, local, and therefore intensely relevant accounts of what the ritual is for and why it is as it is. The diverse explications of the rituals inserts local and contemporary issues and concerns into Muslims' understanding of the rituals, and so, of what it means to be Muslim. The fact that ritual is at the heart of shared Islam means that "Islam" is often intensely relevant to Muslims' lives.

It seems to others, especially in ritual-starved Euro-America, that there is a plethora of Islamic rites. But the Koiné rituals of Islam, are, compared to other religions, relatively few, despite their daily, yearly, and lifetime periodicity. This taciturn ritual discourse gives space for Muslims to generate practices that, wherever they are, feel they need. Additionally, the Koiné rituals' disentanglement from the solar calendar amplifies the scope that Muslims have felt to supplement the canonical rituals with rites of spring; of birth, maturity, coupling, and death; of agricultural promotion and pestilence defense; of initiation, and of course of additional rites of devotion, discipline, membership, and faith. These additional and relevant rituals – as anyone who has attended the wedding of Muslim friends in diverse places can attest – have arisen and still arise in the distinct experiential worlds of Muslims. They are inflected by the Muslims' location (in all senses of the word), their education, their gender, and their distinctive needs, desires, and objects of gratitude.

For all these reasons the phenomenon we call "Islam" is, and always has been, multifaceted and locally differentiated from others' versions of Islam. These distinctive features, sometimes surprising, sometimes shocking to

[2] A. B. Seligman, "Ritual, the Self, and Sincerity," and A. K. Reinhart, "What to Do with Ritual Texts"; see also A. B. Seligman et al., *Ritual and Its Consequences.*

[3] C. Humphrey and J. Laidlaw, *The Archetypal Actions of Ritual*; A. K. Reinhart, "Ritual Action and Practical Action."

Muslims from elsewhere, are what we have called the Dialect aspect of Islam, and they are always present in every temporal manifestation of Islam, in the Islam of every Muslim. These aspects profoundly constitute, at one level, the flexibility and adaptability of Islam to all the various environments in which it is found; at the same time, these Dialect elements are profoundly important to the affective commitment of Muslims to Islam. It is precisely these Dialect understandings, appropriations, and practices that make Islam meaningful and consequential – to men and women, young and old, Africans and Americans, Arabs and Afghans, prosperous and penurious, and all the other diversities that make up Islamic humanity.

In sum, however counterintuitive it seems, it is the disciplined set of shared Islamic practices and beliefs that generates Islam's diversity. Limitations generate space; discursive terseness generates interpretative prolixity. The limited set of what we have called the "cognates" of Islamic symbolic language also, however, mean that these commonly shared features are dense with significance – they draw Muslims and Muslim practice toward them. This density is the reason that Sufi shrines – clearly a part of the local Dialect – are justified not just as "this is holy, this is a good thing, this is a powerful place," but as "this place is like Medinah where the Prophet lived and is buried."[4] The practices of the formative period Muslims generated, and then authorized, new practices in post-formative times. That authorization of a new view, practice, or interpretation nonetheless reinforces the centrality of the Prophet and his time, of the Koiné features of Islam. So, when the magical locale, or the Dialect sacred sites, cease to attract Muslims, the symbolic mass of the Prophet's locale and life still remains in place. It draws new interpretations – political liberationist ones, or gender equalitarian ones, for instance, into its orbit.[5] It is the sheer praxic and discursive mass

4 "But think about this, for the last 15 centuries people lived a more relaxed lifestyle in terms of the number of religious restrictions, and they were satisfied with their beliefs and muslim identity. These people came from the desert two hundred years ago and now want to export their culture and brand it as the only way to be a muslim. We have our own heritage and culture which we are now losing to the culture of the saudis. Why should we accept that? Just because some preacher got brainwashed and was handed few thousand dollars?

"Islam, or any religion, is a belief system. As a mature adult, you are entitled to your own beliefs and interpretations of holy texts. This is why you should not allow someone to tell you what to believe in. you should find out for yourself.

"I just remembered one thing. If you are not allowed to visit shrines then what is the purpose of going to medina. The only thing there is the shrine of prophet muhammad." N. Zahran, "Is Visiting Holy Shrines (Dargahs) or Graves Haraam in Islam?"

5 Asra Nomani seems to have found in Mecca the key to her understanding of Islam: in her visit to the Kaaba, men and women venerated the Kaaba together, the women unveiled. See A. Q. Nomani, *Standing Alone in Mecca*.

of the Koiné elements of Islam that have kept Islam from atomizing and blowing apart into different cults, denominations, or religions.[6]

The story of the Nation of Islam (NOI) illustrates the way the Dialect becomes more and more allied with the Koiné Islam. The Nation of Islam began as an African-American cult holding almost nothing in common with Koiné and Cosmopolitan Islam except an allegiance to *the idea of* "Islam," "the Qur'ān," and "Allah." The NOI was founded in the early 1930s, and was remarkably successful among African-Americans in the 1950s and early 1960s. By the early 1970s, however, its founding figure gone and the ideology of racial segregation waning, the allegiance to those three Koiné morphemes – Islam, Qur'ān, Allah – drew the Nation into Islamic orthopraxy. Renamed the "World Community of Al-Islam" (WCI) the group came to required Standard Islamic *ṣalāh*, Ramadan fasting, Qur'ānic study, and all the usual Koiné practices of Islam henceforth. Now, in the 2000s, for the most part WCI has been absorbed into "Sunnī Islam." And, as if to reiterate the point, when Louis Farrakhan recreated a new NOI and its cultic beliefs in the mid-1990s, within a decade it too was drawn to orthoprax Islamic observance. Farakhan's group too now fasts Ramadan, makes the hajj pilgrimage, and professes many standard Islamic doctrines.[7]

Yet it is not merely the weight of Koiné Islam that keeps Muslims together and constructs an integral Islam. As we saw with Hajji Shariatullah in Bengal, the bearers of the Cosmopolitan Islam – an Islam inculcated in Cosmopolitan institutions like madrasas, or in Cosmopolitan centers, Cairo, Delhi, or Mecca/Medinah itself – help hold Muslims together when their practices grow too divergent. These *ʿilm*-bearers serve as prods, shepherds, and censors, guiding Muslims who know only the Dialect, or who know the Koiné imperfectly, toward a more standard, less localized form of Islam, just as English and writing teachers in state schools from the US to India guide English speakers away from "fixin' to" as a tense marker, and "isn't it" as an all-purpose interrogative, toward a more "standard" English. The Cosmopolitans' prestige, as bearers of Qur'ān, interpreters of *sharīʿah*, and masters of *ʿilm*, gives them gravitas and symbolic power enabling them often to prune the most "idiolectic" features of Dialect Islam, and to exemplify and impose Standard Islam. Their mythology of an Islam removed from present time and particular places lifts them above the fray and makes their Islam seem stable, unchanging, transcendent, eternal.

[6] The utter marginality of Bahais, Druzes, Ahmadis, and other Islam-derived religious groups only emphasizes the point.

[7] "Farrakhan Welcomed in Holy City"; "Fasting Is Prescribed."

Nonetheless, the Cosmopolitans' mythology of "an Islam of Everywhere and Nowhere" runs aground on the shoals of everyday life and, aside from utopian cultists like the ISIS crowd who can delude themselves that they've achieved transcendent identity with the time and community of the Prophet, most Muslims are in fact firmly rooted in the here and now, and they continue to inflect their Islam with relevance and reflexivity.

Time spent on Muslim chat and blog sites, and thousands of conversations over the years, confirms that most chatters and bloggers and commentators – most Muslims in fact – are not out to create a mythic alternate to their own time and place, but instead wish to bring Islam's truths to bear on their particular lived worlds. In the process they are also very much intermingling their lived world with their understanding of Islam. Most of these contemporary engaged Muslims – despite their polite deference to those who might be more learned – claim the right to interpret Islam in a way that makes sense to them. Islam, they insist, is relevant, and by insisting on this claim, they make it so.

All this explains why claims that "Islam is a violent religion," or "Islam is a religion of peace" are not wrong but not right either.[8] Muslims who live in a world of violence deploy Islamic conceptual resources to justify a violent response. Muslims who live in an orderly and amicable environment are free to draw on the wealth of Islamic texts, practices, and ideals that evoke, demand, and idealize peace, tolerance, and irenicism. If Islam were intrinsically violent, it would be impossible to explain the data showing that countries with Islamic majority populations are, if anything, somewhat less violent than other countries. If Islam made Muslims terrorists, it would be impossible to explain the "missing martyrs" who are so obviously absent from the world.[9]

Yet to say of ISIS members that they are not Muslims is absurd: they fast, they pray, they pay *zakāt*, they are committed to the notion of *sharīʿah*, to the example (or one example) of the Prophet, and so on. But it is clear from the rest of the Muslim world's response – both the expert Cosmopolitans who have in their thousands condemned ISIS, and the average Muslims who have neither flocked to Iraq and Syria, nor given any sign of desiring ISIS values in their own countries (including Muslim-minority countries like the US and France) – that ISIS is a very tiny Dialect, one almost certainly doomed to disappear within the greater, more diverse and accepting Islamic *ummah*. It

[8] The "literature" on this topic is absurdly large and, for reasons that should be clear to readers, utterly unhelpful. An interesting Christian theological take can be found at S. Guthrie, "Islam: Inherently Violent or Peaceful?"

[9] C. Kurzman, *The Missing Martyrs*.

may be that the ideological support and great wealth of Gulf Arabs, particularly in Arabia, will maintain the ossified revolution of Wahhabism for a while, but it is becoming clear even to them that *takfīrī* Islam is dangerous, and worse, irrelevant. More and more even Gulf Arabs are coming to view the intolerant variety of Islam as incompatible with the values of the Koiné and the teachings of the Cosmopolitans – that is, of Islam itself.

There is no essence of Islam, no "true" Islam, in the world, but neither is Islam merely the sum of 1.5 billion Muslims' actions, or the totality of millions of diverse regional "islams." Islam is not (merely) a discourse; more importantly, it is a praxis. While the praxis is relatively stable in the domain of ritual, the appropriation of those rituals and the discussion of them is immensely diverse. Lived Islam is the native instantiation of practices and commitments to which Muslims pledge allegiance, which orient their lives, and which for them make the transcendent into the immanent. Some of those practices are widely shared; some are quite restricted in their application; some of the ideas seem to be constitutive of being Muslim – not least the very notion of "Islam" itself – some belong to the arcane but prestigious world of Muslim religious experts and *ʿilm*-bearers. To say of someone that he or she is a Muslim tells us that they have an allegiance, in various degrees, to some subset of these notions, but it does not tell us the reality of their faith and practice – what exactly they believe, what exactly they do, what their stance is toward the ever-changing reality in which we live. Lived Islam is, like life itself, irremediably heterogeneous, unstable, dynamic, creative, and enriching. It is no longer possible to see it otherwise.

Bibliography

Abdul Bari, Muhammad. "The Fara'idi Movement." *Pakistan Historical Society* 8 (1955): 197–208.

"The Reform Movement in Bengal." In *A History of the Freedom Movement (Being the Story of Muslim Struggle for the Freedom of Hind-Pakistan) 1707–1947*, edited by Pakistan Historical Society Board of Editors, 542–555. Karachi: Pakistan Historical Society, 1957.

Abdul-Jabbar, Kareem, and Peter Knobler. *Giant Steps*. New York: Bantam Books, 1983.

Abdurrahman, Münir. *Papa'ların tarih boyunca İslâm-Türk düşmanlığı*. 1st ed. Istanbul: Yağmur Yayınları, 1967.

Abū l-Baqā', Ayyūb b. Mūsá al-Ḥusaynī al-Kufawī (1094/1683). *al-Kulliyāt; mu'jam fī al-muṣṭalaḥāt wa-l-furūq al-lughawiyyah*. Edited by 'Adnān Darwīsh and Muḥammad al-Miṣrī. 5 vols. Damascus: Wizārat al-Thaqāfah wa-l-Irshād al-Qawmī, 1974.

Açıkel, Fethi. "The Twilight of 'the Holy Articulation': Nationalism, Capitalism and Islam; Authoritarian Strategies of National Building and Capitalist Modernization in Turkey." PhD diss., University of Essex, 1999.

Ahmad, Imtiaz, ed. *Ritual and Religion Among Muslims in India*. New Delhi: Manohar, 1981.

Ahmad, Imtiaz, and Helmut Reifeld, eds. *Lived Islam in South Asia: Adaptation, Accommodation, and Conflict*. New Delhi: Social Science Press, 2004.

Ahmad, Mahmud. *Economics of Islam: A Comparative Study*. Lahore: M. Ashraf, 1947.

Āl-i Aḥmad, Jalāl. *Lost in the Crowd*. 1st English ed. Washington, DC: Three Continents Press, 1985.

Ali, Kecia. "Progressive Muslims and Islamic Jurisprudence: The Necessity for Critical Engagement with Marriage and Divorce Law." In *Progressive Muslims: On Justice, Gender and Pluralism*, edited by Omid Safi, 163–189. Oxford: Oneworld, 2003.

Ali, Sheikh Rustum. *Oil, Turmoil, and Islam in the Middle East*. New York: Praeger, 1986.

"An Appeal to the Ulama in Morocco – A Man's Outcry and Speech." Last accessed January 7, 2020. www.dailymotion.com/video/x2zod43.

Anderson, Benedict. *Imagined Communities: Reflections on the Origin and Spread of Nationalism*. Rev. and extended ed. London: Verso, 1991.

Anderson, Betty. "Jordan: Prescription for Obedience and Conformity." In *Teaching Islam: Textbooks and Religion in the Middle East*, edited by Eleanor Abdella Doumato and Gregory Starrett, 71–88. Boulder, CO: Lynne Rienner, 2007.

Anderson, Perry. *The Origins of Postmodernity*. London: Verso, 1998.

Anjum, Ovamir. "Islam as a Discursive Tradition: Talal Asad and His Interlocutors." *Comparative Studies of South Asia, Africa and the Middle East* 27, no. 3 (2007): 656–672.

Antoun, Richard T. *Muslim Preacher in the Modern World: A Jordanian Case Study in Comparative Perspective*. Princeton, NJ: Princeton University Press, 1989.

Appleby, Joyce Oldham. *The Relentless Revolution: A History of Capitalism*. New York: W. W. Norton & Co., 2010.

Asad, Talal. *The Idea of an Anthropology of Islam*. Washington, DC: Center for Contemporary Arab Studies, Georgetown University, 1986.

Genealogies of Religion; Discipline and Reasons of Power in Christianity and Islam. Baltimore, MD: The Johns Hopkins University Press, 1993.

On Suicide Bombing. Wellek Library Lectures. New York: Columbia University Press, 2007.

Atran, Scott. *Talking to the Enemy: Faith, Brotherhood, and the (Un)making of Terrorists*. 1st ed. New York: Ecco Press, 2010.

Atran, Scott, Hammad Sheikh, and Angel Gomez. "Devoted Actors Sacrifice for Close Comrades and Sacred Cause." *Proceedings of the National Academy of Sciences* 111, no. 50 (2014): 17702–17703.

Aydin, Cemil. *The Idea of the Muslim World: A Global Intellectual History*. Cambridge, MA: Harvard University Press, 2017.

Al-Azmeh, Aziz. *Islams and Modernities*. 2nd ed. London: Verso, 1996.

Bailey, Richard W. *Images of English: A Cultural History of the Language*. Ann Arbor, MI: The University of Michigan Press, 1991.

Baldwin, James E. *Islamic Law and Empire in Ottoman Cairo*. Edinburgh: Edinburgh University Press, 2017.

Barkow, Jerome H. "Muslims and Maguzawa in North Central State, Nigeria: An Ethnographic Comparison." *Canadian Journal of African Studies* 7, no. 1 (1973): 59–76.

Behrends, Andrea, Sybille Müller, and Isabel Dziobek. "Moving in and out of Synchrony: A Concept for a New Intervention Fostering Empathy through Interactional Movement and Dance." *The Arts in Psychotherapy* 39, no. 2 (2012): 107–116.

Bein, Amit. *Ottoman Ulema, Turkish Republic: Agents of Change and Guardians of Tradition*. Stanford, CA: Stanford University Press, 2011.

Bell, Daniel. *The Coming of Post-Industrial Society: A Venture in Social Forecasting*. New York: Basic Books, 1976.

Bellah, Robert N. *Religion in Human Evolution: From the Paleolithic to the Axial Age*. Cambridge, MA: Belknap Press of Harvard University Press, 2011.

Bellah, Robert N., and Hans Joas. *The Axial Age and Its Consequences*. Cambridge, MA: Belknap Press of Harvard University Press, 2012.

Berger, Morroe. *Islam in Egypt Today: Social and Political Aspects of Popular Religion.* Princeton Studies on the Near East. Cambridge, UK: Cambridge University Press, 1970.

Berreby, David. "Engineering Terror." *New York Times*, 2010. Last accessed February 24, 2014. www.nytimes.com/2010/09/12/magazine/12FOB-IdeaLab-t .html?searchResultPosition=1; a version of this article appeared in print on September 12, 2010, on page MM22 of the *Sunday Magazine.*

Birnbaum, Eleazar. "The Transliteration of Ottoman Turkish for Library and General Purposes." *JAOS* 87 (1987): 122–156.

Bourdieu, Pierre. *Distinction: A Social Critique of the Judgement of Taste.* Translated by Richard Nice. Cambridge, MA: Harvard University Press, 1984 [1979].

Bowen, John R. "Salat in Indonesia: The Social Meanings of an Islamic Ritual." *Man* 24, no. 2 (1989): 600–619.

"On Scriptural Essentialism and Ritual Variation: Muslim Sacrifice in Sumatra and Morocco." *American Ethnologist* 19, no. 4 (1992): 656–671.

Muslims Through Discourse: Religion and Ritual in Gayo Society. Princeton, NJ: Princeton University Press, 1993.

Boyd, James. "Zoroastrianism: Avestan Scripture and Rite." In *The Holy Book in Comparative Perspective*, edited by Frederick M. Denny and Rodney L. Taylor, 109–125. Columbia, SC: University of South Carolina Press, 1985.

Boyunağa, Yılmaz. *Dost ve düşman gözü ile Türk-İslâm sentezi.* Istanbul: Yağmur Yayınevi, 1970.

Brown, Daniel W. *Rethinking Tradition in Modern Islamic Thought.* Cambridge Middle East Studies 5. New York: Cambridge University Press, 1996.

Brown, Jonathan. *The Canonization of al-Bukhārī and Muslim: The Formation and Function of the Sunnī Ḥadīth Canon.* Islamic History and Civilization. Studies and Texts v. 69. Leiden: Brill, 2007.

Misquoting Muhammad: The Challenge and Choices of Interpreting the Prophet's Legacy. London: Oneworld, 2014.

Brown, Nathan. "Genesis of a New Curriculum." In *Teaching Islam: Textbooks and Religion in the Middle East,* edited by Eleanor Abdella Doumato and Gregory Starrett, 125–138. Boulder, CO: Lynne Rienner, 2007.

Bucaille, Maurice. *La Bible, le Coran et la science: les Écritures saintes examinées à la lumière des connaissances modernes.* Riyadh: International Islamic Federation of Student Organizations, 2005.

Buitelaar, Marjo. *Fasting and Feasting in Morocco: Women's Participation in Ramadan.* Oxford: Berg Publishers, 1993.

Bulliet, Richard W. *Islam: The View from the Edge.* New York: Columbia University Press, 1994.

The Case for Islamo-Christian Civilization. New York: Columbia University Press, 2004.

Burke, Peter. *Popular Culture in Early Modern Europe.* Rev. reprint ed. Aldershot, England: Ashgate, 1994.

Carmichael, David L., Jane Hubert, Brian Reeves, and Audhild Schanche, eds. *Sacred Sites, Sacred Places.* London and New York: Routledge, 1994.

Casanova, Jose, Talal Asad, and Abdullahi al-Naʿim. "Religion, Law, and the Politics of Human Rights" (September 29, 2009). Last accessed August 2, 2019. http://blogs

.ssrc.org/tif/wp-content/uploads/2009/11/Talal-Asad-and-Abdullahi-An-Naim-in-conversation.pdf.

Casey, Maurice. *Aramaic Sources of Mark's Gospel.* Society for New Testament Studies Monograph Series. Cambridge and New York: Cambridge University Press, 1998.

Çayır, Kenan. "Islamic Novels: A Path to New Muslim Subjectivities." In *Islam in Public: Turkey, Iran and Europe*, edited by Nilüfer Göle and Ludwig Ammann, 191–223. Istanbul: Bilgi University Press, 2006.

Cesari, Jocelyne. *When Islam and Democracy Meet: Muslims in Europe and in the United States.* 1st ed. New York: Palgrave Macmillan, 2004.

Cetinsaya, Gokhan. "Rethinking Nationalism and Islam: Some Preliminary Notes on the Roots of 'Turkish-Islamic Synthesis' in Modern Turkish Political Thought." *The Muslim World* 89, no. 3–4 (1999): 350–376.

Chernoff, John. "The Pilgrimage to Mecca: An Excerpt from *A Drummer's Testament.*" *Chicago Review* 34, no. 3 (Summer 1984): 68–93.

Christian, William A. *Local Religion in Sixteenth-Century Spain.* Princeton, NJ: Princeton University Press, 1981.

Cohen, E. E., R. Ejsmond-Frey, N. Knight, and R. I. Dunbar. "Rowers' High: Behavioural Synchrony Is Correlated with Elevated Pain Thresholds." *Biology Letters* 6, no. 1 (February 2010): 106–108.

Cohen, Emma, Roger Mundry, and Sebastian Kirschner. "Religion, Synchrony, and Cooperation." *Religion, Brain & Behavior* (2013): 1–11.

Cook, M. A. *Commanding Right and Forbidding Wrong in Islamic Thought.* Cambridge and New York: Cambridge University Press, 2000.

Crapanzano, Vincent. *The Hamadsha: A Study in Moroccan Ethnopsychiatry.* Berkeley, CA: University of California Press, 1973.

Curtis, Edward E. *Black Muslim Religion in the Nation of Islam, 1960–1975.* Chapel Hill: University of North Carolina Press, 2006.

Das, Veena. "For a Folk-Theology and Theological Anthropology of Islam [reply to F. Robinson]." *Contributions to Indian Sociology* 18, no. 2 (1984): 293–300.

Denny, Frederick. *An Introduction to Islam.* New York: Macmillan 1985.

Deringil, Selim. *The Well-Protected Domains: Ideology and the Legitimation of Power in the Ottoman Empire, 1876–1909.* London and New York: I.B. Tauris, 1998.

DeWeese, Devin A. *Islamization and Native Religion in the Golden Horde: Baba Tükles and Conversion to Islam in Historical and Epic Tradition.* Hermeneutics: Studies in the History of Religions. University Park, PA: Pennsylvania State University Press, 1994.

Dickinson, Eerik. "Ibn al-Ṣalāḥ, al-Shahrazūrī and the *Isnād.*" *Journal of the American Oriental Society* 122, no. 3 (2002): 481–505.

Dorroll, Philip. "'The Turkish Understanding of Religion': Rethinking Tradition and Modernity in Contemporary Turkish Islamic Thought." *Journal of the American Academy of Religion* 82, no. 4 (December 2014): 1033–1069.

Douglas, Mary. *Natural Symbols.* 2nd ed. New York: Pantheon Books, 1982 [1970, 1973].

Doumato, Eleanor Abdella. "Saudi Arabia: From 'Wahhabi' Roots to Contemporary Revisionism." In *Teaching Islam: Textbooks and Religion in the Middle East*, edited by Eleanor Abdella Doumato and Gregory Starrett, 153–176. Boulder, CO, and London: Lynne Rienner, 2007.

Dressler, Markus. *Writing Religion: The Making of Turkish Alevi İslam*. New York: Oxford University Press, 2013. http://dx.doi.org/10.1093/acprof:oso/9780199969401.001.0001.

Dressler, Markus, and Arvind-pal Singh Mandair. *Secularism and Religion-Making*. Reflection and Theory in the Study of Religion. Oxford and New York: Oxford University Press, 2011.

Duijzings, Ger. "Kosovo: The End of a 'Mixed' Pilgrimage." *International Institute for the Study of Islam in the Modern World (ISIM) Newsletter* 3 (1999): 1 [continued on p. 20].

Dunn, Ross E. *The Adventures of Ibn Battuta: A Muslim Traveler of the 14th Century*. Berkeley, CA: University of California Press, 1986.

Dwyer, Daisy Hilse. *Law and Islam in the Middle East*. New York: Bergin & Garvey Publishers, 1990.

Eaton, Richard Maxwell. *Sufis of Bijapur, 1300–1700: Social Roles of Sufis in Medieval India*. Princeton, NJ: Princeton University Press, 1977.

Eccel, Chris. "The Kinship-Based Cult of Muhammad among the Hamd of the Hawran." *Der Islam* 63 (1986): 324–333.

Efendī, Dāmād, and Muḥammad ʿAbdallāh b. Sulaymān Shaykhīzādeh (1078/1667). *Majmaʿ al-anhur fī sharḥ multaqá al-abḥūr*. 2 vols. Beirut: Dār li-Iḥyāʾ al-Turāth al-ʿArabī, n.d. [Istanbul 1317]. [*Multaqá al-abḥur* of Burhānaddīn Ibrāhīm b. Muḥammad al-Ḥalabī 956/1549; with *Durur al-mutaqá* of ʿAlāʾaddīn Muḥammad b. ʿAlī al-Ḥaṣkafī (1088/1677) on the margin.]

Eickelman, Dale F. *Moroccan Islam: Tradition and Society in a Pilgrimage Center*. Modern Middle East series (Austin, Tex.) no. 1. Austin: University of Texas Press, 1976.

Knowledge and Power in Morocco: The Education of a Twentieth-Century Notable. Princeton, NJ: Princeton University Press, 1985.

"Changing Interpretations of Islamic Movements." In *Islam and the Political Economy of Meaning*, edited by William R. Roff, 13–30. Berkeley, CA, & Los Angeles: University of California Press, 1987.

Eliade, Mircea. *Patterns in Comparative Religion*. Translated by Rosemary Sheed. New York: Sheed & Ward, 1958. [*Traité d'histoire des religions* [1948].]

El-Nawawy, Mohammed, and Sahar Khamis. *Islam Dot Com: Contemporary Islamic Discourses in Cyberspace*. Palgrave Macmillan series in International Political Communication. 1st ed. New York: Palgrave Macmillan, 2009.

el-Zein, Abdul Hamid M. *The Sacred Meadows: A Structural Analysis of Religious Symbolism in an East African Town*. Evanston, IL: Northwestern University Press, 1974.

"Beyond Ideology and Theology: The Search for the Anthropology of Islam." *Annual Review of Anthropology* 6 (1977): 227–254.

Endress, Gerhard. *An Introduction to Islam*. Translated by Carole Hillenbrand. Edinburgh: Edinburgh University Press, 1988.

Erdem, Gazi, ed. "A Special Issue on the Presidency of Religious Affairs in Turkey: Diyanet – Introduction." *The Muslim World* 98, no. 2–3 (2008): 159–163.

Esack, Farid. *Qurʾān, Liberation & Pluralism: An Islamic Perspective of Interreligious Solidarity against Oppression*. Oxford, England, and Rockport, MA: Oneworld, 1997.

Esposito, John L., and Hossein Askari. *Islam and Development: Religion and Sociopolitical Change*. Contemporary Issues in the Middle East. 1st ed. Syracuse, NY: Syracuse University Press, 1980.

Esposito, John L., ed. *Islam and Politics*. 1st ed, Contemporary Issues in the Middle East. Syracuse, NY: Syracuse University Press, 1984.

The Oxford Encyclopedia of the Modern Islamic World. 4 vols. New York: Oxford University Press, 1995.

The Oxford Encyclopedia of the Modern Islamic World [Online]. New York: Oxford University Press, 2009.

Etzioni, Amitai. *Security First: For a Muscular, Moral Foreign Policy*. New Haven: Yale University Press, 2007.

Ewing, Katherine. "Malangs of the Punjab: Intoxication or Adab as the Path to God?" In *Moral Conduct and Authority: The Place of Adab in South Asian Islam*, edited by Barbara Daly Metcalf, 357–371. Berkeley, CA: University of California Press, 1984.

Faraj, Muḥammad ʿAbd al-Salām. *The Neglected Duty: The Creed of Sadat's Assassins and Islamic Resurgence in the Middle East*. Translated by Johannes J. G. Jansen. New York and London: Macmillan, 1986.

"Farrakhan Welcomed in Holy City" (January 25, 1998). *Final Call*. Last accessed January 8, 2020. https://worldfriendshiptour.noi.org/mecca.html.

"Fasting Is Prescribed" (July 9, 2014). *Final Call*. Last accessed January 8, 2020. www.finalcall.com/artman/publish/Health_amp_Fitness_11/article_101599.shtml.

Federspiel, Howard M. *Persatuan Islam: Islamic Reform in Twentieth-Century Indonesia*. Cornell University. Monograph series. Ithaca, NY: Modern Indonesia Project, Cornell University, 1970.

Feener, R. Michael. *Islam in World Cultures: Comparative Perspectives*. Religion in Contemporary Cultures. Santa Barbara, CA: ABC-CLIO, 2004.

Ferguson, Charles A. "Diglossia." *Word* 15 (1959): 325–340.

"The Arabic Koine." *Language* 35, no. 4 (1959): 616–630.

Fischer, Michael M. J., and Mehdi Abedi. *Debating Muslims: Cultural Dialogues in Postmodernity and Tradition*. Madison, WI: University of Wisconsin Press, 1990.

Flood, Finbarr Barry. "Between Cult and Culture: Bamiyan, Islamic Iconoclasm, and the Museum." *The Art Bulletin* 84, no. 4 (December 2002): 641–659.

Frank, Erica, Jennifer Carrera, and Shafik Dharamsi. "Political Self-Characterization of U.S. Medical Students." *J Gen Intern Med* 22, no. 4 (April 2007): 514–517.

Frankl, P. J. L. "The Observance of Ramaḍān in Swahili-land." *Journal of Religion in Africa* 26, no. 4 (1996): 416–434.

Gade, Anna M. *Perfection Makes Practice: Learning, Emotion, and the Recited Qurʾān in Indonesia*. Honolulu: University of Hawai'i Press, 2004.

Gambetta, Diego, and Steffen Hertog. "Engineers of Jihad." Sociology Working Papers (2007–10). Last accessed August 2, 2019. http://www.nuff.ox.ac.uk/users/gambetta/engineers%20of%20jihad.pdf.

Geaves, Ron. *Islam and Britain: Muslim Mission in an Age of Empire*. London and New York: Bloomsbury Academic, 2018.

Geertz, Clifford. *The Religion of Java*. Chicago: University of Chicago Press, 1960.

Islam Observed: Religious Development in Morocco and Indonesia. The Terry lectures, Yale University, v. 37. New Haven: Yale University Press, 1968.

Gellens, Sam I. "The Search for Knowledge in Medieval Muslim Societies: A Comparative Approach." In *Muslim Travelers: Pilgrimage, Migration, and the Religious Imagination*, edited by Dale F. Eickelman and James Piscatori, 50–65. Berkeley, CA: University of California Press, 1990.

Gerber, Haim. *State, Society, and Law in Islam: Ottoman Law in Comparative Perspective*. Albany: State University of New York Press, 1994.

Islamic Law and Culture, 1600–1840. Studies in Islamic Law and Society. Leiden: Brill, 1999.

Gesink, Indira Falk. "'Chaos on Earth:' Subjective Truths versus Communal Unity in Islamic Law and the Rise of Militant Islam." *American Historical Review* (2003): 710–724.

Gräf, Bettina, and Jakob Skovgaard-Petersen. *Global Mufti: The Phenomenon of Yusūf al-Qaradāwī*. New York: Columbia University Press, 2009.

Graham, William A. *Beyond the Written Word: Oral Aspects of Scripture in the History of Religion*. Cambridge and New York: Cambridge University Press, 1987.

Green, Nile. *Islam and the Army in Colonial India: Sepoy Religion in the Service of Empire*. Cambridge Studies in Indian History and Society. Cambridge: Cambridge University Press, 2009.

Grehan, James. *Twilight of the Saints: Everyday Religion in Ottoman Syria and Palestine*. Oxford: Oxford University Press, 2014.

Guthrie, Stan. "Islam: Inherently Violent or Peaceful? Scholar Warren Larson Has a Surprising Answer to This Difficult Question" (February 9, 2015). Last accessed August 2, 2019. http://www.christianitytoday.com/ct/2015/february-web-only/islam-inherently-violent-or-peaceful.html.

Güvenç, Bozkurt. *Türk-İslam sentezi*. 1st ed. İstanbul: Sarmal Yayınevi, 1991.

Haines, Charles Reginald. *Islam as a Missionary Religion*. London and New York: E & JB Young [for the] Society for Promoting Christian Knowledge, 1889.

Haj, Samira. *Reconfiguring Islamic Tradition: Reform, Rationality, and Modernity*. Cultural Memory in the Present. Stanford, CA: Stanford University Press, 2009.

Hall, David D., ed. *Lived Religion in America: Toward a History of Practice*. Princeton, NJ: Princeton University Press, 1997.

Hamès, Constant. "L'Usage talismanique du Coran." *Revue de l'Histoire des Religions* 218, no. 1 (2001): 83–95.

Hamès, Constant, ed. *Coran et talismans. Textes et pratiques magiques en milieu musulman*. Paris: Karthala, 2007.

Hammoudi, Abdellah. *Master and Disciple: The Cultural Foundations of Moroccan Authoritarianism*. Chicago: University of Chicago Press, 1997.

A Season in Mecca: Narrative of a Pilgrimage. Translated by Pascale Ghazaleh. New York: Hill and Wang, 2006.

Harrison, Christopher. *France and Islam in West Africa, 1860–1960*. African Studies Series, no. 60. Cambridge and New York: Cambridge University Press, 1988.

Hasluck, F. W. *Christianity and Islam Under the Sultans*. 2 vols. Oxford: The Clarendon press, 1929. Edited by Margaret Masson Hardie Hasluck.

Hering, B. B. *Studies on Indonesian Islam*. Occasional paper (James Cook University of North Queensland, Centre for Southeast Asian Studies), no. 19. Townsville, Qld., Australia: Centre for Southeast Asian Studies, James Cook University of North Queensland, 1986.

Heyworth-Dunne, J. *An Introduction to the History of Education in Modern Egypt*. London: Luzac and Co., 1939.

Hirschkind, Charles. *The Ethical Soundscape: Cassette Sermons and Islamic Counterpublics*. Cultures of History. New York: Columbia University Press, 2006.

Hock, Hans Henrich. *Principles of Historical Linguistics*. Trends in Linguistics; Studies and Monographs 34. Edited by Werner Winter. Berlin: Mouton de Gruyter, 1986.

Hodgson, Marshall G. S. *The Venture of Islam: Conscience and History in a World Civilization*. 3 vols. Chicago: University of Chicago Press, 1974.

Rethinking World History: Essays on Europe, Islam, and World History. Studies in Comparative World History. Cambridge and New York: Cambridge University Press, 1993.

Holm, John A. *Pidgins and Creoles: [Volume 1] Theory and Structure*. Cambridge: Cambridge University Press, 1988.

Hughs, Aron W. *Theorizing Islam: Disciplinary Deconstruction and Reconstruction*. Sheffield, UK, and Bristol, CT: Equinox, 2012.

Humphrey, Caroline, and James Laidlaw. *The Archetypal Actions of Ritual: A Theory of Ritual Illustrated by the Jain Rite of Worship*. Oxford: Oxford University Press, 1994.

Huq, Maimuna. "Reading the Qur'an in Bangladesh: The Politics of 'Belief' among Islamist Women." *Modern Asian Studies* 42 (2008): 457–488.

Hymes, Dell. "Pidginization and Creolization of Languages." Proceedings of a Conference Held at the University of the West Indies, Mona, Jamaica, April 1968. Cambridge UK, 1971.

Ibn Baṭṭūṭah, Muḥammad ʿAbdallāh (770/1368–1369). *The Travels of Ibn Baṭṭūṭah (A.D. 1325–1354)*. Translated by H. A. R. Gibb [completed by C. F. Beckingham]. Haklyut Society Series II; no. 110, 117, 141, 178 ed. 5 vols. London: Cambridge University Press for the Haklyut Society, 1956–2002. Tr. of *Tuḥfat al-nuẓẓār fī gharāʾib al-amṣār wa-ʿajāʾiib al-afsār* [v1:1956; v2:1959; v3:1971; v4:1994; v5 [Index] 2002].

Ibn Taymiyyah, Taqīaddīn Aḥmad (728/1328). *Kitāb iqtiḍāʾ al-ṣirāṭ al-mustaqīm mukhālafat aṣḥāb al-jaḥīm*. Edited by Muḥammad Ḥāmid al-Fiqī. Cairo: Maktabat al-Sunnah al-Muḥammadiyyah, 1369/1950.

Ibn Taimīya's Struggle against Popular Religion: With an Annnotated Translation of His Kitāb iqtiḍāʾ aṣ-ṣirāṭ al-mustaqīm mukhālafat aṣḥāb al-jaḥīm. Translated by Muhammad Umar Memon. The Hague: Mouton, 1976.

Thalāth rasāʾil fī al-jihād. Edited by Muḥammad ibn ʿAbdallāh Abu Suʿaylik and Ibrāhīm ʿAlī. 1st ed. Amman: Dār al-Nafāʾis, 1993.

İzmirli, İsmail Hakkı. *İslâm-Türk ansiklopedisi = Muḥîṭ al-maʿârif al-Islâmiyyah al-Turkiyyah*. Istanbul: Asari ʿİlmiye Kütüphanesi Neşriyatı, 1359 [1940].

Jackson, Sherman A. Jackson. "Ibn Taymiyyah On Trial in Damascus." *Journal of Semitic Studies* 39, no. 1 (Spring 1994): 41–85.

Jacobsen, Kate Ostergaard. "*Ramadan* in Morocco: An Analysis of the Interaction of Formal and Local Traditions." *Temenos* 32 (1996): 113–135.

Jong, F. de, and Bernd Radtke, eds. *Islamic Mysticism Contested: Thirteen Centuries of Controversies and Polemics*, Islamic History and Civilization: Studies and Texts, vol. 29. Leiden and Boston: Brill, 1999.

Kafesoğlu, İbrahim. *Türk İslâm sentezi*. Istanbul: Aydınlar Ocağı, 1985.

Kaptein, N. J. G. *Muḥammad's Birthday Festival: Early History in the Central Muslim Lands and Development in the Muslim West Until the 10th/16th Century*. Leiden and New York: Brill, 1993.

Katz, Marion Holmes. *The Birth of the Prophet Muhammad: Devotional Piety in Sunni Islam*. Culture and Civilisation in the Middle East. London: Routledge, 2006.

Kepel, Gilles. *Allah in the West: Islamic Movements in America and Europe*. Translated by Susan Milner. Mestizo spaces = Espaces métissés. Stanford, CA: Stanford University Press, 1997.

Khalid, Adeeb. "Ottoman Islamism between the Ümmet and the Nation." *Archivum Ottomanicum* 19 (2001): 197–211. Special issue on "Late Ottoman Religion."

Khan, Muin-ud-din Ahmad. *History of the Fara'idi Movement in Bengal (1818–1906)*. Pakistan Historical Society Publication, no. 41. Karachi: Pakistan Historical Society, 1965.

Kister, M. J. "'You Shall only Set out for Three Mosques': A Study of an Early Tradition." *Le Muséon* 82 (1969): 1–8.

Kuran, Timur. *The Long Divergence: How Islamic Law Held Back the Middle East*. Princeton, NJ: Princeton University Press, 2011.

Kuruvilla, Carol. "5 Things You Need to Know About Sharia Law" (July 15, 2016). Last accessed August 2, 2019. https://www.cairoklahoma.com/blog/5-things-you-need-to-know-about-sharia-law/.

Kurzman, Charles. *The Missing Martyrs: Why There Are So Few Muslim Terrorists*. Oxford and New York: Oxford University Press, 2011.

Lambek, Michael. *Knowledge and Practice in Mayotte: Local Discourses of Islam, Sorcery, and Spirit Possession*. Toronto: University of Toronto Press, 1993.

"Localising Islamic Performances in Mayotte." In *Islamic Prayer across the Indian Ocean: Inside and Outside the Mosque*, edited by David J. Parkin and Stephen Cavana Headley, 63–97. Richmond, UK: Curzon, 2000.

Landau, Jacob M. *Radical Politics in Modern Turkey*. Social, Economic, and Political Studies of the Middle East, v. 14. Leiden: Brill, 1974.

Lane, Edward William. *An Account of the Manners and Customs of the Modern Egyptians*. 5th corrected ed. New York: Dover Publications, 1973 [1860].

Launay, Robert. "The Birth of a Ritual: The Politics of Innovation in Dyula Islam." *Savanna* 6, no. 2 (1977): 145–154.

Beyond the Stream: Islam and Society in a West African Town. Comparative Studies on Muslim Societies. Berkeley, CA: University of California Press, 1992.

Lawrence, Bruce B. "Citizen Ahmed among the Believers: Salvation Contextualized in Indonesia and Egypt." In *Between Heaven and Hell: Islam, Salvation, and the Fate of Others*, edited by Muhammad Hasan Khalil, 288–311. Oxford: Oxford University Press, 2012.

The Koran in English: A Biography. Lives of Great Religious Books. Princeton, NJ: Princeton University Press, 2017.

Lester, Herbert C. "Hinduism: Veda and Sacred Texts." In *The Holy Book in Comparative Perspective*, edited by Frederick M. Denny and Rodney L. Taylor, 126–147. Columbia, SC: University of South Carolina Press, 1985.

Lévi-Strauss, Claude. *Myth and Meaning [the 1977 Massey Lectures]*. New York: Schocken Books, 1979 [1978].

Lewis, Bernard. *Islam and the West*. New York: Oxford University Press, 1993.

———. "What Went Wrong? The Clash between Islam and Modernity in the Middle East." *The Atlantic* (January 2002). Last accessed January 8, 2020. www.theatlantic.com/magazine/archive/2002/01/what-went-wrong/302387.

———. *The Crisis of Islam: Holy War and Unholy Terror*. Modern Library ed. New York: Modern Library, 2003.

———. *What Went Wrong? The Clash between Islam and Modernity in the Middle East*. 1st Perennial ed. New York: Perennial, 2003.

Lewis, Bernard, and Buntzie Ellis Churchill. *Islam: The Religion and the People*. Indianapolis: Wharton Press, 2009.

Lewis, Geoffrey. *The Turkish Language Reform: A Catastrophic Success*. Oxford linguistics. Oxford and New York: Oxford University Press, 1999.

Lincoln, Bruce. *Holy Terrors: Thinking about Religion after September 11*. 2nd ed. Chicago: University of Chicago Press, 2006.

Little, Donald P. "The Historical and Historiographical Significance of the Detention of Ibn Taymiyya." *International Journal of Middle East Studies* 4, no. 3 (July 1973): 311–327.

———. "Did Ibn Taymiyya Have a Screw Loose." *Studia Islamica* 41 (1975): 93–111.

Loeffler, Reinhold. *Islam in Practice: Religious Beliefs in a Persian Village*. Albany, NY: State University of New York Press, 1988.

Lukens-Bull, Ronald A. "Between Text and Practice: Considerations in the Anthropological Study of Islam." In *Defining Islam: A Reader*, edited by Andrew Rippen, 37–57. London: Equinox, 2007.

MacDonald, Duncan B. *Development of Muslim Theology, Jurisprudence and Constitutional Theory*. New York: Charles Scribner's, 1926.

Magnarella, Paul J. *Human Materialism: A Model of Sociocultural Systems and a Strategy for Analysis*. Gainesville: University Press of Florida, 1993.

Mahmood, Saba. "Rehearsed Spontaneity and the Conventionality of Ritual: Disciplines of *Ṣalāt*." *American Ethnologist* 28, no. 4 (2001): 827–853.

———. *Politics of Piety: The Islamic Revival and the Feminist Subject*. Princeton, NJ: Princeton University Press, 2005.

Makdisi, George. *The Rise of Colleges: Institutions of Learning in Islam and the West*. Edinburgh: Edinburgh University Press, 1981.

Malcolm X. *The Autobiography of Malcolm X*. New York: Ballantine Books, 1973.

Malony, Elliot C. *Semitic Interference in Marcan Syntax*. SBL Dissertation Series 51. Chico, CA: Scholars Press, 1981.

al-Maqrīzī, Aḥmad ibn ʿAlī, and Adel Allouche. *Mamluk Economics: A Study and Translation of al-Maqrīzī's Ighāthah [al-ummah bi-kashf al-ghummah]*. Translated by Adel Allouche. Salt Lake City, UT: University of Utah, 1994.

Marcus, Julie. *A World of Difference: Islam and Gender Hierarchy in Turkey*. Asian Studies Association of Australia; Women in Asia publication series. London and New Jersey: Zed, 1992.

Mariani, Ermete. "Cyber-Fatwas, Sermons, and Media Campaigns: Amr Khaled and Omar Bakri Muhammad in Search of New Audiences." In *Producing Islamic Knowledge: Transmission and Dissemination in Western Europe*, edited by Martin van Bruinessen and Stefano Allievi, 142–168: Routledge, 2011.

Marranici, Gabriele. *The Anthropology of Islam*. Oxford and New York: Berg, 2008.

Marshall, T. H. *Class, Citizenship, and Social Development: Essays.* 1st ed. Garden City, NY: Doubleday, 1964.

Martin, Richard C., ed. *Islam in Local Contexts.* Contributions to Asian Studies vol. 17. Leiden: Brill, 1982.

Martin, Vanessa A. *Islam and Modernism: The Iranian Revolution of 1906.* London: I.B. Tauris, 1989.

Masuzawa, Tomoko. *The Invention of World Religions, or, How European Universalism Was Preserved in the Language of Pluralism.* Chicago: University of Chicago Press, 2005.

Matheson, V., and A. C. Milner. *Perceptions of the Haj: Five Malay Texts.* Research Notes and Discussions, Paper No. 46. Singapore: Institute of Southeast Asian Studies, 1984.

Mawdūdī, Abū l-ʿAlāʾ. *Naḥwá al-dustūr al-Islāmī.* Cairo: Maṭbaʿah al-Salafiyyah, 1373/1953–1954.

Mayer, Peter. *Tombs and Dark Houses: Ideology, Intellectuals and Proletarians in the Study of Contemporary Indian Islam.* Adelaide: University of Adelaide, Centre for Asian Studies, 1977.

McLuhan, Marshall. *Understanding Media: The Extensions of Man.* 1st ed. New York: McGraw-Hill, 1964.

Mechran, Golnar. "Iran: A Shi'ite Curriculum to Serve the Islamic State." In *Teaching Islam: Textbooks and Religion in the Middle East,* edited by Eleanor Abdella Doumato and Gregory Starrett, 53–70. Boulder, CO, and London: Lynne Rienner, 2007.

Mernissi, Fatima. *The Veil and the Male Elite: A Feminist Interpretation of Women's Rights in Islam.* Reading, MA: Addison-Wesley Pub. Co., 1991.

Messick, Brinkley. "The Mufti, the Text and the World: Legal Interpretation in Yemen." *Man New Series* 21, no. 1 (1986): 102–119.

Metcalf, Barbara D. "The Pilgrimage Remembered: South Asian Accounts of the Hajj." In *Muslim Travelers,* edited by Dale F. Eickelman and James Piscatori, 85–107. Berkeley and Los Angeles: University of California Books, 1990.

"Living Hadith in the *Tablighi Jamaʿat.*" *Journal of Asian Studies* 52, no. 3 (August 1993): 584–608.

Minault, Gail. "Some Reflections on Islamic Revivalism vs. Assimilation among Muslims in India [reply to F. Robinson]." *Contributions to Indian Sociology* 18, no. 2 (1984): 301–305.

Munson Jr., Henry L. *Religion and Power in Morocco.* New Haven: Yale University Press, 1993.

Murad, Hasan Qasim. "Ibn Taymiya on Trial: A Narrative Account of His *Miḥan.*" *Islamic Studies* 18, no. 1 (Spring 1979): 1–32.

Musa, Aisha Y. *Ḥadīth as Scripture: Discussions on the Authority of Prophetic Traditions in Islam.* 1st ed. New York: Palgrave Macmillan, 2008.

Muslim, Abū l-Ḥusayn Ibn al-Ḥajjāj al-Qushayrī al-Nīsābūrī (261/875). *Ṣaḥīh Muslim bi-sharḥ al-Nawawī.* 18 vols. plus index. Beirut: Dār al-Kutub al-ʿIlmiyyah, n.d.

Nadel, S. F. *Nupe Religion.* London: Routledge & Kegan Paul, 1954.

Naipaul, V. S. *Among the Believers: An Islamic Journey.* New York: Alfred A. Knopf, 1981.

Beyond Belief: Islamic Excursions among the Converted Peoples. London: Little Brown and Co., 1998.

Na'Na, Seif. "[Palestine]: A Conflict of Historical Narratives." In *Teaching Islam: Textbooks and Religion in the Middle East*, edited by Eleanor Abdella Doumato and Gregory Starrett, 139–152. Boulder, CO, and London: Lynne Rienner, 2007.

Nandy, Ashis. "The Politics of Secularism and the Recovery of Religious Tolerance." In *Mirrors of Violence: Communities, Riots and Survivors in South Asia*, edited by Veena Das, 321–345. Delhi: Oxford University Press, 1990.

Narayanan, Vashudha. "Shared Ritual Spaces: Hindus and Muslims at the Shrine of Shahul Hamid in South India." *Religious Studies News* 41 (February 1998): 15, 30, 41.

"Religious Vocabulary and Regional Identity: A Study of the Tamil *Cirappuranam*." In *Beyond Turk and Hindu: Rethinking Religious Identities in Islamicate South Asia*, edited by David Gilmartin and Bruce B. Lawrence, 74–97. Gainesville: University Press of Florida, 2000.

Nelson, Cynthia. "Religious Experience, Sacred Symbols, and Social Reality." *Humaniora Islamica* 2 (1974): 253–266.

Nelson, Kristina. *The Art of Reciting the Qur'an*. [New] ed. Cairo and New York: American University in Cairo Press, 2001 [1st ed. 1985].

Nizami, Ashraf F. *Namaz: The Yoga of Islam*. 2nd revised ed. Baroda: Nizami, 1977.

Nomani, Asra Q. *Standing Alone in Mecca: An American Woman's Struggle for the Soul of Islam*. 1st ed. San Francisco: Harper San Francisco, 2005.

Norris, H. T. *Ṣūfī Mystics of the Niger Desert: Sīdī Maḥmūd and the Hermits of Aïr*. Oxford: Clarendon [Oxford University] Press, 1990.

Ölçen, Ali Nejat. *İslam'da karanlığın başlangıcı ve Türk Islam sentezi*. Ankara: Ekin Yayınevi, 1991.

O'Meara, Simon. *Space and Muslim Urban Life at the Limits of the Labyrinth of Fez*. Culture and Civilization in the Middle East 12. New York: Routledge, 2007.

Orsi, Robert A. *The Madonna of 115th Street: Faith and Community in Italian Harlem, 1880–1950*. New Haven: Yale University Press, 1985.

Gods of the City: Religion and the American Urban Landscape. Religion in North America. Bloomington, IN: Indiana University Press, 1999.

Between Heaven and Earth: The Religious Worlds People Make and the Scholars Who Study Them. Princeton, NJ: Princeton University Press, 2005.

Parkin, David J., and Stephen Cavana Headley, eds. *Islamic Prayer across the Indian Ocean: Inside and Outside the Mosque*. Curzon Indian Ocean Series. Richmond, UK: Curzon, 2000.

Peacock, James L. *Muslim Puritans: Reformist Psychology in Southeast Asian Islam*. Berkeley, CA: University of California Press, 1978.

Purifying the Faith: The Muhammadijah Movement in Indonesian Islam. The Kiste and Ogan Social Change Series in Anthropology. Menlo Park, CA: Benjamin/Cummings Pub Co., 1978.

Pearson, Michael N. *Pilgrimage to Mecca: The Indian Experience, 1500–1800*. Princeton, NJ: Markus Wiener, 1996.

Peletz, Michael G. *Social History and Evaluation in the Interrelationship of Adat and Islam in Rembau, Negeri Sembilan*. Singapore: Institute of Southeast Asian Studies, 1981.

Peters, F. E. *The Hajj*. Princeton, NJ: Princeton University Press, 1994.

Piamenta, M. *Islam in Everyday Arabic Speech*. Leiden: Brill, 1979.

Pipes, Daniel. *In the Path of God: Islam and Political Power*. New York: Basic Books, 1983.

Polanyi, Karl. *The Great Transformation*. New York and Toronto: Farrar & Rinehart, 1944.

Poliakov, Sergei Petrovich, and Martha Brill Olcott. *Everyday Islam: Religion and Tradition in Rural Central Asia*. Translated by Anthony Olcott. Armonk, NY: M.E. Sharpe, 1992.

Qalʿājī, Muḥammad Rawwās. *Muʿjam lughat al-fuqahāʾ*. Beirut: Dār al-Nafīs, 1996/1416.

Rahnema, Ali. *Superstition as Ideology in Iranian Politics: From Majlesi to Ahmadinejad*. Cambridge Middle East Studies 35. Cambridge: Cambridge University Press, 2011.

Rapoport, Yossef, and Shahab Ahmed. *Ibn Taymiyya and His Times*. Studies in Islamic Philosophy. Karachi: Oxford University Press, 2010.

Rāzī, Najm al-Din ʿAbd Allāh ibn Muḥammad. *The Path of God's Bondsmen from Origin to Return (Merṣād al-ʿebad men al-mabdaʾ elá'l-maʿād): A Sufi Compendium*. Translated by Hamid Algar. Persian Heritage Series, no. 35. [Corrected and updated] ed. North Haledon, NJ: Islamic Publication International, 2003.

Redfield, Robert. *Peasant Society and Culture*. Chicago: University of Chicago Press, 1956. Published together with *The Little Community*, Phoenix Books, University of Chicago Press, 1960.

The Little Community, and Peasant Society and Culture. Phoenix Books. Chicago: The University of Chicago Press, 1960.

Reeves, Edward B. "Power, Resistance, and the Cult of Muslim Saints in a Northern Egyptian Town." *American Ethnologist* 22, no. 2 (1995): 306–323.

Regourd, Anne. "Usages talismaniques du Coran." In *Livres de parole, Torah, Bible, Coran*, edited by Annie Berthier and Anne Zali, 187–193. Paris: Bibliothèque National de France, 2005. Avec la collaboration de Laurent Héricher, d'Annie Vernay-Nouri et de Geneviève Voitelriz.

Reinhart, A. Kevin. "'Like the Difference between Heaven and Earth': Ḥanafī and Shāfiʿī Discussions of *Farḍ* and *Wājib*." In *Studies in Islamic Legal Theory*, edited by Bernard Weiss, 205–234. Studies in Islamic Law and Society. Leiden: Brill, 2001.

"[The Quran in Islamic] Jurisprudence." In *The Blackwell Companion to the Qur'ān*, edited by Andrew Rippen, 434–439. London: Blackwell, 2006.

"Legitimacy and Authority in Islamic Discussions of 'Martyrdom Operations/Suicide Bombings.'" In *Enemy Combatants, Terrorism, and Armed Conflict Law: A Guide to the Issues*, edited by David K. Linnan, 167–183. Westport, CT: Praeger, 2008.

"Fundamentalism and the Transparency of the Arabic Qurʾān." In *Rethinking Islamic Studies: From Orientalism to Cosmopolitanism*, edited by Carl W. Ernst and Richard C. Martin, 97–113. Columbia, SC: University of South Carolina Press, 2010.

"Ritual Action and Practical Action: The Incomprehensibility of Muslim Devotional Action." In *Islamic Law in Theory: Studies on Jurisprudence in honor of Bernard Weiss*, edited by A. Kevin Reinhart and Robert Gleave, 55–103. Leiden: Brill, 2014.

"What to Do with Ritual Texts: Islamic *Fiqh* Texts and the Study of Islamic Ritual." In *Islamic Studies in the Twenty-First Century: Transformations and Continuities*, edited by Léon Buskins and Annemarie van Sandwijk, 67–86. Amsterdam: Amsterdam University Press, 2016.

Rezvan, E. A. "The Qur'ān and Its World: VII. Talisman, Shield, and Sword." *Manuscripta Orientalia* 4, no. 3 (1998): 24–34.

Ridgeon, Lloyd V. J. *Sufis and Salafis in the Contemporary Age*. New York: Bloomsbury Academic, 2015.

Rippin, Andrew, and Jan Knappert. *Textual Sources for the Study of Islam*. Chicago: University of Chicago Press, 1986.

Roald, Anne Sofie. "Tarbiya: Education and Politics in Islamic Movements in Jordan and Malaysia." PhD thesis, Lund University, 1994.

Robinson, Francis. "Islam and Muslim Society in South Asia [review of works of Imtiaz Ahmad]." *Contributions to Indian Sociology* 17, no. 2 (1983): 185–201.

"Islam and the Impact of Print in South Asia." In *Islam and Muslim History in South Asia*, 66–104. New Delhi and New York: Oxford University Press, 2000.

"What Went Wrong? (Book Review)." *The Times Literary Supplement* no. 5219, (April 11, 2003): 26–27.

Rosen, Lawrence. *Varieties of Muslim Experience: Encounters with Arab Political and Cultural Life*. Chicago: University of Chicago Press, 2008.

Roy, Asim. *The Islamic Syncretistic Tradition in Bengal*. Princeton, NJ: Princeton University Press, 1983.

Roy, Olivier. *Globalized Islam: The Search for a New Ummah*. The CERI series in Comparative Politics and International Studies. New York: Columbia University Press, 2004.

Ryan, Patrick J. "Imale: Yoruba Participation in the Muslim Tradition: A Study of Clerical Piety." Published by Scholars Press for Harvard Theological Review, 1977.

Said, Edward. "Impossible Histories: Why the Many Islams Cannot be Simplified." *Harpers* (2002): 69–74.

Saidi, Tamim. "Islam and Culture: Don't Mix Them Up" (February 15, 2008). Last accessed August 2, 2019. https://www.minnpost.com/community-voices/2008/02/islam-and-culture-dont-mix-them. This article originally appeared on Engage Minnesota's website.

Sarıcan, Bayram. *1930'lardan günümüze Bursa'da dinî hayat; görduklerim—duyduklarım—yaşadıklarım hatıralar*. Hatırat Serisi 1. Istanbul: Düşünce Kitabevi, 2003. Yayına Hazırlayan: Mustafa Öcal.

Schimmel, Annemarie. *Islamic Calligraphy*. Iconography of Religions. Section 22: Islam. Fasc. 1 [Institute of Religious Iconography, State University Groningen]. Leiden: Brill, 1970.

Schott, Ben. "Dial-a-Fatawa." *New York Times* (May 12, 2009). Last accessed February 4, 2015. http://schott.blogs.nytimes.com/2009/05/12/dial-a-fatwa.

Schulz, Dorothea E. "Evoking Moral Community, Fragmenting Muslim Discourse: Sermon Audio-Recordings and the Reconfiguration of Public Debate in Mali." *Journal for Islamic Studies* 27 (2007): 39–72.

Sedgwick, Mark. *Against the Modern World: Traditionalism and the Secret Intellectual History of the Twentieth Century*. New York: Oxford University Press, 2004.

Seligman, Adam B. "Ritual, the Self, and Sincerity." *Social Research* 76 (Winter 2009): 1073–1096.

Seligman, Adam B., Robert P. Weller, Michael J. Puett, and Bennett Simon. *Ritual and Its Consequences: An Essay on the Limits of Sincerity*. Oxford and New York: Oxford University Press, 2008.

al-Shāfiʿī, Muḥammad b. Idrīs (204/820). *al-Risālah*. Edited by Aḥmad Muḥammad Shākir. Cairo: Maktabat Dār al-Turāth, 1979/1399. 2nd printing.

Shahrur, Muhammad. *The Qurʾan, Morality and Critical Reason: The Essential Muhammad Shahrur*. Leiden and Boston: Brill, 2009. [Selected writings with an introduction from, and translated by, Andreas Christmann, and an interview between Shahrur and Dale F. Eickelman.]

Sharif, Jaʿfar, and G. A. Herklots. *Islam in India or the Qanūn-i-Islām: The Customs of the Musalmāns of India; Comprising a Full and Exact Account of Their Various Rites and Ceremonies from the Moment of Birth to the Hour of Death*. New edition revised and rearranged, with additions by William Crooke. New Delhi: Oriental Reprint, 1921 [1832].

Sidky, M. H. "*Malang*, Sufis, and Mystics: An Ethnographic and Historical Study of Shamanism in Afghanistan." *Asian Folklore Studies* 49, no. 2 (1990): 274–301.

Simmel, Georg, and Kurt H. Wolff, eds. *The Sociology of Georg Simmel*. Glencoe, IL: Free Press, 1950.

Smith, Jane. *An Historical and Semantic Study of the Term Islam as Seen in a Sequence of Quran Commentaries*. Harvard Dissertations in Religion no. 1. Missoula, MT: Scholars Press, 1975.

Smith, Jonathan Z. "Religion, Religions, Religious." In *Critical Terms for Religious Studies*, edited by Mark Taylor, 269–284. Chicago: University of Chicago Press, 1998.

Smith, Wilfred Cantwell. "Some Similarities and Differences between Christianity and Islam: An Essay in Comparative Religion." In *The World of Islam: Studies in Honour of Philip K. Hitti*, edited by James Kritzeck and R. Bayley Winder, 47–59. London and New York: Macmillan and St. Martin's Press, 1959.

"The Historical Development in Islam of the Concept of Islam as an Historical Development." In *Historians of the Middle East*, edited by Bernard Lewis and P. M. Holt, 484–502. Historical Writing on the Peoples of Asia. London: Oxford University Press, 1962.

The Meaning and End of Religion: A New Approach to the Religious Traditions of Mankind. New York: Macmillan, 1963.

Soloveitchik, Haym. "Migration, Acculturation, and the New Role of Texts in the Haredi World." In *Accounting for Fundamentalisms: The Dynamic Character of Movements*, edited by Martin E. Marty and R. Scott Appleby, 197–235. Fundamentalism project, v. 4. Chicago: University of Chicago Press, 1994.

"Rupture and Reconstruction: The Transformation of Contemporary Orthodoxy." *Tradition* 28, no. 4 (1994): 64–130.

Soroosh, Abdolkarim. "The Evolution and Devolution of Religious Knowledge." In *Liberal Islam*, edited by Charles Kurzman, 244–255. London: Oxford University Press, 1998.

Reason, Freedom and Democracy in Islam: Essential Writings of Adbolkarim Soroush. Translated and edited with a critical introduction by M. Sadri and A. Sadri. London: Oxford University Press, 2000.

Starrett, Gregory. "The Political Economy of Religious Commodities in Cairo." *American Anthropologist* 97, no. 1 (1995): 51–68.

Putting Islam to Work: Education, Politics, and Religious Transformation in Egypt. Berkeley, CA: University of California Press, 1998.

Steenbrink, Karel A. *Dutch Colonialism and Indonesian Islam: Contacts and Conflicts, 1596–1950.* Currents of Encounter, v. 7. Amsterdam and Atlanta, GA: Rodopi, 1993.

Stewart, Devin J., Baber Johansen, and Amy Singer. *Law and Society in Islam.* Princeton Series on the Middle East. Princeton, NJ: Markus Wiener Publishers, 1996.

The Story of English. British Broadcasting Corporation. Television Service; Meridian Education Corporation; MacNeil/Lehrer Productions; International Tele-Film Enterprises; Visual Education Centre; Films for the Humanities (Firm); Films Media Group; Kineticvideo.com (Firm), 2007.

Strathern, Andrew, and Pamela J. Stewart. *Contesting Rituals: Islam and Practices of Identity-Making.* Durham, NC: Carolina Academic Press, 2005.

Stroumsa, Guy G. *A New Science: The Discovery of Religion in the Age of Reason.* Cambridge, MA: Harvard University Press, 2010.

Styers, Randall. *Making Magic: Religion, Magic, and Science in the Modern World.* Reflection and Theory in the Study of Religion. New York: Oxford University Press, 2004.

al-Ṭabarī, Abū Jaʿfar Muḥammad b. Jarīr (310/923). *Jāmiʿ al-bayān ʿan tāʾwīl al-Qurʾan.* 30 vols. Cairo: Muṣṭafá al-Bābī al-Ḥalabī wa-Awlāduh, 1388/1968.

Talmon-Heller, Daniella. *Islamic Piety in Medieval Syria: Mosques, Cemeteries and Sermons under the Zangids and Ayyūbids (1146–1260).* Jerusalem Studies in Religion and Culture. Leiden and Boston: Brill, 2007.

Taylor, Charles. *A Secular Age.* Cambridge, MA: Belknap Press of Harvard University Press, 2007.

Tayob, Abdulkader. "Dialectical Theology in the Search for Modern Islam." In *Islamic Studies in the Twenty-First Century: Transformations and Continuities,* edited by Léon Buskens and Annemarie van Sandwijk, 161–182. Amsterdam: Amsterdam University Press, 2016.

Tilly, Charles. *Citizenship, Identity and Social History.* International Review of Social History Supplement. New York: Cambridge University Press, 1996.

Identities, Boundaries, and Social Ties. Boulder, CO: Paradigm Publishers, 2005.

Timuroğlu, Vecihi. *12 Eylül'ün eğitim ve kültür politikası: Türk-İslam sentezi.* Anakara: Başak Yayınları, 1991.

Toprak, Binnaz. "Religion as State Ideology in a Secular Setting: The Turkish-Islamic Synthesis." In *Aspects of Religion in Secular Turkey,* edited by Malcolm Wagstaff, 10–16. Occasional Papers no. 40. Durham: Centre for Middle Eastern and Islamic Studies, University of Durham, 1990.

Trimingham, J. Spencer. *Islam in Ethiopia.* London and New York: Oxford University Press, 1952.

Trudgill, Peter. "Standard English: What It Isn't." In *Standard English: The Widening Debate,* edited by Tony Bex and Richard J. Watts, 117–128. London: Routledge, 1999.

Trudgill, Peter, and Jean Hannah. *International English: A Guide to the Varieties of Standard English.* London: Edward Arnold, 1982.

Türkyilmaz, Zeynep. "Anxieties of Conversion: Missionaries, State and Heterodox Communities in the Late Ottoman Empire." UCLA, 2010.

Udovitch, Abraham L. "An Eleventh Century Islamic Treatise on the Law of the Sea." *Annales islamologiques* 27 (1993): 37–54.

Ukeles, Raquel Margalit. "Innovation or Deviation: Exploring the Boundaries of Islamic Devotional Law." Harvard University, 2006.

Varisco, Daniel Martin. *Islam Obscured: The Rhetoric of Anthropological Representation*. Contemporary Anthropology of Religion. 1st ed. New York: Palgrave Macmillan, 2005.

Reading Orientalism: Said and the Unsaid. Publications on the Near East. Seattle, WA: University of Washington Press, 2007.

Viswanathan, Gauri. *Outside the Fold: Conversion, Modernity, and Belief*. Princeton, NJ: Princeton University Press, 1998.

Waardenburg, Jacobus Diederik Jan. *L'islam dans le miroir de l'occident*. Paris: Mouton & Co., 1963.

Waardenburg, Jean J. "Changes of Perspective in Islamic Studies over the Last Decades." *Humaniora Islamica* 1 (1973): 247–260.

Muslims as Actors: Islamic Meanings and Muslim Interpretations in the Perspective of the Study of Religions. Religion and Reason, v. 46. Berlin and New York: Walter de Gruyter, 2007.

Waldman, Marilyn Robinson. "The Popular Appeal of the Prophetic Paradigm in West Africa." In *Islam in Local Contexts*, edited by Richard C. Martin, 110–114. Contributions to Asian Studies. Leiden: Brill, 1982.

Webb, Edward. "The 'Church' of Bourguiba: Nationalizing Islam in Tunisia." *Sociology of Islam* 1, no. 1 (2013): 17–40.

Weiss, B. "Medieval Muslim Discussions of the Origin of Language." *Zeitschrift der Deutschen Morgenländischen Gesellschaft* 124, no. 1 (1974): 33–41.

Wensinck, A. J. *The Muslim Creed: Its Genesis and Historical Development*. London: Frank Cass & Co., 1965 [1932].

A Handbook of Early Muhammadan Tradition. Leiden: Brill, 1971.

Westermarck, Edward. *Ritual and Belief in Morocco*. London: Macmillan and Co. Limited, 1926.

White, Jenny B. *Islamist Mobilization in Turkey: A Study in Vernacular Politics*. Studies in Modernity and National Identity. Seattle, WA: University of Washington Press, 2002.

Muslim Nationalism and the New Turks. Princeton Studies in Muslim Politics. Princeton, NJ: Princeton University Press, 2013.

Wilson, M. Brett. "The Failure of Nomenclature: The Concept of 'Orthodoxy' in the Study of Islam." *Comparative Islamic Studies* 3, no. 2 (2007): 169–194.

Translating the Qur'an in an Age of Nationalism: Print Culture and Modern Islam in Turkey. Oxford: Oxford University Press, 2014.

Wolfe, Michael. *The Hadj: An American's Pilgrimage to Mecca*. London: Secker & Warburg, 1994.

One Thousand Roads to Mecca: Ten Centuries of Travelers Writing about the Muslim Pilgrimage. 1st ed. New York: Grove Press, 1997.

Woodward, Mark R. *Islam in Java: Normative Piety and Mysticism in the Sultanate of Yogyakarta*. Monographs of the Association for Asian Studies, no. 45. Tucson, AZ: University of Arizona Press, 1989.

"Textual Exegesis as Social Commentary: Religious, Social, and Political Meanings of Indonesian Translations of Arabic Hadith Texts." *Journal of Asian Studies* 52, no. 3 (August 1993): 565–583.

Yijiu, Jin. "The Qur'ān in China." In *Islam in Local Contexts*, edited by Richard Martin, 95–101. Contributions to Asian Studies, no. 17. Leiden: Brill, 1982.

Zadeh, Travis E. *The Vernacular Qur'an: Translation and the Rise of Persian Exegesis.* Qur'anic Studies Series, vol. 7. Oxford and London: Oxford University Press in association with the Institute of Ismaili Studies, 2012.

Zahran, Nedel. "Is Visiting Holy Shrines (Dargahs) or Graves Haraam in Islam?" Last accessed August 2, 2019. https://www.quora.com/Is-visiting-holy-shrines-dargahs-or-graves-haraam-in-Islam.

Zenkovsky, Serge A. *Pan-Turkism and Islam in Russia.* Russian Research Center Studies, no. 36. Cambridge, MA: Harvard University Press, 1960.

Zuckermann, Ghil'ad. "A New Vision for 'Israeli Hebrew': Theoretical and Practical Implications of Analysing Israel's Main Language as a Semi-Engineered Semito-European Hybrid Language." *Journal of Modern Jewish Studies* 5, no. 1 (2006): 57–71.

Index